13th International Conference Mobile Learning 2017

AA004905

Budapest, Hungary
10 – 12 April 2017

Editors:

Inmaculada Arnedillo Sanchez
Pedro Isaias
Luis Rodrigues

ISBN: 978-1-5108-4797-2

Printed from e-media with permission by:

Curran Associates, Inc.
57 Morehouse Lane
Red Hook, NY 12571

CURRAN ASSOCIATES INC. proceedings.com

Some format issues inherent in the e-media version may also appear in this print version.

Copyright© (2017) by International Association for Development of the Information Society (IADIS)
All rights reserved.

Printed by Curran Associates, Inc. (2017)

For permission requests, please contact International Association for Development of the Information Society (IADIS) at the address below.

International Association for Development of the Information Society (IADIS)
Rua Sao Sebastiao Da Pedreira
No. 100, 30, 1050-209
Lisbon, Portugal

Phone: 351 21 3151373
Fax: 351 21 3151244

secretariat@iadis.org

Additional copies of this publication are available from:

Curran Associates, Inc.
57 Morehouse Lane
Red Hook, NY 12571 USA
Phone: 845-758-0400
Fax: 845-758-2633
Email: curran@proceedings.com
Web: www.proceedings.com

PROCEEDINGS OF THE 13th INTERNATIONAL CONFERENCE

MOBILE LEARNING 2017

BUDAPEST, HUNGARY

10 - 12 APRIL, 2017

Organised by

iadis

international association for development of the information society

Copyright 2017

IADIS Press

All rights reserved

This work is subject to copyright. All rights are reserved, whether the whole or part of the material is concerned, specifically the rights of translation, reprinting, re-use of illustrations, recitation, broadcasting, reproduction on microfilms or in any other way, and storage in data banks. Permission for use must always be obtained from IADIS Press. Please contact secretariat@iadis.org

Edited by Inmaculada Arnedillo Sánchez and Pedro Isaías

Associate Editor: Luís Rodrigues

TABLE OF CONTENTS

FULL PAPERS

SHORT PAPERS

REFLECTION PAPERS

POSTERS

DOCTORAL CONSORTIUM

FOREWORD

These proceedings contain the papers and posters of the 13th International Conference on Mobile Learning 2017, which was organised by the International Association for Development of the Information Society, in Budapest, Hungary, 10 - 12 April 2017.

The Mobile Learning 2017 Conference seeks to provide a forum for the presentation and discussion of mobile learning research which illustrate developments in the field. In particular, but not exclusively, we aim to explore the theme of mobile learning under the following topics:

- Learning analytics and mobile learning
- Cloud computing and mobile learning
- Pedagogical approaches, models and theories for mLearning
- mLearning in and across formal and informal settings
- Strategies and challenges for integrating mLearning in broader educational scenarios
- User Studies in mLearning
- Learner mobility and transitions afforded by mlearning
- Socio-cultural context and implications of mLearning
- Mobile social media and user generated content
- Enabling mLearning technologies, applications and uses
- Evaluation and assessment of mLearning
- Research methods, ethics and implementation of mLearning
- Innovative mLearning approaches
- Tools, technologies and platforms for mLearning
- mlearning: where to next and how?

The Mobile Learning 2017 received 104 submissions from more than 27 countries. Each submission has been anonymously reviewed by an average of 4 independent reviewers, to ensure that accepted submissions were of a high standard. Consequently only 19 full and short papers were approved, which means an acceptance rate of 18%. A few more papers were accepted as reflection papers, posters, panels and doctoral consortium. An extended version of the best papers will be published in the International Journal of Mobile and Blended Learning (ISSN: 1941-8647).

Besides the presentation of full, short, reflection, doctoral papers and posters, the conference also features a Keynote presentation from and internationally distinguished researcher. We would therefore like to express our gratitude to Professor Dragan Gasevic, Chair in Learning Analytics and Informatics, The University of Edinburgh, Scotland, for accepting our invitation as keynote speaker.

The conference also includes two Panel presentations entitled "Electrodermal Activity Monitoring: the Gamification of Meditation and Mindset" by Dr. Jake McNeill and Dr. Emma Wertz, Kennesaw State University, USA, and a panel entitled "Current and Future Research Trends in Mobile Learning" presented by A/Professor Pedro Isaías, The University of Queensland, Australia.

A successful conference requires the effort of many individuals. We would like to thank the members of the Program Committee for their hard work in reviewing and selecting the papers that appear in this book. We are especially grateful to the authors who submitted their papers to this conference and to the presenters who provided the substance of the meeting. We wish to thank all members of our organizing committee.

Last but not least, we hope that everybody has enjoyed Budapest and their time with colleagues from all over the world, and we invite you all to next edition of the International Mobile Learning in 2018.

Inmaculada Arnedillo Sánchez, Trinity College Dublin, Ireland
Program Chair

Pedro Isaías, The University of Queensland, Australia
Conference Chair

Budapest, Hungary
April 2017

PROGRAM COMMITTEE

PROGRAM CHAIR

Inmaculada Arnedillo Sánchez, Trinity College Dublin, Ireland

CONFERENCE CHAIR

Pedro Isaías, The University of Queensland, Australia

COMMITTEE MEMBERS

Abdallah Tubaishat, Zayed University, United Arab Emirates
Adamantios Koumpis, Universität Passau, Germany
Alessandro Pagano, University of Bari, Italy
Alex Voychenko, IRTC, Ukraine
Anastasios Economides, University of Macedonia, Greece
Anastasios Karakostas, ITI CERTH, Greece
Anastopoulou Stamatina, University of the Aegean, Greece
Andreas P. Schmidt, Karlsruhe University of Applied Sciences, Germany
Anna Riccioni, University of Bologna, Italy
Antoanela Naaji, Vasile Goldis Western University, Romania
Antonio Panaggio, Ministry of Education, University and Research (MIUR), Italy
Bahtijar Vogel, Malmö University, Sweden
Boriss F. Misnevs, Transport and Telecommunication Institute, Latvia
Brendan Tangney, The University of Dublin, Trinity College Dublin, Ireland
Carmen Holotescu, University "Ioan Slavici" of Timisoara, Romania
Charalampos Karagiannidis, University of Thessaly, Greece
Chiara Rossitto, Department of Computer and Systems Sciences, DSV, Stockholm University, Sweden
Chiu-Kuo Liang, Chunghua University, Taiwan
Christos Bouras, University of Patras, Greece
Claudia Steinberger, University of Klagenfurt, Austria
Daniyar Sapargaliyev, University of Wolverhampton, UK
Demetrios Sampson, Curtin University, Australia
Dumitru Dan Burdescu, University of Craiova, Romania
Elisabetta Parodi, Lattanzio Learning Spa, Italy
Emad Bataineh, Zayed University, United Arab Emirates
Euripides Loukis, University of the Aegean, Greece
Franz Lehner, University of Passau, Germany
George Magoulas, Birbeck College, UK
Giuliana Dettori, ITD-CNR, Italy
Gulcan Ercetin, Bogazici University, Turkey

Gwo-Dong Chen, National Central University, Taiwan
Gwo-Jen Hwang, National Taiwan University of Science and Technology, Taiwan
Hannu-Matti Jarvinen, Tampere University of Technology, Finland
Helen Farley, University of Southern Queensland, Australia
Inge de Waard, The Open University, UK
Ivana Marenzi, University of Hanover, Germany
Jalal Nouri, Stockholm University, Sweden
Jane Sinclair, University of Warwick, UK
Jirarat Sitthiworachart, Walailak University, Thailand
Jo Herstad, University of Oslo, Norway
Jocelyn Wishart, University of Bristol, UK
Johan Stymne, Stockholm University, Sweden
Jozef Hvorecky, Vysoka Skola Manazmentu, Slovakia
Juan Manuel Santos-Gago, University of Vigo, Spain
Judith Seipold, London Mobile Learning Group (LMLG), UK
Jun-Ming Su, National University of Tainan, Taiwan
Kateryna Synytsya, IRTC ITS, Ukraine
Kuo-Liang Ou, National Hsin-chu University of Education, Taiwan
Lam-for Kwok, City University of Hong Kong, Hong Kong
Larissa Zaitseva, Riga Technical University, Latvia
Louise Mifsud, Oslo and Akershus University College of Applied Science, Norway
Luca Tateo, Aalborg University, Denmark
Luis Anido-Rifon, University of Vigo, Spain
Marcus Specht, Open University of The Netherlands, The Netherlands
Marguerite Koole, University of Saskatchewan, Canada
Maria Uther, University of Winchester, UK
Marina Rui, University of Genova, Italy
Mario Vacca, Italian Ministry of Education, Italy
Mercedes Fisher, Milwaukee Area Technical College (MATC), USA
Mike Joy, University of Warwick, UK
Mudasser Wyne, National University, USA
Nicolaos Protogeros, University of Macedonia, Greece
Oleksiy Voychenko, International Research And Training Center (IRTC), Ukraine
Oskar Pettersson, Linnaeus University, Sweden
Otto Petrovic, University of Graz, Austria
Oytun Sözüdoğru, Cyprus Science University, Cyprus
Paul Hayes, National College of Ireland, Ireland
Petra Poulova, University of Hradec Kralove, Czech Republic
Phillip Benachour, Lancaster University, UK
Pramod Pathak, National College of Ireland, Ireland
Qing Tan, Athabasca University, Canada
Ray Yueh Min Huang, National Cheng Kung University, Taiwan
Rebecca Hogue, University of Ottawa, Canada
Roza Dumbraveanu, "Ion Creangă" Pedagogical State University, Moldova
Saku Ekanayake, University of Peradeniya, Sri Lanka
Sara Zoccoli, Italian Ministry of Education, Italy
Sergio Ilarri, University of Zaragoza, Spain
Shen Ruimin, Shanghai Jaitong University, China
Shenguan Yu, Beijing Normal University, China

Song Yanjie, The Education University of Hong Kong, Hong Kong
Stephen McNeill, Kennesaw State University, USA
Tamara Powell, Kennesaw State University, USA
Teresa Cerratto-Pargman, Stockholm University, Sweden
Thrasyvoulos Tsiatsos, Aristotle University of Thessaloniki, Greece
Ting-Ting Wu, National Yunlin University of Science and Technology, Taiwan
Tony Hall, National University of Ireland, Ireland
Tzung-shi Chen, National University of Tainan, Taiwan
Werner Beuschel, Tech. Hochschule Brandenburg, Germany
Yanmin Zhu, Shanghai Jiao Tong University, China
Yannis P. Psaromiligkos, Technological Education Institute of Piraeus, Greece
Zsolt Nagy, University of Nyiregyhaza, Hungary

KEYNOTE LECTURE

STATE AND DIRECTIONS OF LEARNING ANALYTICS ADOPTION

By Professor Dragan Gasevic,
Chair in Learning Analytics and Informatics, The University of Edinburgh, Scotland

Abstract

The analysis of data collected from user interactions with educational and information technology has attracted much attention as a promising approach for advancing our understanding of the learning process. This promise motivated the emergence of the new field learning analytics and mobilized the education sector to embrace the use of data for decision-making. This talk will first introduce the field of learning analytics and touch on lessons learned from some well-known case studies. The talk will then identify critical challenges that require immediate attention in order for learning analytics to make a sustainable impact on learning, teaching, and decision making. The talk will conclude by discussing a set of milestones selected as critical for the maturation of the field of learning analytics. The most important take away from the talk will be that:

- systemic approaches to the development and adoption of learning analytics are critical,
- multidisciplinary teams are necessary to unlock a full potential of learning analytics,
- capacity development at institutional levels through the inclusion of diverse stakeholders is essential for full learning analytics adoption.

PANEL

ELECTRODERMAL ACTIVITY MONITORING: THE GAMIFICATION OF MEDITATION AND MINDSET

by Jake McNeill, Ph.D. and Emma Wertz, Ph.D.
Kennesaw State University, Georgia, USA

Abstract

Galvanic Skin Response (GSR) technology allows users to monitor their response to stress while engaged in various tasks. The PIP, from Galvanic, Inc., is an integrated Bluetooth app that can measure stress levels and relaxation in a closed loop system. Moreover, PIP's diverse apps offer competition and gamification of the users' relaxation levels, as one can learn to adapt behavior to achieve desired performance.
This panel will discuss PIP's various mobile learning uses and case studies when incorporating the device in: K-12 and higher education schools and universities in the United States; corporate wellness; and Public Relations research, theory testing, and work with corporate partners. Topics, such as stress levels in the classroom and workplace will be discussed. Original PIP case studies, including client campaigns and fear appeal research, will be presented. The panel will also include real-time demonstrations.

Keywords: Electrodermal activity monitoring, cognitive neurorehabilitation, biometric user interfaces, galvanic skin response, health and gaming.

References

Darnell, S. S. (2015). "EngageMe: The Design and Implementation of a Reflective Tool for Evaluating Student Engagement". All Dissertations. Paper 1790.

Chaturvedi, H. (2015). "Virtual humans and Photorealism: The effect of photorealism of interactive virtual humans in clinical virtual environment on affective responses". All Theses. Paper 2249.

Hurley, R. A., Hutcherson, D. E., Tonkin, C. E., Dailey, S. B., & Rice, J. C. (2015). "Measuring physiological arousal towards packaging: tracking electrodermal activity within the consumer shopping environment," Journal of Applied Packaging Research: Vol. 7: No. 3, Article 5.

PANEL

CURRENT AND FUTURE RESEARCH TRENDS IN MOBILE LEARNING

by A/Professor Pedro Isaías,
The University of Queensland, Australia

Abstract

Mobile learning is benefiting from several advances in technology that promote its accessibility. Responsive design, which adapts content to different device sizes and resolution, can critically improve the learner experience. Moreover with the use of Artificial Intelligence and Big Data analytics it is possible to have a depiction of the students' interests and preferences and enhance the personalisation of learning. In terms of customisation, the introduction of geo-location features in Learning Management Systems have also allowed students to receive learning content per their location.

The mounting popularity of mobile devices' use has driven educational institutions to promote Bring Your Own Device policies, which are not without challenges, but do seem to enable the dissemination of mobile learning and empower students to take control over the devices where content is delivered and created. Mobile learning is also responsible for fostering collaboration and social learning by allowing students to communicate with peers worldwide. The use of mobile devices for education constitutes a challenge for the variety of distractions they can provide. Hence maintaining the engagement of the user is essential in this context. The use of augmented reality and gamification promises to endow mobile learning with appealing learning scenarios that will encourage the active participation of the learners and maintain their involvement.

Full Papers

DESIGN OF A PROTOTYPE MOBILE APPLICATION TO MAKE MATHEMATICS EDUCATION MORE REALISTIC

Dawid B. Jordaan, Dorothy J. Laubscher and A. Seugnet Blignaut
TELIT-SA, North-West University, Vanderbijlpark Campus, South Africa

ABSTRACT

To enter the world of work, students require skills which include flexibility, critical thinking, problem solving, collaboration and communication. The use of mobile technologies which are specifically created for a context could stimulate motivation in students to recognise the relevance of Mathematics in the real world. South Africa in particular is a suitable location to use mobile learning across distance due to its viability, affordability and availability as opposed to web-based technology. The design team developed an app for financial Mathematics based on the principles of realistic mathematics education (RME) for mathematics teachers to use with their students. The paper describes the design process and general usability aspects of the formative evaluation of the prototype app for financial Mathematics. The authors suggest that a graphic artist becomes part of the design team to enhance the visual attractiveness of the app.

KEYWORDS

Realistic Mathematics Education (RME); mobile applications; Distance Education (DE); Android; interactivity; user interface

1. INTRODUCTION

The rapidly changing information society influences the roles of learners and teachers (Gravemeijer, 2012). Future jobs require what Gravemeijer (2012) refers to as 21st century skills, which include "flexibility, critical thinking, problem solving, collaboration, and communication." Gravemeijer (2012) emphasizes the importance of addressing these demands by investigating educational practices that may nurture these goals. Heck et al. (2007) are of the opinion that the use of mobile technology could increase motivation as well as performance in learners. Also, the use of real-life contexts stimulate motivation because the relevance of Mathematics can be seen in the real world (Risnawati et al., 2014).

Various reasons are offered for poor performance in Mathematics, which include: when topics are taught (Fauzan et al., 2013), inaccurate learning material, inadequate or outdated teaching methods, poor forms of assessment, students' anxiety about Mathematics (Widjaja and Heck, 2003); and students' negative attitudes towards Mathematics (Widjaja and Heck, 2003).

Mobile learning is a field that is rapidly expanding and it affords new possibilities to improve learning, especially in a distance education (DE) environment (Kizito, 2012). South Africa in particular is a suitable location to use mobile learning in distance education due to its viability and affordability as opposed to web-based technology (Kizito, 2012). The portability of mobile technology allows learners to work creatively and collaboratively (Zaranis et al., 2013). When used correctly, technology could promote critical thinking, improve problem solving skills and facilitate collaboration (Stols, 2012). Further research is required to determine how the mobile phone can effectively be used in testing in DE (Kizito, 2012).

This paper investigates the need for, and the design and development of, a mobile application which would assist Mathematics teacher-students in making their teaching, as well as their students' learning more realistic in terms of the context in which the learning takes place.

2. LITERATURE REVIEW

2.1 Realistic Mathematics Education

Mathematics teachers are challenged to develop Mathematics education that is in line with the dynamic conceptions of symbolizing and the development of meaning (Bakker et al., 2003). The role of the teacher is essential to understand how to teach effectively with technology (Drijvers, 2012). Digital tasks should be designed in such a way that students are encouraged to develop their own Mathematics. The teacher should guide the process and should know when to further explore a topic or concept and when to cease to investigate a topic (Drijvers et al., 2013).

The traditional approach to teaching Mathematics still dominate in many classrooms today (Fauzan et al., 2013). This approach is characterized by teachers who actively explain material and provide examples and exercises, while learners listen, write and perform the tasks the teacher requires (Gravemeijer, 2012, Widjaja and Heck, 2003). The social norms of traditional classrooms dictate that the teachers' answers are always correct and that students should follow given procedures to reach correct answers, which are more important than reasoning (Gravemeijer, 2012). Learners seldom have the opportunity to understand the rationale behind algorithms that are taught to them (Risnawati et al., 2014). Such a traditional approach to teaching Mathematics is held responsible for the poor quality of Mathematics Education and students' negative attitude towards Mathematics (Fauzan et al., 2013, Widjaja and Heck, 2003). Another consequence of traditional teaching is that when students solve word problems, high level cognitive and metacognitive processes are often absent (Mousoulides et al., 2007).

Reform from the traditional approach demands that curricula, teaching materials and assessment need to be adapted (Zulkardi, 2000). Freudenthal (1968), often regarded as the father of Realistic Mathematics Education (RME), opposes the traditional idea that the end result of the work of mathematicians is the starting point for Mathematics Education (Gravemeijer and Doorman, 1999). RME is regarded as a domain-specific instruction theory for the teaching and learning of Mathematics (Drijvers et al., 2013). The RME-based teaching and learning process promotes learner-centred learning (Fauzan et al., 2013). Problem solving through modelling leads to the design of activities that allow for students to deal with non-routine problem situations that demand the development of important mathematical ideas which can be extended, explored and refined in other problem situations (Mousoulides et al., 2007). Technological tools create new prospects for problem solving in Mathematics (Doorman et al., 2007). A corner stone of RME is that students are encouraged to not only receive information, but also question and process information (Widjaja and Heck, 2003), actively participate in the educational process and develop mathematical tools and insights (Drijvers et al., 2013).

2.2 Mobile Learning

Mobile technology offers a new generation of learning to students of all ages without being bound by place and time (Alzaza and Yaakub, 2010). Mobile learning (mLearning) is becoming more popular within formal education as its benefits offer cost-efficiency, portability; instant connectivity; and context sensitivity. Mobile learning assists students to create social interaction; it promotes collaborative learning, interactivity and instant feedback as well as collaboration between peers; it improves their knowledge structure; their learning achievements and motivation (Mouza and Barrett-Greenly, 2015). Domingo and Garganté (2016) further point out that students are more willing to engage when learning with mobile technology; their desire to accomplish educational tasks also increases with the use of mobile technology, and it helps learners to become more self-directed in their learning. Mobile communication in education is a solution with a selection of prospects and challenges (Kommers and Hooreman, 2009).

mLearning applications have various educational benefits: they can be used as study aids; can be accessed from almost anywhere; and with the aid of location capabilities, students can use location-based information (Cheon et al., 2012). Mobile technology applications supplement higher education by extending traditional educational platforms and encouraging distance learning or using settings outside of the classroom (Al-Emran et al., 2016). Content applications that make use of personalized instruction can facilitate academic growth and self-efficacy among students (Mouza and Barrett-Greenly, 2015).

3. METHOD

This research relates to the first phase of a four-phased qualitative design-based research process where four teacher-students in the Open Distance Education (ODL) program of the North-West University (NWU), Potchefstroom Campus participated in individual interviews. They shared their perceptions and experiences on support teachers' need in order to effectively implement the RME principles in their teaching practice. The teacher-students confirmed that their own students inter alia (i) had problems with certain areas of Mathematics, (ii) suffered challenges with the integration of the content across the curriculum, (iii) were excited about the affordances that mobile learning could bring to Mathematics education, and (iv) experienced challenges to link school Mathematics to real life problems, e.g. handling their own finances. The researchers decided to zoom in on the aspect of financial Mathematics for the content aspect of the mobile application (app) because all the participants mentioned this area as troublesome to their students.

The context in which the app will be used should form the anchor for the development of the content (Widjaja and Heck, 2003). The app was specifically designed for teacher-students enrolled in an open distance learning (ODL) teacher professional development programme through the Unit of Open Distance Learning (UoDL) at the North-West University at the Potchefstroom Campus. They were all established Mathematics teachers at semi-rural schools in the North-West Province, South Africa, and enrolled for a BEd Honours programme. The design of the application was based on RME principles: (i) guided reinvention (or progressive mathematisation); (ii) emergent modelling; and (iii) didactical phenomenology (Andresen, 2007). The process of guided reinvention began with a real-life problem which was then mathematised (Gravemeijer and Doorman, 1999). The aim with the app was to guide these teacher students to become comfortable with using technology in teaching and learning, as well as to enable them to interact with their learners on RME.

3.1 Creating the App

Software engineering is the application of engineering to the design, development, implementation, testing and maintenance of software in a systematic method. The objective of software engineering is to produce software systems to customers in a cost effective way. Once installed these systems should display characteristics such as efficiency, reliability, maintainability, robustness, portability and so on (Sommerville, 2016). The software process is a set of activities and associate results which produce a software product. Software specification, development, validation and evolution are fundamental process activities common to all software processes.

Software development models are processes or methodologies used for the development of software projects. There are many development models that have been developed in order to achieve different objectives. The models specify the various stages of the process and the order in which they are carried out (Sommerville, 2016). Examples of software development models are: Evolutionary Prototyping Model; Spiral Method (SDM); Iterative and Incremental Method; Extreme programming (Agile development); Waterfall model; Prototype model; Rapid application development model and so on (Whitten and Bentley, 2007). Choosing the right model for developing a software product or application is very important as the model determine where and when the development and testing processes are carried out.

For the development of our app, which we name *Financial Maths App*, we decided to use the Prototype Model because of the advantages that this model offer: Users are actively involved in the development; Since a working model of the system is provided, the users get a better understanding of the system being developed; Errors can be detected much earlier; Rapid user feedback is available leading to better solutions; Missing functionality can be identified easily; and Confusing or difficult functions can be identified (Whitten and Bentley, 2007). The basic idea is that instead of freezing the requirements (as required by many other models) before a design or coding can proceed, a prototype is built to understand the requirements based on the currently known requirements. By using this prototype, the client can get an "actual feel" of the system, since the interactions with the prototype can enable the client to better understand the requirements of the desired system. The prototype is usually not a complete system and many of the details are not built into the prototype. The goal is to provide a system with overall functionality. Figure 1 depicts the phases in the development of a prototype.

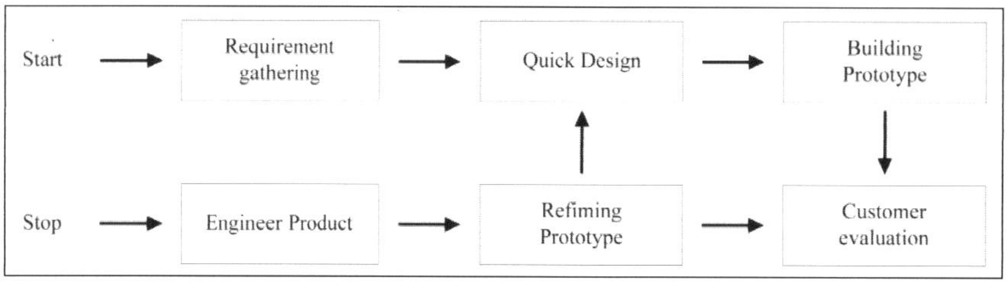

Figure 1. Prototyping model (Whitten and Bentley, 2007).

3.2 Creating the App

Background. While the first author of this paper was the designer of the app, the second author was the content specialist and also responsible for the various design documents, and the third author was the expert on the use of technology in teaching and learning. Together they formed a tight project team. They obtained ethics clearance for this research from the Ethics Committee of the North-West University (NWU-HS-2014-0267).

Requirement (Step 1). The first step in creating an app was to develop a clearly defined purpose for the mobile app: we had to determine what the app should be able to do; what its primary appeal would be; which concrete problem it was going to address; and what part of life it aimed to improve. Detail design documents were created which outlined the standards, planning design, development, and ongoing evaluation of the project (Fleisch and Schöer, 2014).

Quick Design (Step 2). Next the foundation of the user interface was laid. This step visually conceptualized the main features and a rough layout and structure of the app. Sketches for the proposed layout and structure of the app were drawn which assisted the team to understand the journey better Figure 2 is an example of such a sketch.

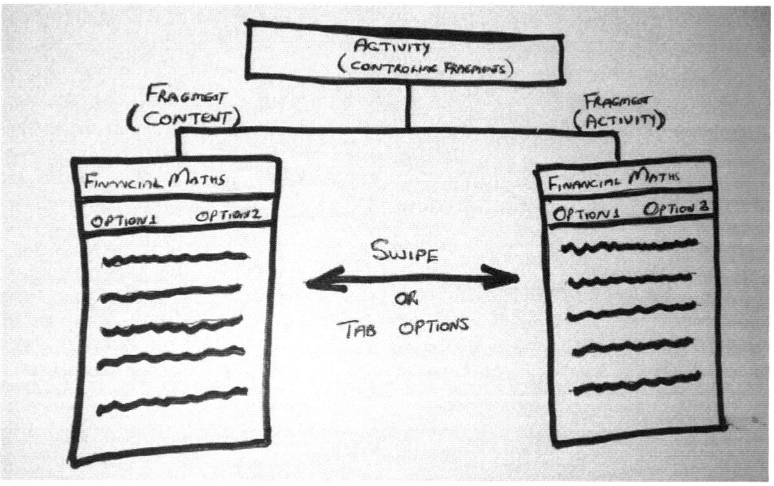

Figure 2. Example of layout sketch (own sketch).

Building Prototype (Step 3). At this stage all the ideas and features culminated as a clear picture of the structure and a storyboard for the project was created. The storyboard provided a road map which illustrated the connections between the different screens and how the user could navigate through the app. The storyboard formed the foundation for the first version of the prototype.

Customer Evaluation (Step 4). The next step involved the testing of the prototype. Friends, family, colleagues, and experts all helped to review the prototype. They were requested to test run the app and give sincere feedback and identify flaws and dead-end links. If possible to monitor how they used the app, one should take note of their actions as these would provide important feedback for user interface (UI) and user experience (UX) evaluation (Molich and Nielsen, 1990). Based on their feedback, the prototype was modified. The aim was to finally specify the app concept before going into the design process. For the *Financial Maths app*, the content author tested the app with two of her Mathematics colleagues who are Mathematics lecturers, as well as with a RME expert.

Refining Prototype (Step 5). Next, individual screen content were designed. The task was to create high-resolution versions of the prototype. All comments from the prototype testers were included in order to design the most suitable user interface. With the screen designs completed and implemented, the actual app concept was complete, all the graphics were inserted, and all text was signed off—the actual design was now implemented and made clickable.

Repeat (Step 2 to 5). The next step was to test the full design once more and collect as much feedback as possible from a variety of users. The new ideas and comments were used to refine the app. A consistent look and feel of the layout was assured and we ensured that it would perform reliably on different devices.

Deployment (Step 6). As the vast majority of the intended students used Android devices (Dahlstrom et al., 2016), the brief was to develop the *Financial Maths app* for Android devices (smart phones and tablets). The *Financial Maths* app was consequently installed on Android devices and tested for functionality in a live environment.

4. USABILITY OF THE APP

4.1 The User Interface

Figure 1 illustrates two scenarios that are realistic and relevant to students at school, from which the concepts of simple and compound interest could develop. Students are not expected to reinvent all the content themselves, and should be guided by the teacher who allows them the opportunity to reflect on their invented strategies (Gravemeijer and Doorman, 1999). Drijvers et al. (2013) suggest that guidance from the teacher will help the progression in a sensible manner, as is suggested in Figure 3.

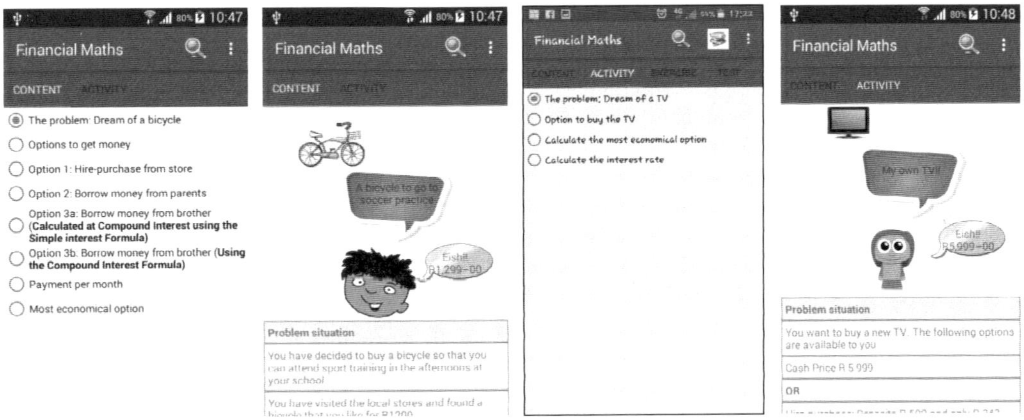

Figure 3. A context that is meaningful and natural is created.

Emergent modelling refers to the development of models from the student's activity which leads to the emergence of formal Mathematics (Gravemeijer and Doorman, 1999). The use of models is encouraged as a bridge between what is abstract to students and what is real (Dolk et al., 2002). Figure 4 illustrates how the use of models has been encouraged in the app. The models too are grounded in the contextual problem and are not derived from the intended Mathematics (Gravemeijer, 1999). The last screenshot in Figure 4 illustrates that students are in various instances given three opportunities to attempt to develop their own strategies to solve a problem before a hint is given.

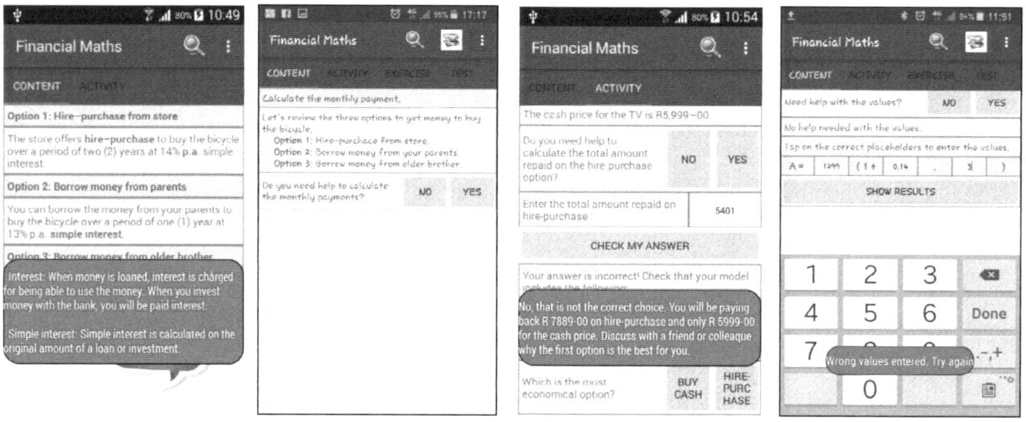

Figure 4. Hints and tips are provided should students require them.

The third principle that was incorporated in the design of the app was didactical phenomenology, which deals with the idea of how mathematical structures can assist in organising phenomena in real life (Zulkardi, 2000). Students are confronted with situations that need to be organised, and in that way students can build concepts (Bakker et al., 2003). The phenomena of personal finances, hire-purchase and interest rates are relevant real-life notions that can be structured with mathematical content (Figure 5).

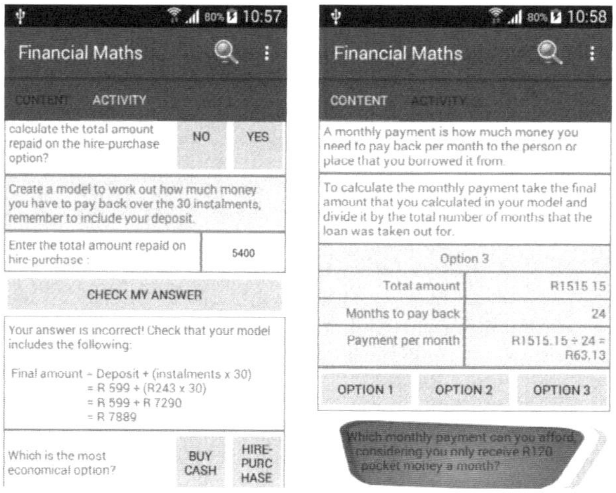

Figure 5. An illustration of the use of models.

4.2 General Usability of the App

The initial design document provided the design team with a broad idea of the content of the app. In the drafts to follow, more particulars are given with regard to the detail of when hints and tips should appear; how many attempts students can make on a solution before receiving help; and words of encouragement when the solutions are correctly worked out. Molich and Nielsen (1990) are of the opinion that general usability evaluations should comprise not more than ten members, and the design team followed this suggestion. The three team members perused and tested the first two prototypes and suggested changes in terms of usability. An RME expert evaluated the third prototype of the app and focused specifically on the inclusion of the RME principles. His evaluation revealed that all the principles of RME were sufficiently addressed in the app and that it should achieve the purpose for which it was designed, namely to make teachers' teaching of Mathematics, and learners' learning experiences more realistic, relevant and experientially real. He suggested that the app be thoroughly tested before being released for student use.

Two more experts in the field of Mathematics education tested the app. Their main suggestion for improving the app was to make the problem situation more visible at the start of the app:

Put something in that sets the scenario more clearly. The start of the app is too vague.

Their evaluation also included comments on why they felt the app was suited to the purpose for which it was created:

It works very well because all the steps are clearly shown. It will help the teachers to teach their learners to follow logical steps in their calculations.

The app included an activity that clearly showed the intertwining of the concepts of compound and simple interest, a key characteristic of RME (Widjaja and Heck, 2003). The Mathematics education experts found this appropriate and necessary:

I like this very much. By including this comparison of concepts you can see wow, it's quicker to use the compound interest formula, and yet you still get the same answer as when repeating the simple interest formula.

They also suggested that the app be extended to other content areas and that it be made available to a wider range of teachers.

5. CONCLUSIONS AND RECOMMENDATIONS

The design of this app has the potential to be extended into a larger project where a variety of problem content areas in Mathematics, at different grade levels, could be addressed. These apps could be made available to any Mathematics teacher who needs assistance with both content as well as the notion of incorporating relevant, real life contexts in their Mathematics teaching.

A comment made by a Mathematics education specialist relates to the need for the development of users of such apps in terms of the integration of technology into their every teaching and learning:

We had a bigger problem working the phone that doing the sums. Let's hope that the students that will be using this app are comfortable with the technology.

Although one of the points of criticism from the subject experts was that the problem scenario was not well articulated, the design team is of the opinion that a more graphic approach would work better. The context and content should be presented with the aid of more graphics and less words.

ACKNOWLEDGEMENT

We would like to thank the National Research Foundation of South Africa for in part supporting this work. Any opinion, findings and conclusions or recommendations expressed in this material are those of the authors and therefore the NRF does not accept any liability in regard thereto.

Thank you also to the teacher-students who shared their needs for the app with us for their patience, dedication and willingness to participate in the study and learn with us.

REFERENCES

Al-Emran, M., et al. 2016. Investigating Attitudes Towards the Use of Mobile Learning in Higher Education. *Computers in Human Behavior,* 56, 93-102.

Alzaza, N.S. & Yaakub, A.R. 2010. Students' Awareness and Requirements of Mobile Learning Services in the Higher Education Environment. *American Journal of Economics and Business Administration,* 3, 95-100.

Andresen, M. 2007. Introduction of a New Construct: The Conceptual Tool "Flexibility". *The Montana Council of Teachers of Mathematics,* 4, 230-250.

Bakker, A., et al. 2003. Design Research on How It May Support the Development of Symbols and Meaning in Mathematics Education. *Onderwijs Research Dagen (ORD).* Kerkrade, The Netherlands.

Cheon, J., et al. 2012. An Investigation of Mobile Learning Readiness in Higher Education Based on the Theory of Planned Behavior. *Computers and Education,* 59, 1054–1064.

Dahlstrom, E., et al. 2016. *2016 Student and Technology Research Study* [Online]. EDUCAUSE Center for Analysis and Research (ECAR) Available: https://library.educause.edu/resources/2016/6/2016-student-and-technology-research-study [Accessed 10 October 2016].

Dolk, M., et al. 2002. Using Multimedia Cases for Educating the Primary School Mathematics Teacher Educator: A Design Study. *International Journal of Educational Research,* 37, 161-178.

Domingo, M.G. & Garganté, A.B. 2016. Exploring the Use of Educational Technology in Primary Education: Teachers' Perception of Mobile Technology Learning Impacts and Applications' Use in the Classroom. *Computers in Human Behavior,* 56, 21-28.

Doorman, M., et al. 2007. Problem Solving as a Challenge for Mathematics Education in the Netherlands. *ZDM Mathematics Education,* 39, 405-418.

Drijvers, P. 2012. Digital Technology in Mathematics Education: Why It Works (or Doesn't). *12th International Congress on Mathematical Education.* Seoul, Korea.

Drijvers, P., et al. 2013. Digital Design: Rme Principles for Designing Online Tasks. *ICMI Study 22: Task Design in Mathematics Education.* Oxford, UK.

Fauzan, A., et al. 2013. The Development of an Rme-Based Geometry Course for Indonesian Primary Schools. *In:* Plomp, T. & Nieveen, N. (eds.) *Educational Design Research - Part B: Illustrative Cases* Enschede: SLO.

Fleisch, B. & Schöer, V. 2014. Large-Scale Instructional Reform in the Global South: Insights from the Mid-Point Evaluation of the Gauteng Primary Language and Mathematics Strategy. *South African Journal of Education,* 34, 1-12.

Freudenthal, H. 1968. Why to Teach Mathematics So as to Be Useful. *Educational Studies in Mathematics,* May 1968, 3-8.

Gravemeijer, K. 1999. How Emergent Models May Foster the Constitution of Formal Mathematics. *Mathematical Thinking and Learning,* 1, 155-177.

Gravemeijer, K. 2012. Aiming for 21st Century Skills. *International Journal for Mathematics in Education,* 4, 30-42.

Gravemeijer, K. & Doorman, M. 1999. Context Problems in Realistic Mathematics Education: A Calculus Course as an Example. *Educational Studies in Mathematics,* 39, 111-129.

Heck, A., et al. Applets for Learning School Algebra and Calculus: Experiences from Secondary School Practice with an Integrated Learning Environment for Mathematics. Electronic Proceedings e+Calculus, 2007 Lisbon. 1st JEM Workshop,.

Kizito, R.N. 2012. Pretesting Mathematical Concepts with the Mobile Phone: Implications for Curriculum Design. *The International Review of Research in Open and Distance Learning,* 13, 38-55.

Kommers, P.A.M. & Hooreman, R.W. 2009. Mobile Phones for Real-Time Teacher Coaching. *Journal of research in innovative teaching,* 2, 80-90.

Molich, R. & Nielsen, J. 1990. Improving a Human Computer Dialogue. *Communications of the ACM,* 33, 338-348.

Mousoulides, N., et al. 2007. From Problem Solving to Modeling – the Emergence of Models and Modelling Perspectives. *Nordic Studies in Mathematics Education,* 12, 23-47.

Mouza, C. & Barrett-Greenly, T. 2015. Bridging the App Gap: An Examination of a Professional Development Initiative on Mobile Learning in Urban Schools. *Computers and Education,* 88, 1-15.

Risnawati, et al. The Development of Realistic Mathematics Eduation-Based Blog at Linear Algebra Course in Uin Suska Riau. International conference on research, implementation and education of Mathematics and Sciences, 18-20 May 2014 Yogyakarta. Yogyakarta State University.

Sommerville, I. 2016. *Software Engineering,* Harlow, England, Addison-Wesley Publishing Company.

Stols, G. 2012. Does the Use of Technology Make a Difference in the Geometric Cognitive Growth of Pre-Service Mathematics Teachers? *Australasian Journal of Educational Technology and Society,* 28, 1233-1247.

Whitten, J.L. & Bentley, L.D. 2007. *Systems Analysis & Design Methods,* Los Angeles, CA, McGraw-Hill.

Widjaja, Y.B. & Heck, A. 2003. How a Realistic Mathematics Education Approach and Microcomputer-Based Laboratory Worked in Lessons on Graphing at an Indonesian Junior High School. *Journal of Science and Mathematics Education in S.E. Asia,* 26, 1-51.

Zaranis, N., et al. 2013. Using Mobile Devices for Teaching Realistic Mathematics in Kindergarten Education *Creative Education* 4, 1-10.

Zulkardi 2000. Realistic Mathematics Education Theory Meets Web Technology *National Conference on Mathematics in ITB* Bandung.

TABLETS AND APPLICATIONS TO TELL MATHEMATICS' HISTORY IN HIGH SCHOOL

Eduardo Jesus Dias, Carlos Fernando Araujo Jr. and Marcos Andrei Ota
Cruzeiro do Sul University, Brazil

ABSTRACT

In this article, we suggest that the history in Mathematics Education combined with *mobile* technology, can provide analysis of concepts, theories and significant logical structures in the process of teaching and learning of Mathematics, as the main objective of this study is to analyze the students' motivation and learning using tablets in the classroom. From a collaborative work, high school students have created applications that told a little the Mathematics' history. A private school situated in the east side of São Paulo city conducted this experiment. With the participation of 4 teachers and 107 students of the first year of the high school, we observed that the tablet generated a stimulating and challenging environment in search of mathematical historical elements to explain concepts and theories so far not questioned by students in conventional classes. The results presented in the study indicate that the use of tablets in the work development was of paramount importance not only in the motivational issue, but also in getting knowledge about some mathematical theories put in its history.

KEYWORDS

Tablet, App, Mathematics, Interdisciplinary, History.

1. INTRODUCTION

In the mathematics' process of teaching and learning, the story is a resource that can bring to the educational setting significant educational benefits for the Discipline. According to Miorim and Miguel (2004), there are arguments that enhance the pedagogical use of history in the Mathematic Education, that is, the story ends up participating in the construction of both epistemological as well as ethical nature of mathematical knowledge.

D'Ambrosio (2008, p.29) argues that, "the mathematics' story is a key element to understand how theories and mathematical practices were created". Therefore, we can highlight that the historical factor contextualizes the Mathematics into the classroom and serves as a parameter to gives life to facts and human needs. In this article, we have a proposal to discuss the use of tablet in the classroom in a collaborative work. In addition as a mediator object can contribute in the construction of mathematical concepts through the creation of applications that offer social issues, historical and cultural in the Mathematics' teaching, through the study of five civilizations (Babylonian, Chinese, Greek, Egyptian and Indian) that influenced the current Mathematics.

> New information and communication technologies become, today, part of a vast instrument historically mobilized for education and learning. It is up to each society to decide what composition, from the set of educational technologies, to mobilize to reach its development goals. (WERTHEIN, 2000, p.77)

According to Teixeira and Brandão (2003) when teachers planned the pedagogical proposal in a way that they view and recognize its potentialities the association between technological resource potential with the area in knowledge may happen. In addition, a teaching and a meaningful learning that meets at characteristics of the current student, in a context of more interactive and dynamic learning will also happen.

The point of this article is that with an inter- disciplinary work involving some areas of knowledge and the use of *mobile* technologies can arouse the curiosity among high school students for Mathematics and make it meaningful? Can we question that the primitive concepts of Mathematics can favor the continuity of the studies of the current Mathematics? In addition, what would be the true contribution of a project in which it participates a group of teachers and students to build applications that enable the development of historical and cultural thinking in the issue of teaching Mathematics with the use of the tablet?

Looking under these aspects, we realize that we could use these devices (tablets and applications) in our research to try to answer these questions, because we intend to use the tablet as a basic tool in achieving the proposed objectives.

Therefore, this article brings the importance of the mathematical discoveries promoted by ancient civilizations and shows that mathematics, besides being a knowledge that adapts over time, also promotes coherent logics that translate social, cultural and intellectual progress. Mathematical historical concepts were objects of debate among the students involved. The use of mobile resources (Tablets) proved to be important not only for students' acceptance and positive evaluation, but also for the possibility of using technology to gather materials in different formats, bringing to the fore active methodologies for the promotion of interdisciplinary activities.

1.1 The history and teaching of Mathematics

In the process of teaching and learning of Mathematics, history is a resource that can bring to the educational setting significant educational benefits to the Discipline. According to Miorim & Miguel (2004), there are arguments that enhance the pedagogical use of history in the Mathematic Education, that is, the story ends up participating in the construction of both epistemological as well as ethical nature of mathematical knowledge.

D'Ambrosio (2008, p.29) argues, "The mathematics' story is a key element to understand how theories and mathematical practices were created". Therefore, we can highlight that the historical factor contextualizes the Mathematics into the classroom and serves as a parameter to gives life to facts and human needs.

According to Miorim & Miguel (2004), story is "a source that enables the development of a critical thinking, a qualification as a citizen and an awareness and an evaluation of different social uses of Mathematics" (MIORIN; MIGUEL, 2004, p.61-62). The Mathematics that influenced much of humanity was born from small towns organization surrounded the Euphrates river, Tigris and Nilo, because in that region agriculture was the base of support for people who lived there and farmed the land. Faced with this, it is possible to believe that history in Mathematics Education meets the social and cultural changes each time, based on individual needs and collective society. Through the need to count, to organize, to draw and to establish logical parameters that generated ways of communication between writing and thinking built the Mathematics. Gomes (2000) says that the signs are important tools for us to understand the human reality in its values, conduct and expectations generated by their everyday experience.

Using the tablet in the classroom, the teacher can explore the concepts of the Mathematics' history, using images that portray historical pictures of the mathematical context, several texts that tell the story of these people, and videos that historically narrate the development of that Science.

2. LITERATURE REVIEW

2.1 The tablet and the project interdisciplinary

The tablet is a tool in clipboard format and promotes easily access to the Internet and other resources such as notes, spreadsheets, and games, reading books, many applications used both for leisure and for job.

Starting from the assumption that our contemporary society is connected a lot to use new Technologies of Information and Communication, this tool meets the individual and social needs of communication, because according to Vygotsky (1991), the use of mediating artefacts between man and nature, or between man and the man himself, would have key role in social and historical development.

In our research, we consider that the interdisciplinary work allied to the history of Mathematics, could be an important resource in the process of teaching and learning of Mathematics that is, based at the collaborative project between students and teachers we can establish analysis more satisfactory of learning primitive Mathematics.

According to Radford (1997, p. 32, cited by MIORIN; MIGUEL, 2004, p.125) "a process whose product is obtained through negotiation of meaning resulting from social activity individuals, within the cultural context that involves them". And the mathematical knowledge in particular, as a "symbolic manifestation of certain sensibilities developed by members of a culture through experiences shared and from which the meaning of the products is produced" (RADFORD,1997, p.30, cited by MIORIN; MIGUEL, 2004, p. 125).

Thus, we realize that a collaborative project that involves people for a socio-cultural investigation will make important historical contributions in the mathematical context supported by the use of a tablet and its auxiliary tools, among which we can mention, for example, the internet and the app.

> The mathematical content with the new technologies, the High School student shows a different attitude in the classroom. Notable are the desire for discovery and the curiosity of young people to know how the device generated a certain graphic image, collaborating significantly in this process of understanding the correlated algebraic and geometric concepts (ARAUJO JR; DIAS, 2012, p.96).

The issue of the use of tablets at school promoted a dynamic differentiated activity in the classroom, in which the need arose to work together with other areas of knowledge. By theme suggested, we consider necessary the interdisciplinary work, as to Goldman (1979, p. 3-25), "an interdisciplinary look at reality allows us to better understand the relationship between its whole and its constituent parts". This show us the importance of methodologies in integrated work between the various specific areas of knowledge, in order to build attitudinal elements (FAZENDA, 1994) at the process in teaching and learning.

According to Ruiz & Bellini (1998), we can see the "interdisciplinary as a result of a non-simplified intellectual attitude of the reality approach. This attitude implies admitting that in every situation there are multiple variables simultaneously interfering" (RUIZ; BELLINI, 1998, p.55).

The interdisciplinary approach of these authors make it clear that this field of study is much more comprehensive and complex than we can imaged. We can say that the social historical context of the interdisciplinary reality will promote a coherent intellectual attitude to human needs, but also the enrichment of the joint work of the specific sciences, promoting an intellectual advance of knowledge as a whole.

3. METHODOLOGY

3.1 The resources in drawing up the app

In the project, participated together with the Mathematics' area the History teachers (P1), Portuguese (P2) and Computing (P3) and more 107 students of 1st year of High School divided in three different classes. They randomly selected five themes of ancient civilizations that contributed to Mathematics. They are Chinese, Babylonian, Indian, Egyptian and Greek. The purpose of the study was to investigate the origins, cultures, religions, economy, social structure and mainly, the mathematical contributions developed by civilizations investigated. They established an activity delivery schedule to compose a final evaluation, as shown in Table 1. Socio-cultural approach is mentioned for the understanding of the work developed by the students and teachers in the interdisciplinary project.

They divided the activity about the general history of civilizations and the history of Mathematics in three basic formatting procedures. They are: 1) source of research; 2) summary and synthesis of theme; and 3) conclusion or overview of the group about the research.

After this procedure, the students delivered the research on the history of the civilizations to teachers (P1) and (P2) for the correction and possible guidance. The students had a period of one more week for the conclusion and final delivery of the work to the researcher teacher.

Table 1. Project activities deliverables schedule.

General History of Civilization	Delivery Time: 1st Half Aug/13
History of Mathematics	Delivery Time: 2nd Fortnight Aug/13
Formatting Applications	Delivery Time: 1st Half Sep/ 13
Finalization and Presentation of Applications	Delivery Time: 2nd Fortnight Sep/ 13

Figure 1. Resources used by students in developing applications. Source: Research Authors.

The questionnaires have closed and open questions about the findings of mathematical concepts from ancient civilizations, comments from students involved in the project.

In the process of application formatting, we asked to students to elect two representatives team to attend meetings and guidelines in the afternoon with the teacher (P3). These meetings took place in institution laboratory, where they discussed the formatting templates of mathematical applications.

In the first meeting held in the second week of August, attended by 30 students representatives, we and the teacher (P3); at that time, it was proposed the development of some objects. They should contain in the application: 1) history of civilization; 2) history of Mathematics; 3) comics; 4) virtual book; 5) animation; 6) quiz or game; 7) group site and 8) tutorial app.

Occurred two more meetings in the first week of September with the students' representatives and we transmitted technical guidelines for the construction of the project. The collaborative teacher (P3) brought at the time virtual tools that students could use in development and formatting application. In Figure 1, we have images of the resources used by students in project.

We can observe the diversity of resources that the collaborative teacher (P3) offered for students create their App (application) with personal characteristics of each group involved. In the work, the teams created a logo (Online Logo Maker) that should portray team's identity. They produced a questionnaire (Quiz Your Friends) for users to respond and thus generate a concept at the end of the study. They developed a website (Wix) with additional information about proposed project in the classroom and told the history of Mathematics in a relaxed way, using resources such as comics (ToonDoo) and animations (Go!Animate). Finally, they delivered the application to the researcher teacher through an interactive resource called qrcode, as each group of students generated a code for their App and so the tablet reader identified and started automatically the application download process on the teacher's artefact. In Google Play Store, there are many readers of these codes; we used the scan, because it read the codes very quickly and safely. We reaffirm that this resource was efficient to give authenticity of the work delivered

In Figure 2, we have the presentation of one of the applications (group: Chinese civilization) developed by the learners of the project, resulting from research and investigations of both the history and mathematical curiosity, but also the exploitation of available resources for the preparation of app.

We may note some features in Figure 2, because girls formed the group and its logo translated well that gender issue that the teamwork established. We also noted that students cited questions about working with abacus, using fractions, the discovery of the number π, the development of geometry, setting the system decimal and positional numbering using sticks as a numerical representation (1 to 9) and zero as a blank space.

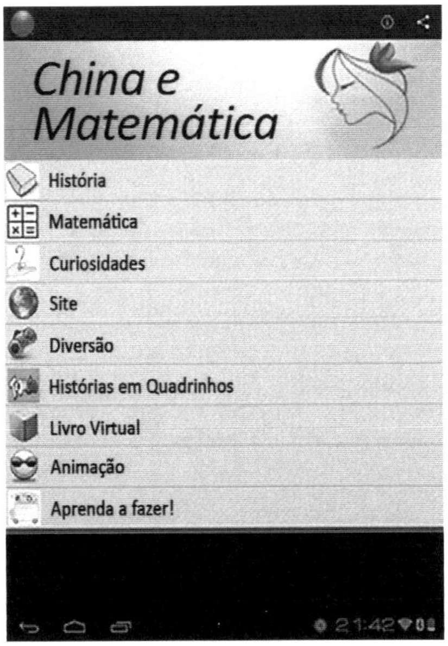

Figure 2. Application developed in group (China). Source: Research Authors.

4. THE SEARCH

4.1 Data and analysis

They focus on the construction of applications developed by students that told about the history of ancient civilizations and how they influence Mathematics to the present day and their contributions in the learning of elementary Mathematics. We assume that it is through this mathematical historical context experienced by students that we will be able to substantiate the contents taught in the classroom. Through a questionnaire with closed questions, observation, reports and analysis of the applications built, it was possible to verify the degree of learning of basic mathematical historical concepts, and its satisfaction and acceptance of the interdisciplinary collaborative work involving the Disciplines of Portuguese, History, Mathematics and Computing. We monitored the construction of the application and it we found that both teachers and students involved in the project brought important contributions in the process of historical mathematical identification using the tablet and the applications produced in collaborative work that generated and allowed the discussion about Mathematics' history.

The students presented the applications through a seminar proposed by the teacher. Students were individually assessed in their expositions, regarding the learning of the observed mathematical concepts.

In Table 2, we have the students responses regarding the issue that talks about the most important discovery of the ancient people searched:

Table 2. Evaluation of the degree of interest in Mathematical discoveries. Source: Research Author.

What most caught your attention in your research, concerning the Mathematical discoveries?	
Replies	**Percentages**
The construction of the number system	39%
Geometry	15%
Curious problems	17%
The drawings and images used for counting and troubleshooting	17%
Arithmetic and Algebra	8%
No fact	3%

That frame shows the students' interest and curiosity in observing writing and numbering system as the starting point of ancient civilizations, because it is through numeration system, that Mathematics is present and grounded in the numerical and social foundations of every civilization, investigations carried out by the groups, it is in the speech of student:

[...] I was intrigued and at the same time surprised when I saw the Chinese numbers, I found it very interesting (Student A).

It is believed that when students did their research and built the application talking about the numerical system, we agreed that the link between the past and the future, according to D'Ambrosio (2008), provokes in the student some discoveries and concepts for his present, of a living and mutable Mathematics, according to the needs of each civilization. The content managed so that the history of Mathematics will better contextualize its teaching with activities that promote a differentiated dynamics in the classroom so that it does not become an unnecessary content for the students. We believe that the history and the use of technologies resources used in this research favored the learning of topics of which the students were previously unaware. As the interdisciplinary project involving the Disciplines of Portuguese, History, Mathematics and Computing, we verified in our questionnaire that students evaluated very positively the work developed with the tablet and the teachers' support.

We also observed that the interdisciplinary activity will be able not only promote a collaborative autonomy between them, but also will promote attitudes and actions in an innovative way regarding mathematics learning, creating concrete relations of reality in which it lives. (FAZENDA, 1994).

Technological interaction promoted by tablet and its applications were essential for other students to do their placements and suggestions in a way to contribute with the continuity of this work.

[...] in the tablet the history and an animation got very interesting as well as the application's activities. The application structure in general got very cool and easy to understand content (Student B).

We note that in this speech the student considers that the structures such as HQ and animations generated by tablet and the applications brought interactive and dynamic elements of motivation action and reaction (LÉVY, 1993). We believed that in these observations the students are in the process of adapting to use the tablets and applications in school dynamics.

We must also to demystify the idea that the teaching of Mathematics is done only unilaterally (teacher – student), that is, there are different ways of learning and not only one.

5. FINAL CONSIDERATIONS

We observed that the majority of applications built shows a Mathematics focus on theory and topics that students have already heard in the classroom. Another fact is the report of its social and cultural importance regarding to the civilization inserted in it.

We think that we were able to answer some of the issues and objectives set out in the work, because the historical mathematical concepts were objects of debate among students involved, and realized that we perceived that they argued about texts and mathematical curiosities established by the groups of the same theme.

The teams have positioned themselves through written arguments and shared between them, thus creating moments of reflection about some historical topics of mathematical content.

The learners expressed the importance of the mathematical discoveries promoted by ancient civilizations and indicated that Mathematics, besides being a knowledge that adapts over time, also promotes coherent logics that reflect our social, cultural, historical and e intellectual progress.

History and mathematical discoveries promote reflections, individual and collective motivations so that everyone shares facts, legends, curiosities and episodes (MIORIM & MIGUEL, 2004). History not only grounds the Mathematics experienced by all of us, but it will also be the basis of future mathematical discoveries in the technological advancement of our civilization. These moments will serve as a point of departure not only for the teacher to contextualize Mathematics, but also so that the teacher can establish with the students an analogy of what they are learning in the classroom.

We also emphasize that the interdisciplinary work associated with the development of classroom applications exposes a motivating structure for students and teachers to explore mathematics in a much more dynamic and challenging way. The use of active methodologies makes it possible to construct new ways of learning, the adoption of mobile devices in the classroom emerges as a facilitator of pedagogical actions to promote learning in the current generation.

It is observed in this article that tablet and its resources were fundamental not only to structure the collective work, but to it also helped direct the interdisciplinary work, impacting positively the discussions, debates and the current understanding of Mathematics taught in the classroom. We reinforce that the participation of collaborating teachers in this project potentiated the effectiveness of the results achieved in this research.

REFERENCES

Araujo Jr, C.F. et. al, 2012. *Tablets at Elementary and Secondary Education: principles and applications.* Terracota, São Paulo, Brazil.

D'Ambrosio, U., 2008. *Concise History of Mathematics in Brazil.* Vozes, Petrópolis, Brazil.

Fazenda, I. C.A., 1994. *Interdisciplinarity history, theory and search.* Papirus, Campinas, Brazil.

Goldman, L., 1979. *Dialectic andculture.* Paz e Terra, Rio de Janeiro, Brazil.

Gomes, H. F., Jan/ Apr 2000, Information Science. *The informational environment and its technologies in the construction of meanings and senses.* Brasília, Brazil, v.29, n.1 Available in: <http://revista. ibict.br/ciinf/index.php/ciinf/issue/archive>. Accessed in: Sep 04th, 2012.

Miorin, M. A. et al, 2004. *History in Mathematics Education: Proposals and challenges.* Autêntica, Belo Horizonte, Brazil.

Radford, L., February 1997, For the Learning of Mathematics. On *Psychology, Historical Epistemology, and the Teaching of Mathematics: towards a Socio-Cultural History of Mathematics.* 17, 1, p.26-33.

Ruiz, A. R. et al., 1998. *Teaching and Knowledge: elements for an action pedagogy.* UEM, Londrina, Brazil.

Teixeira, A. C. et al, 2003. *Educational Software: the difficult start.* New Technologies in Education, 1.1: P.1-7.

Vygotsky, L., 1991. *Thought and language.* 3.ed. M. Fontes, São Paulo, Brazil.

Werthein, J., May/Aug.2000. Magazine Information Science. *The Information Society and its challenge.* Brasília, Brazil, v. 29, n.2, p. 71-77.

ASSESSING THE POTENTIAL OF LEVELUP AS A PERSUASIVE TECHNOLOGY FOR SOUTH AFRICAN LEARNERS

Nhlanhla A. Sibanyoni and Patricia M. Alexander
School of Computing, UNISA,
Pretoria, South Africa

ABSTRACT

Good study behaviour after school hours is an important way of improving learners' chances of success. Learners, once they reach high school, particularly require support that will assist them to study effectively outside the classroom. South African schools are under pressure to improve results in mathematics but besides the homework that schools set, it is difficult for them to motivate the learner to do any additional study of mathematics after school. This suggests that schools could take advantage of technology to create good study behaviour by introducing mobile phones as a persuasive technology. The ubiquity of mobile phones has raised interest in their usage as educational tools and how best to leverage them both during school hours and outside the classroom. However, research in mobile learning argues that mobile phones might enhance learning but might easily distract learners unless there is some control and structure. This paper is based on preliminary research done for a PhD thesis and does not include all the results of the data already collected. The paper conceptualises the first phase of research to assess a specific initiative incorporating the LevelUp application to motivate good studying behaviour outside the classroom for grade 11 learners studying mathematics using their mobile phones or tablets.

KEYWORDS

Persuasive technology, Mathematics, Mobile phones, Motivation.

1. INTRODUCTION

South Africa performance has consistently been rated amongst the worst in mathematics teaching on the world, and the learners' performance was the lowest of all 21 middle-income countries that were compared. This was reported in the Third International Mathematics and Science Study (TIMMSS) when South Africa participated in years 1995, 1999 and 2011 studies (Howie 2003; McCarthy & Oliphant 2013). The teaching of mathematics and numeracy is however key to South Africa achieving its goal of developing a knowledge economy (Howie 2003). Another challenge that South Africa is facing involves providing equally good mathematics teaching to all members of its multicultural society (total population estimated at 55 million in 2016). The extent of the mathematics performance problem has been found to vary in different schools and regions of South Africa (Basic Education 2016).

In response to these challenges, a 10 Key Pillars strategy was developed in 2014 in one of the South African provinces and targets lower income and rural schools as part of intervention to support the development of quality basic education. Information Communication and Technology (ICT) in Education was identified as one of the key pillars and identifies connectivity, content, ICT infrastructure and equipment, teacher development, and efficient technical support and management as being needed (Lesufi 2014).

Various educational applications that were used in a school setting have raised considerable interest in the past; however more recently educators and developers have become interested in educational applications that bridge the gap between the school environment and outside-the-classroom environments. In support of this, learners in the schools participating in a 2014 pilot study were provided with free Wi-Fi and tablets (Lesufi 2014). This provides an opportunity for educational application developers to evaluate and improve their applications. Several promising educational applications developed by South Africans, such as Dr Math and LevelUp, are being introduced to schools. Hence further empirical research is required to assess the effectiveness of these applications. Dr Math was a project that used Mxit, an instant messenger application that ran on non-smartphones to enable participants to send instant messages to each other. Dr Math used the popular and very affordable Mxit application because teenagers were already using Mxit to communicate to friends. It is a platform that enables high school learners to obtain Mathematics homework assistance on their mobile phones from tutors based at a South African University (Butgereit 2007). LevelUp is described in Section 4.1.

The aim of the full study is to draw attention to persuasive technology, using Fogg Behaviour Model (FBM) and take into consideration intrinsic and extrinsic motivation to encourage good study behaviour for secondary level schools learner outside the classroom. This paper is based on preliminary research done for a PhD thesis and does not include all the results of the data already collected. The paper conceptualises the first phase of the research to assess the potential of a specific initiative incorporating the LevelUp application is effective to motivate good studying behaviour outside the classroom for grade 11 learners studying mathematics using their mobile phones or tables.

2. METHODOLOGY

This research uses a case study methodology using mixed methods. LevelUp is the application being used to encourage learners to put in an additional effort to study Mathematics after school hours; Data is being collected from one school and this combination forms the case being studied. Data has already been collected by interviewing developers. This paper concentrates on observations in the form of demonstrations of the app. Feedback from learners will in the coming months be obtained in the school environment using observations, focus groups and questionnaires. Hence this paper reports on motivational theory and its application in persuasive technology.

3. LITERATURE REVIEW

3.1 Mobile learning

The literature review shows that there are a number of studies relating to mobile learning in Mathematics with studies that are concerned with learners outside the classroom as the subjects (Cheung & Slavin 2013; Crompton & Burke 2014) and others that focus on device and software as primary topics (Pereira & Rodrigues 2013). The main purpose of these studies was to provide user friendly applications and to focus on various technology-related areas of research such as wireless mobile, pervasive computing for learning and ubiquitous computing in learning (Crompton & Burke 2014; Chiang et al. 2016).

A recent development is the provision of learner support in school and outside the classroom facilitated by games embedded in mobile technology to provide motivational effects (Koutromanos & Avraamidou 2014; Su & Cheng 2015). We live in a mobile society, where learners are continuously on the move; hence, the focus of ICT in education should be on learner mobility and learning (Sharples, Taylor, & Vavoula 2006). Sharples, Corlett and Westmancott (2002) claim that learning also needs to take place whenever there is a break in the formal education routine with its pre-specified times and places. Formal education cannot provide people with all the knowledge and skills they require throughout their lifetimes. Examples of these extra-curricular learning needs are: addressing immediate problems outside the school boundaries, sharing ideas with peers, participating in continuing vocational and professional development. Mobile technology makes this learning feasible and tools, such as mobile phones, can support learning anytime, anywhere. The use of mobile technology for ubiquitous study has been found to be valued by learners and provides them with a sense of freedom (Su & Cheng 2015; Marçal, Andrade, & Viana 2016).

3.2 Persuasive technology

Many children and adults, regardless of their social strata or culture origin, are apathetic, feel alienated or are irresponsible (Ryan & Deci 2000). This results in a passive attitude or lack of engagement in certain aspects of life. This study focuses on addressing this lack of engagement specifically in terms of learner activity outside the classroom and after school hours. It studies only learners who have to wait for hours for their parents to fetch them at school and learners who walk home (in other words learners who probably spend an extended period after school with very little adult supervision or structured activities). In a school setting learners are expected, and at times pressured to regard studying activities as being meaningful and rewarding. Although studying can be presented as interesting and enjoyable, it is difficult to ensure that the learners view these activities in the same way as leisure activities - as fun. This is because studying requires sustained effort and motivation may be small (Brophy 2004).

Studies of persuasive technology focus on how technology can be used to influence people's attitudes and motivate behaviour. Examples are: motivating people to exercise according to a schedule; motivating a driver to listen to the news; mobile phone applications to remind friends to keep contact with their peers (Oinas-kukkonen & Harjumaa, 2008). Nakajima and Lehdonvirta (2013) argue that it is difficult to change a habit even when you are aware of the benefits of making and acting on the ideal choice as, for example, sticking to a diet.

Professor BJ Fogg founded the persuasive tech lab at Stanford University, where he still directs research into the design of computer technology to change people's behaviour (Laja 2013; Fogg 2016). The Fogg Behaviour Model (FBM) shown in Figure 1 proposes that for a behaviour to occur three elements, namely, motivation, ability and a trigger, must come together simultaneously (Fogg 2009).

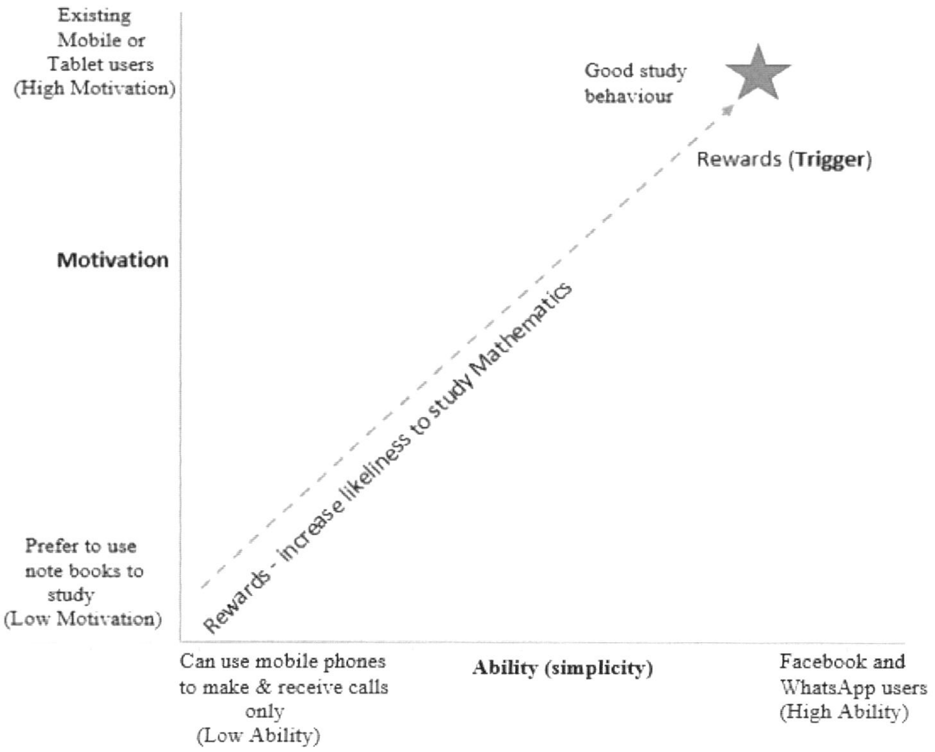

Figure 1. The fogg behaviour model (Fogg 2009).

4. DISCUSSION

4.1 Example of Level as a persuasive technology

The developers of the LevelUp application aim to bring learner study behaviour in Mathematics outside the classroom to the top right of Figure 1. Since the learners are already motivated to use mobile phones or tablets or computers, it is assumed that they will find it easy to use the LevelUp app for studying Mathematics on their mobile devices (ability). By rewarding the learners for using LevelUp for Mathematics with airtime and data (trigger), the developers expect to influence them to prefer to spend time using LevelUp instead of on other apps such as Facebook or WhatsApp. However, it is important to note that there are learners who are already highly motivated, but who cannot use mobile phones (possibly because they are difficult to use, unaffordable or not easy to access). As shown in Figure 1 these learners are likely to give up easily. On the other hand the FMB model predicts that learners who are not interested in studying mathematics using mobile devices, for example those who prefer to use paper or note books, will have low motivation, even though they can use mobile phones or tablets easily when making and receiving calls and accessing Facebook or WhatsApp (easy to use). It is expected that such learners will be irritated when requested to study Mathematics using LevelUp.

4.2 Motivation

To be motivated means to be moved to perform a behaviour; motivation is a reason for our behaviour or action (Spanias, Photini & Middleton 1999; "Oxford University Press" 2015). A person who feels energized or stimulated toward a behaviour or action is deemed be motivated (Ryan & Deci 2000).

Ryan and Deci (2000) explain that motivation has two types, namely, intrinsic and extrinsic motivation. Both of these sources of motivation can shape the development and practice of education in an individual.

Intrinsic motivation refers to an action or behaviour that is performed because it is inherently interesting, satisfying or enjoyable. A person who is intrinsically motivated voluntarily acts for the fun or challenge (Ryan & Deci 2000). For example, learners with intrinsic motivation have the determination or aspiration to participate in learning "for its own sake", and their learning goals tend to focus on understanding and mastery of concepts (Middleton 1995). Thus, learners who are motivated intrinsically engage in tasks using learning methods that differ from those of other learners because they are achieving an understanding of their own learning potential. This motives them to increase time on task, perform more difficult tasks, increase creativity, be self-monitoring, find different ways of processing information and do all of this without an extrinsic motivator (Middleton 1995; Spanias & Middleton 1999).

Extrinsic motivation relates to achievement that is motivated by external factors. In other words, the person performs a task to obtain tangible rewards or due to pressure from someone else. Extrinsic motivation can manifest itself in different ways; for example a learner who does his homework fearing parental sanctions does so in order to achieve the separable outcome of avoiding sanctions. Similarly, a learner who does homework because it will lead to a particular career path is not doing it because she finds it interesting but for its instrumental value (Ryan & Deci 2000).

In a study conducted by Gonzalez-Dehass et al. (2005), teachers rated learners whose parents monitored, enforced, or helped with homework as showing less initiative, autonomy, persistence and satisfaction in doing their schoolwork. The study also discovered that learners reported being extrinsically motivated and dependent on external sources for academic guidance and evaluation when their parents were involved in monitoring, enforcing, or helping with homework. The study suggests that parents who are involved with their children's schoolwork should be less controlling and that better ways of parental involvement should be sought.

4.3 LevelUp application

The reward system is the heart of LevelUp app, as it is intended to encourage learners to test their knowledge through daily challenges in exchange for rewards (The Reach Trust 2016). The LevelUp reward system works similarly to leading South African loyalty programmes, such as Discovery Vitality (Discovery 2016). The app encourages learner engagement by immediately awarding 500 tokens just for signing up, and by welcoming the learner with positive messages such as "Congratulations and AWESOME, let's go!" The initial screen explains to the learner on how to earn more tokens. Each level tells the learner how many tokens are needed to move to the next level, the tokens rewarded thus far and the number of daily challenges. Challenges include solving Mathematics problems and answering questions on politics, health and entertainment as part of a quiz. Once the learner submits a correct answer she or he earns points.

The learner needs to accumulate enough tokens to redeem them for coupons for products (these are basic household items like toiletries) or for airtime at a large supermarket chain. Hence virtual rewards are converted into concrete rewards. The process to redeem the coupons, where they can be redeemed and the number of tokens required per product or for airtime is explained in order to enable a quick coupon cash-in time. The type of reward and indeed the monetary value has in the case of LevelUp been chosen bearing in mind the fact that the learners are in greatest need of Maths motivation in SA are those from families where money is extremely tight. In fact the award of air time is essential to facilitate further use of LevelUp.

5. RESULTS

How does persuasive technology facilitate learners study behavior after school, that's where level up comes in?

Developer 1: We have strong belief that the South African school system is not perfect, we feel that learners are not always given the chance that they deserve, while it is good to address the school system it's not the only way we can do this. There is an opportunity to provide extra support for learners outside of the traditional school system. That's what we try to do, we are based on the assumption that learners are eager to learn they just needed to be given the opportunities. We were trying to use technology and trying to distribute our solutions, so they can so this at home with the phone that they already own.

Do you think it is working as it should?

Developer 2: Not completely, I think we were a little overly optimistic about the enthusiasm that the learners show. We did realize that a lot of them are just very jaded and they don't quite take the opportunity that we give them in the way that we hoped. It turns out they look at the tool and they like ah this is still work. Part of it is also our short coming where we feel we can make the app more interesting. There's the saying that you can lead a horse to water but you can't make it drink. We did inspire quite a few people, we have a few people that follow along and do their challenges every day and see the opportunity that this presents to them but a lot of people also play for a few days and then quit

Developer 3: I think at a technical level it's working as it should, so we don't' have any technical issues with the way the product works. We haven't had the take up of the product that we'd have like to have, so technically we've done fine but we spent quite a lot of money on marketing and we've visited a lot of schools, while the feedback has been very good from the people using the product we haven't had the scale that we'd have like to have seen and that's been disappointing. It seems clear that we still haven't solved the demand problem even though we have incentives there. The majority of learners are not demanding the product that we are offering so that has been frustrating.

How does level up rewards system encourage learner's self-study?

Developer 4: It's not tied to the classroom it's completely self-study, they have to get motivated on their own account, they have to sign up, they have to start doing the challenges on a regular bases. The challenges are fairly short and fairly simple in a way, some of them used to be really hard, we found that too many people were getting frustrated that way so we made the challenges easier.

Even if there were rewards?

Developer 5: Yes, I think there's only so much you can do on a relatively small device where you don't have your computer nearby. The way the challenges are now the learners get something out of it, first of all they practice their reading comprehension, which alone is a practice I think is good for them. Then we add some follow up links like if you wanna know more about this, we used to have classroom content in the app and we removed that recently because it was quite expensive for us and we felt that wasn't so popular with the learners. Mostly it was because that content was from a third party and it was that terribly well proof read, it wasn't good quality and we had to pay for it, as a business it didn't make sense anymore. I think learners had the opportunity of drilling deeper and understanding more about a topic, I'm not sure how many learners used that opportunity.

6. CONCLUSION

Using the FBM, LevelUp app designers should first define the desired behaviour that the learners should achieve. In this study, learners should use LevelUp. This will help LevelUp developers to identify what discourages learners from studying Mathematics using their mobile phones or tablets. For example, it will be instructive if learners are found not to be using the app but are using their mobile phones or tablets for social purposes.

The advantage of using FBM is to gain insight into the psychological element that is lacking, that is whether motivation, ability or a trigger is missing. The disadvantage of using this model without considering the intrinsic or extrinsic motivation, is that learners' intrinsic motivation could be undermined. For example, if rewards are not available learners might lose interest in using LevelUp as they have developed a habit of expecting to be rewarded for doing any task.

The results from the interview with the developers show that the developers are not sure why the learners are not really motivated to use LevelUp on their mobile phones or tablets. The importance of the full study whose first concepts are explained in this paper is to help developers to understand motivation and thereafter to build persuasive educational apps that are sensitive to learner's intrinsic and extrinsic motivation. An example is apps that can reinforce intrinsic motivation and hence help to increase learners' creativity. However the theory recommends that tasks should not be too easy and adults should not help too much by providing answers or by trying to increase ability or extrinsic motivation too actively (too many reminder messages).

The next part of the empirical research of this study will be based on observation and feedback from learners in a single class regarding an existing mobile app (LevelUp). For future research, design science research studies should be conducted with more diverse sample data using FBM in conjunction with intrinsic and extrinsic motivation.

REFERENCES

Anon, 2015. Oxford University Press. Available at: http://www.oxforddictionaries.com/ definition/english/motivation [Accessed April 25, 2015].

Anon, 2016. The Reach Trust. Available at: http://mylevelup.mobi/ [Accessed February 23, 2016].

Basic Education, 2016. *National Senior Certificate - School Performance Report*,

Brophy, J., 2004. *Motivating Students to Learn Second Edition* Second., London: Lawrence Erlbaum Associates.

Butgereit, L., 2007. Math on Mxit: The Medium is the Message. *CSIR Researchspace*, (Accessed: 2014-10-10). Available at: http://researchspace.csir.co.za/ dspace/bitstream/10204/1785/1/Butgereit1_2007.pdf.

Cheung, A.C.K. & Slavin, R.E., 2013. The effectiveness of educational technology applications for enhancing mathematics achievement in K-12 classrooms : A. *Educational Research Review*, 9, pp.88–113.

Chiang, F.K. et al., 2016. Research and trends in mobile learning from 1976 to 2013: A content analysis of patents in selected databases. *British Journal of Educational Technology*, 47(6), pp.1006–1019.

Crompton, H. & Burke, D., 2014. Review of trends in mobile learning studies in mathematics: A meta-analysis. In *Communications in Computer and Information Science*. pp. 304–314.

Fogg, B.J., 2009. A behavior model for persuasive design. In *Persuasive '09: Proceedings of the 4th International Conference on Persuasive Technology*. California: ACM. Available at: http://captology.stanford.edu/projects/behaviordesign.html.

Fogg, B.J., 2016. BJ Fogg's Behavior Model. Available at: http://www.behaviormodel.org/ [Accessed February 15, 2017].

Gonzalez-Dehass, A.R., Willems, P.P. & Holbein, M.F.D., 2005. Examining the relationship between parental involvement and student motivation. *Educational Psychology Review*, 17(2), pp. 99–123.

Howie, S.J., 2003. Language and other background factors affecting secondary pupils â€™ performance in Mathematics in South Africa. *African Journal of Research in SMT Education*, 7, pp.1–20.

Koutromanos, G. & Avraamidou, L., 2014. The use of mobile games in formal and informal learning environments: a review of the literature. *Educational Media International*, 51(1), pp.49–65.

Laja, P., 2013. How to Use Behavioral Design for Boosting Conversions (Using The Fogg Behavior Model). Available at: https://conversionxl.com/how-to-use-behavioral-design-for-boosting-conversions-using-the-fogg-behavior-model/ [Accessed February 15, 2017].

Lesufi, P., 2014. *Media Statement*, South Africa.

Marçal, E., Andrade, R. & Viana, W., 2016. Mobile Phone Text Messaging to Increase Student Participation : An Experience in a Blended Course. *ACM*, pp.239–245.

McCarthy, J. & Oliphant, R., 2013. *Mathematics Outcomes in South African Schools. What are the facts? What should be done?*, Available at: http://www.cde.org.za/images/pdf/MATHEMATICS OUTCOMES IN SOUTH AFRICAN SCHOOLS.pdf.

Middleton, J.A., 1995. A study of intrinsic motivation in the Mathematics classroom : A personal constructs approach. *Journal for Research in Mathematics Education*, 26(3), pp.254–279.

Nakajima, T. & Lehdonvirta, V., 2013. Designing motivation using persuasive ambient mirrors. *ACM*, 17(1), pp.107–126.

Oinas-kukkonen, H. & Harjumaa, M., 2008. Towards deeper understanding of persuasion in software and Information Systems. *IEEE Conference Publication*, pp.200–205.

Pereira, O.R.E. & Rodrigues, J.J.P.C., 2013. Survey and analysis of current mobile learning applications and technologies. *ACM Computing Surveys*, 46(2), p.27:1-27:35.

Ryan, R.M. & Deci, E.L., 2000. Intrinsic and extrinsic motivations: Classic definitions and new directions. *Contemporary Educational Psychology*, 25(1), pp.54–67.

Ryan, R.M. & Deci, E.L., 2000. Self-determination theory and the facilitation of intrinsic motivation, social development, and well-being. *The American Psychologist*, 55(1), pp.68–78.

Sharples, M., Corlett, D. & Westmancott, O., 2002. The design and implementation of a mobile learning resource. *Personal and Ubiquitous Computing*, 6(3), pp.220–234.

Sharples, M., Taylor, J. & Vavoula, G., 2006. A theory of learning for the mobile age. In R. Andrews & C. Haythornthwaite, eds. *The Sage Handbook of Elearning Research*. London: Sage Publications, pp. 221–247.

Spanias, Photini A & Middleton, J.A., 1999. Motivation for achievement in mathematics : findings , generalizations, and criticisms of the research. *Journal for Research in Mathematics Education*, 30(1), pp.65–88.

Su, C.H. & Cheng, C.H., 2015. A mobile gamification learning system for improving the learning motivation and achievements. *Journal of Computer Assisted Learning*, 31(3), pp.268–286.

#GOTTACATCHEMALL: EXPLORING POKEMON GO IN SEARCH OF LEARNING ENHANCEMENT OBJECTS

Annamaria Cacchione[1], Emma Procter-Legg[2] and Sobah Abbas Petersen[3]
[1]*Universidad Complutense de Madrid, Facultad de Filologia, Av.da Complutense sn, 28040 Madrid, Spain*
[2]*Independent; Abingdon, Oxon, UK*
[3]*SINTEF Technology and Society, Trondheim, Norway*

ABSTRACT

The Augmented Reality Game, Pokemon Go, took the world by storm in the summer of 2016. City landscapes were decorated with amusing, colourful objects called Pokemon, and the holiday activities were enhanced by catching these wonderful creatures. In light of this, it is inevitable for mobile language learning researchers to reflect on the impact of this game on learning and how it may be leveraged to enhance the design of mobile and ubiquitous technologies for mobile and situated language learning. This paper analyses the game Pokemon Go and the players' experiences according to a framework developed for evaluating mobile language learning and discusses how Pokemon Go can help to meet some of the challenges faced by earlier research activities.

KEYWORDS

Pokemon Go, MALL, Learning, Augmented Reality, Gamification, Situated learning.

1. INTRODUCTION

During the early summer of 2016, you didn't need to be a Pokemon Go player to realize that world demography underwent a seismic shift with the introduction of Pokemon Go. Our surroundings have been augmented by the introduction of this colorful new species of not-fully-human-beings, the Pokemon, that many humans want to catch, train and somehow dominate. According to Wikipedia, the game has reportedly been downloaded by more than 130 million people worldwide since its launch (August 2016).

The successful reboot of the Pokemon into augmented reality – they existed before in the late 90's[1]– has sparked the interest of mobile learning researchers and learning technologists in general: what can we borrow from this phenomenon that has caught the interest of so many people of all ages, to improve the learning process? What are its more interesting features in terms of "learning enhancements"? Is Augmented Reality the actual trigger of this success or is there something else we should consider? Moreover, how can the main features of the game be incorporated into other environments specifically built for learning purposes?

In this paper we aim to analyse the Pokemon Go (henceforth PG) game within the learning/teaching perspective and, in particular, within the mobile learning and MALL paradigms. We will apply the evaluation framework for mobile language learning that we developed in (Cacchione et al. 2015), in order to identify key factors – especially those related to neuroscience – which influence its effect, impact and success. A comparison between PG and Geocashing will illustrate the evolution of the concept of location-based games – a concept that is very close to that of situated learning that we have explored in several previous works. Finally, we will summarize our findings, also trying to depict possible further scenarios integrating the elements that our analysis has shown to be particularly interesting and effective.

[1]According to the Independent in 2007 Pokemon was the 2nd highest selling game franchise, behind Mario, with 155 million games sold. https://web.archive.org/web/20070112150103/http://news.independent.co.uk/world/science_technology/article2141636.ece

2. THE POKEMON GO EXPERIENCE

Pokémon Go is a free, location-based augmented reality game developed for mobile devices. Players use GPS on their mobile device to locate, capture, battle, and train virtual creatures (a.k.a. Pokémon), which appear on screen overlaying the image seen through the device's camera. This makes it seem like the Pokemon are in the same real-world location as the player.

(a) (b)

Figure 1. (a) A Pokestop corresponding to a piece of street art, a mural of a robot; (b) The robot on the wall of a school in Campobasso suburbs.

The basic playing mode is very easy: just search for a Pokemon and trying to catch it with the Pokeball, which you flick aiming at the circle that appears over its head. When you run out of Pokéballs, you can collect more from PokéStops, which are usually found in towns and cities or places of interest, see Figure 1. From level 5, you can access gyms and join teams to battle. If you want to be a PG expert player, you can study strategies and discuss moves with other users both on and offline. Moreover, there are many external (i.e. not directly linked to the game) support pages and tutorials on the Internet, both by Niantic (Pokemon Go company) and user generated groups. Many of them offer crowd-sourced tools, like maps, to help users find Pokemon in their area of interest. Similar to many other games, you don't have to be an expert player to enjoy PG and you can play it at several levels. You could open the app and enjoy the theme tune while following your avatar around in the real/virtual space and see which Pokemon appear in your surroundings. You might have fun by taking pictures of your friends with Pidgey on their shoulders while drinking beer in the pub. Or, of course, you could organize hunting expeditions with your Whatsapp PG group. The entry level is very easy and intuitive: just download the app, create your avatar and start exploring. It's a simple concept, but builds in complexity as you progress through the levels of the game.

In Figure 2, you see AnnaSibel encountering two Pokemon: Zubat (on the left) and Paras. Clicking on Zubat, it enters AnnaSibel's room and flies over the computer monitor (picture 2). Then Zubat is caught with the Pokeball (the white and red ball under AnnaSibel in the 1st picture).

The user-friendliness of the game is surely one of its success factors. But what are the others? First of all, the game is beautiful: the environments are colorful, detailed, graphically curate. The overall impression is almost that of a 3D space. The user identity is customizable and you can choose how you want to appear in the game (name, hair, eyes, outfit). The soundtrack is nice and there are good sound effects for commands too. Pages tracking your records – the Pokedex, i.e. the inventory of Pokemon you caught, the tools collected etc. – are easy to browse.

When you meet a Pokemon for the first time, it is astonishing: seeing a little screaming creature flying in your kitchen is amazing. Then you want to take a selfie with it before catching it – and sending it to your skeptical friends. Afterwards, when you are more familiar with the game, the surprise effect diminishes but never fades away, it is frequently reinforced by encountering new types of monsters.

Then, there is the "activity factor": you have to walk around instead of just standing there or lying on the sofa, and nobody else can catch a Pokemon for you - you have to take action. That gives you a reason for going out for a walk – there have been news reports of people losing a significant amount of weight by playing PG. It also gives you a reason to talk to other people who you might otherwise not meet: to give and receive hints, to know how to beat stronger ones, or to know where the nearest Pokestops are.

Pokestops are key points for socializing. They are special sites of interest – monuments, statues, portals etc. – where you can get Pokeballs and other useful tools. They are geo-localized like all the rest, but they open up and release their tools only when you get close enough to them. That's why you find groups of people hanging around Pokestops with their smartphones talking to each other about the game. Poke stops also improve the knowledge of the sites, allowing (better: forcing) you to discover corners of your city you would have never seen otherwise.

(a) (b)

Figure 2. (a) The avatar AnnaSibel meets two Pokemon; (b) Zubat flies over AnnaSibel's computer monitor.

3. EXPERIENCES FROM MOBILE ASSISTED LANGUAGE LEARNING

Language learning and technologies to support language learning have been influenced in many ways though mobile and ubiquitous technologies; from electronic dictionaries to lists of pictures and words in our pockets (Joseph, Binstead, & Suthers, 2005); from capturing and sharing language content (Pemberton, Winter, & Fallahkair, 2010) to creative conversations with friends, teachers and other language learners (Petersen, Procter-Legg, & Cacchione, 2014). Perceptions of MALL have evolved from a focus on the device itself to the social and collaborative experiences of the learners. The affordances of mobile and ubiquitous technologies today have taken us beyond a single learner and her mobile phone to multiple learners interacting to experience unique and personalized learning experiences through a seamless blend of technologies and concepts such as mobile devices, social networks, cloud computing and gamification. In (Kukulska-Hulme, 2010), and (Kukulska-Hulme, 2009), Kukulska-Hulme provides an overview of interesting and game changing applications of technologies that have influenced MALL. One of the trends identified by Kukulska-Hulme is situated and immersive learning, where learners interact with their immediate surroundings and collaborate with people to create their own individualised learning experiences.

However, it was noted that the pervasiveness of the devices alone may not be enough to facilitate real interactions between people. This was confirmed through some of our own studies with LingoBee, a crowd-sourced, situated, mobile and collaborative language learning app (SIMOLA, 2012). It is indeed the creative use of the affordances of the technology and the devices that lead to a culture of learning where interactions play a central role.

LingoBee was designed to engage language learners to collect interesting and colloquial language content during their everyday activities and share them with other learners through a cloud-based repository. During the studies, the app was introduced to the learners as a part of their language courses, encouraging them to bridge the classroom learning with their daily activities (Procter-Legg, Petersen, & Cacchione, 2014). Learners captured and shared content using their mobile phones and other learners could annotate, edit and comment on them, often leading to a conversation among several learners.

We noticed that the learners needed prompting and careful design of learning-related activities to stimulate the use of the app. In addition, it was hard to sustain the use of it beyond the studies due to a number of reasons such as the sheer volume and influence of other social networks (Procter-Legg et al., 2014). Nevertheless, it was evident from the interviews with learners that while they liked the affordances of LingoBee, they still expected the app to include features to nudge or stimulate learners to use it. Some of the challenges that were identified from the evaluations can be summarised as below:

- Learners found it difficult to interact with native speakers or other learners in the real world as the technology was designed for collaboration and social interaction through LingoBee's cloud-based repository.
- Explicit features for motivating learners (e.g. such as gamification, rewards for contributions, etc.) to use the app were not included as it was assumed that social networking norms such as "like" or "flag" or the possibility to contribute and enhance an existing contribution (wiki functionality) would serve as intrinsic motivation to learners.
- As with other mobile learning applications, the context in which learning takes place or what triggered it continues to be a challenge. When a learner makes a contribution to the repository, referred to as a "LingoBee moment" (Adlard, Ottway, & Procter-Legg, 2012), we know the time, GPS location and whether the learner contributed multimedia or something about the environment. However, it was still inadequate to understand what may have triggered the learning and the best way to enhance deep learning and retention.

4. AUGMENTED REALITY AND MALL

"Put simply, augmented reality is a technology that overlays computer generated visuals over the real world through a device camera – bringing your surroundings to life and interacting with sensors such as location and heart rate to provide additional information" (Ramirez, 2014).

PG has brought Augmented Reality (AR) to our neighborhoods, schools and cities and both children and adults have been swept off their feet like never before. AR has existed for many years; in 1968, Ivan Sutherland developed the first head-mounted system using computer-generated graphics to show users wireframe drawings. In 1990, Boeing's Tim Caudell coined the term "Augmented Reality" to describe an electronic system that guides workers to install electrical cables and fuselage in aircrafts. AR has been a part of the entertainment industry since the 1990s and in 2000, Hirokazu Kato created ARToolkit, an open source software library to support the creation of AR applications. More recently, AR has become accessible for individual consumers and smaller scale development companies through Google Glass, Reckon Jet, Solos and similar products from other companies. PG has no doubt impacted the future of AR technology and its role in future mobile applications.

AR applications in language learning and education in general has, until now, been limited, perhaps due to the limitations of the technology (Jain, Manweiler, & Choudhury, 2015). Affordances of AR technology in classrooms were reported by Pemberton and Winter (Pemberton & Winter, 2009) where they identified the benefits of spatial 3D representations of molecules and atoms in learning biology. Examples of using AR with mobile devices include overlays of building in Oslo for urban design by Architecture students (Liestøl & Morrison, 2015). Cook has written about augmented reality and location-based field trips based on the CONTSENS project (Cook, 2010). In the EU MIRROR project focused on reflection and learning, mixed reality was used to provide a scenario or a situation as a problem that the user had to solve, to train civil protection workers to manage crisis situations (Di Loreto, Mora, & Divitini, 2013).

A possible reading of PG in terms of novelty and innovation potential, directly related to its impact on the audience, is that "it is the ultimate mash-up", having combined three key innovative technological components into one single highly attractive and engaging environment: games and gamification, virtual reality and the Internet of Things (IoT) (Buff, 2016). Pokémon Go takes IoT and lets you put virtual things into it and seamlessly combines them into a coherent story in an impressive way. Although PG does not use the concept of IoT in the traditional way where we imagine sensors, its power no doubt lies in the unique mash-up of technologies that have previously existed only separately, and put together in an irresistible packaging.

5. EVALUATION OF PG FROM A LEARNING PERSPECTIVE

In this section we try to evaluate the game to identify its potentialities from an educational perspective. In other words, we want to see if PG can be exploited as a good learning environment – or, better, which of its peculiar features can be identified as successful learning elements, to be "exported" to other learning environments too. We will apply the evaluation framework developed in 2015 for mobile learning applications (Cacchione, Procter-Legg, Petersen, & Winter, 2015). The framework is composed of a set of factors of different nature – neuroscientific, technological, organisational and pedagogical – and aims to provide a comprehensive account of what plays a major role in ensuring effective learning via mobile devices. Even if we are hereby comparing objects of a different nature – a game app and a possible learning app – the comparison is made possible by a couple of relevant factors: a) they are both mobile, context and situation-oriented; b) they both promote interactivity among users, and therefore are social-oriented. We of course cannot evaluate PG's pedagogical features because it was not built for learning purposes, but we will focus on the neuro-scientific aspects, by examining the set of criteria schematized in the diagram below and linking them to the technological features.

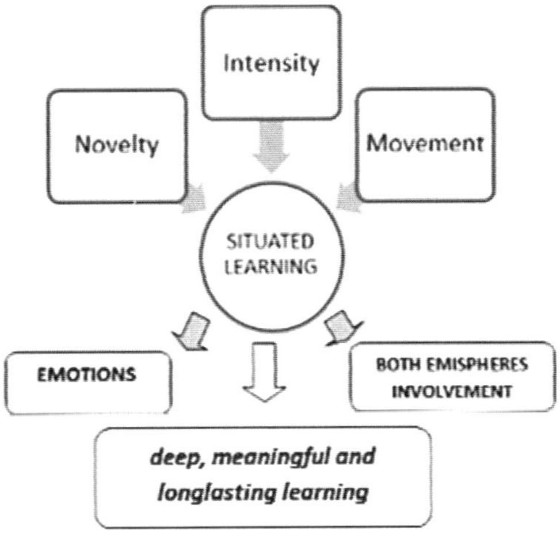

Figure 3. Evaluation framework for Mobile Language Learning.

At first glance, all the criteria included in the evaluation framework, presented in Figure 3, seem to be present in PG. Situated learning (in circle in the middle) is an instructional approach developed by Lave and Wenger (Lave & Wenger, 1991), following the work of Dewey, Vygotsky and others (Clancey, 1995), who claim that students are more inclined to learn by actively participating in the learning experience. Situated learning essentially is a matter of creating meaning from the real activities of daily living. It can obviously occur without any technological support, but the ICT revolution of the last decade caused its very explosion, essentially due to the advent of mobile devices and smartphones in particular. Technology development allowed situational learning to make a big step forward: when the user enters a new site/context/situation, new contents pop up from reality surrounding him/her. That is one of the main peculiar AR features: the real life experience is enriched by new objects popping up from where we turn our attention to. This is PG's way of providing the user with game-object, i.e. Pokemon. Therefore, we can affirm PG to be strongly situated.

Situated learning is promoted by novelty, intensity and movement. PG is the game of the moment: no doubt about its novelty. If, on one side, all its components are not so innovative taken per se and individually, they do are as they are integrated into one single game. According to Phingbodhipakkiya, the game is one continuous playscape (Phingbodhipakkiya, 2016). Our brains love novelty, and the same dopaminergic reward pathway that's accessed when we talk about ourselves is also activated when we experience new things. Activation of this pathway directs individuals to repeat what they just did to get more rewards. In the case of Pokémon Go, you're experiencing new things every single time you play the game, and that drives you to go to new locations, so you can find new Pokemon.

Movement is constitutive of PG, because only very few Pokemon are available at your home. You have to search for them in the streets and in the squares, and that's why some news reported of many PG players having lost weight by playing every day; e.g. (Eastaugh, 2016). Getting out of the house to play stimulates real world communication and interaction, finding Pokemon collaboratively (Hirsh-Pasek & Golinkoff, 2016). An example of this is people at PokeStops talking to each other and the collaboration and play sessions across generations such as a mother and child catching Pokemon. PG has mobilised communities and brought local history to the forefront; people have learned new things about their geographical areas and their neighborhoods (Butcher, 2016).

Intensity is given by the environment structure and by its "furnishing". There are plenty of interesting stimuli such as PokeStops and gyms, besides, of course, Pokemon themselves. As said before, the environment is colorful and well designed so to offer an intense and entertaining experience. Nevertheless, intensity is more questionable than other characteristics. It is difficult to assess, as it is more linked to personal, subjective perception and, furthermore, tends to vary from user to user and from event to event.

As shown in the diagram above, all the considered features are put in relationship with deep, meaningful and long-lasting learning. The diagram shows in fact that novelty, intensity, movement are constitutive of situated learning and that situated learning is linked to/can generate emotions. Emotions are directly connected to good learning, where good means deep, meaningful and long-lasting – and this result can be obtained by involving both the brain hemispheres, like emotions can actually do.

Emotions is one of the factors that really affect learning through the release of the relevant chemicals such as dopamine in the brain, and activity and emotions can improve the synaptic connections, thus enhancing the learning (Zull, 2004) and (Bajaj, Bellotti, Berta, & de Gloria, 2016). The emotional impact is layered by the factors described above and by others, e.g. the personalized avatars, making the game more personal and more real. Research has shown that virtual responses activate the same neural networks as real experiences, in the same way that images of rewards and real rewards are perceived almost identically in the brain. PG takes cues from the actual environment and couples them with the virtual world for greater impact. For example, if you're near a body of water you might catch a Magikarp, and if you're in the subway you might catch a Rattata [*Magicarp is a carp-fish and Rattata a rat, AN*] — this water/land congruence increases your sense of delight and accomplishment. Bundling emotions strengthens the positive association with the game and keeps you hooked.

Furthermore, emotions are fed by the social and collaborative dimension: PG stimulates dialogue among users to find the best solutions. The social and collaborative dimension has been described as one that is important for learning, as seen in some multiplayer games (Bajaj et al., 2016). PG players exchange information about sites and Pokemon presence. PG players are a community; they have dedicated pages on social networks and informal groups of friends living and playing in the same area. This aspect is related to creative ways of problem solving, e.g. collaboratively. One of the first players to catch all the Pokemon was a Singaporian, who did not leave Singapore to achieve his goal. He asked friends who were abroad to help him catch some Pokemon that were only found in specific parts of the world, e.g. Australia or New Zealand, by using his account. However, when accused of cheating, his claimed he was just solving a problem in creative ways ("First Singaporean to catch all 145 Pokemon admits getting help from overseas friends," 2016).

All the elements composing the diagram are therefore included in PG, and can both explain its success and provide the basis for building a learning environment with similar features. Our evaluation can be defined as positive, and can offer suggestions to exploit PG-like objects for learning purposes.

6. CONCLUSION

This paper provides an analysis of PG according to an evaluation framework previously developed in order to identify key factors for language learning – especially neuroscience related – influencing its effect, impact and success. We draw from our previous experiences with LingoBee and other mobile language learning technologies and identify how the challenges that were experienced earlier by our learners may be resolved and how the learning experiences may be improved using AR technology. In this respect, PG and the playful experiences have no doubt provided new energy and stimulations to designers of learning technologies. PG also shows the maturity of AR technology, which will encourage more researchers and developers to work with AR applications.

Regarding the PG learning potential, its structural features make it very suitable to promote situated learning in users. Novelty, intensity and movement are core characteristics of PG and allow for the generation of emotions that can strongly favour the learning process. As already highlighted, PG players reported to have learnt a lot about places and monuments they have never noted before. This kind of learning occurs spontaneously, is totally embedded in the game and, as it is driven by the pleasure of discovery, it is expected to last and form stable knowledge. That corresponds to the ideal form of learning that AR and SL -based apps like PG could effectively promote.

It should be noted that the PG phenomenon is relatively new and therefore lacks detailed analytics and scientific evaluations as a support for learning. Our future work will include analyzing the features in PG in more detail from the perspective of the neuroscience of learning and involving more PG players for an in-depth understanding of their experiences.

In spite of the enormous success of PG during the summer of 2016, there have been reports of players getting bored and expressions of relief from players when they have reached a certain level or caught all the Pokemon (seen the last "Gotcha"). It is ironic that the game manages to engage the players so intensely for a while, yet it has not always managed to sustain that engagement in a lasting way. Perhaps the thrill of going up a level wears off after a while and the end state of the game is a natural end. If PG has had a lasting behaviour change on the players is to be seen. It would be interesting to see if the PG players that had been more active than usual continue their level of activity after completing the game. In language learning, we need learners to acquire good learning habits that last over a long time; i.e. a behaviour and attitude change. So, perhaps the aim and thus the design of the technology may be different for a game or an app to support situated language learning. A last observation can be made about a powerful side effect of PG, strictly related to its situationality. One of the main benefits of situated mobile language learning is the acquisition of colloquial vocabulary and immersion in the culture. Pokemon GO certainly provides an immersive environment for the players where they will at least enhance their vocabulary with "Gotcha"!

REFERENCES

Adlard, R., Ottway, T., & Procter-Legg, E. (2012). Crowdsourcing with the Lingobee App: A Study in facilitating pollination across language and culture in self-directed learning. *International Journal of Computer-Assisted Language Learning and Teaching (IJCALLT), 2*(4).

Bajaj, N., Bellotti, F., Berta, R., & de Gloria, A. (2016). A Neuroscience based approach to Game Based Learning Design. In R. Bottino, J. Jeuring, & R. C. Veltkamp (Eds.), *Games and Learning Alliance: 5th International Conference, GALA 2016* (pp. 445-454): Springer.

Buff, T. (2016). Peek-a-boo, Pikachu: how the augmented reality of Pokémon Go could transform learning. Retrieved from https://www.agylia.com/blog/mobile/how-the-augmented-reality-of-pokemon-go-could-transform-learning

Butcher, A. (2016, 14 July). Pokémon Go See the World in Its Splendor. *New York Times*. Retrieved from http://www.nytimes.com/2016/07/17/opinion/sunday/pokemon-go-see-the-world-in-its-splendor.html?action=click&contentCollection=Asia%20Pacific&module=RelatedCoverage&region=Marginalia&pgtype=article&_r=2

Cacchione, A., Procter-Legg, E., Petersen, S. A., & Winter, M. (2015). A proposal for an integrated evaluation framework for mobile language learning: Lessons learned from SIMOLA - Situated mobile language learning. *Journal of Universal Computer Science, 21*(10), 1248-1268.

Clancey, W. J. (1995). *A tutorial on situated learning*. Paper presented at the International Conference on Computers and Education, Taiwan. http://konstruktivismus.uni-koeln.de/didaktik/situierteslernen/clancey_situated_learning.PDF

Cook, J. (2010). Mobile Phones as Mediating Tools within Augmented Contexts for Development *International Journal of Mobile and Blended Learning, 2*(3).

Di Loreto, I., Mora, S., & Divitini, M. (2013). Supporting Crisis Training with a Mobile Game System. In M. Ma, M. Oliveira, S. A. Petersen, & J. B. Hauge (Eds.), *Serious Games Development and Applications* (Vol. 8101, pp. 165-177). Berlin Heidelberg: Springer.

Eastaugh, S. (2016, 29/07/2016). British Pokemon Go player says catching 'em all shed pounds. *CNN Online*. Retrieved from http://edition.cnn.com/2016/07/29/health/pokemon-go-sam-clark-lost-weight/

First Singaporean to catch all 145 Pokemon admits getting help from overseas friends. (2016, 19 August). *The Star Online*. Retrieved from http://www.thestar.com.my/news/regional/2016/08/19/first-singaporean-to-catch-all-145-pokemon-admits-getting-help-from-overseas-friends/

Hirsh-Pasek, K., & Golinkoff, R. M. (2016). Pokémon Go: A window into how we might reimagine learning #BecomingBrilliant. Retrieved from https://www.brookings.edu/blog/education-plus-development/2016/07/19/pokemon-go-a-window-into-how-we-might-reimagine-learning-becomingbrilliant/

Jain, P., Manweiler, J., & Choudhury, R. R. (2015). *OverLay: Practical Mobile Augmented Reality*. Paper presented at the MobiSys'15, Florence, Italy. http://synrg.csl.illinois.edu/papers/overlay.pdf

Joseph, S., Binstead, K., & Suthers, D. (2005). *Photostudy: Vocabulary Learning and Collaboration on Fixed and Mobile Devices.* Paper presented at the 3rd IEEE International Workshop on Wireless and Mobile Technologies in Education, Tokushima, Japan.

Kukulska-Hulme, A. (2009). Will Mobile Learning change Language Learning. *ReCALL, 21*(2), 157-165.

Kukulska-Hulme, A. (2010). Learning Cultures on the Move: Where are we heading? *Educational Technology and Society, 13*(4), 4-14.

Lave, J., & Wenger, E. (1991). *Situated Learning: Legitimate Peripheral Participation*: Cambridge University Press.

Liestøl, G., & Morrison, A. (2015). The Power of Place and Perspective. In A. de Souza e Silva & M. Sheller (Eds.), *Mobility and Locative Media: Mobile Communication in Hybrid Spaces* (pp. 207-): Routeledge.

Pemberton, L., & Winter, M. (2009). *Collaborative Augmented Reality in Schools*. Paper presented at the 8th International Conference on Computer Supported Collaborative Learning, CSCL2009, Rhodes, Greece.

Pemberton, L., Winter, M., & Fallahkair, S. (2010). Collaborative Mobile Knowledge Sharing for Language Learners. *Journal of the Research Centre for Educational Technology, 6*(1).

Petersen, S. A., Procter-Legg, E., & Cacchione, A. (2014). LingoBee: Engaging Mobile Language Learners Through Crowd-Sourcing. *International Journal of Mobile and Blended Learning, 6*(2).

Phingbodhipakkiya, A. (2016). The Neuroscience of Pokemon GO. Retrieved from http://blog.ed.ted.com/2016/08/01/the-neuroscience-of-pokemon-go/

Procter-Legg, E., Petersen, S. A., & Cacchione, A. (2014). LingoBee Mobile App: Connecting to Language Learners through Technology. In S. Leone (Ed.), *Synergic Integration of Formal and Informal E-Learning Environments for Adult Lifelong Learners* (pp. 199-221): IGI Global.

Ramirez, M. (2014). Emerging trends in Augmented Reality Retrieved from https://www.jisc.ac.uk/blog/emerging-trends-in-augmented-reality-15-jul-2014

SIMOLA. (2012). Situated Mobile Language Learning. Retrieved from http://itrg.brighton.ac.uk/simola.org/

Zull, J. E. (2004). The Art of Changing the Brain. *Educational Leadership, 62*(1), 68-72

A FRAMEWORK FOR FLIPPED LEARNING

Jenny Eppard and Aicha Rochdi
Zayed University, UAE

ABSTRACT

Over the last few decades, with the rapid developments of mobile technology, the advent of Web 2.0 sites, and the expansion of social media, there has been an incremental use of technology in the classroom. One of the approaches for technological integration into the classroom is via flipped learning. This pedagogical method has become increasingly popular and there is a growing body of literature that is investigating the implementation of this teaching methodology in the various classrooms. The present paper is an overview of the research related to the flipped classroom. The goals are threefold: a) to provide a synthesis of the definitions of the concept of the flipped learning as used in field b) to review the various theories and models that may explain the theoretical underpinnings for flipped classroom; and c) to develop a tentative framework based on the literature.

KEYWORDS

Flipped learning. inverted learning, mobile learning.

1. INTRODUCTION

Over the last few decades, with the rapid developments of mobile technology, the advent of Web 2.0 sites, and the expansion of social media, there has been an incremental use of informational technology in the classroom to meet the needs of twenty-first century students. Indeed, these students "prefer to access subject information on the internet, where it is more abundant, more accessible, and more up-to-date" (Paige, Hickok, and Patrick, 2004, p. 11).

One of the approaches for technological integration into the classroom is via flipped learning. This pedagogical method has become increasingly popular in the educational arena. There is a growing body of literature that is investigating the implementation of this concept especially in the area of STEM subjects (science, technology, engineering and mathematics). In a survey, Bishop and Verleger (2013) researched flipped learning and listed 39 blog posts and online articles that focus around the flipped classroom as well as 11 websites that promote the flipped classroom or provide resources to help educators flip their classroom. Yarbro, Arfstrom, McKnight and Mcknight (2014) referred to the Flipped Learning Networks community of practice which showed that there has been a significant increase in the number of members. In 2012, there were 2,500 members to 10,000 in 2013 and then another jump to more than 20,000 members in 2014.

Another example of this increase appears in a simple Google search. According to these same scholars, when they carried out a Google search they found that the term "flipped learning" resulted in 244,000 hits in June, 2014. When we put in the term "flipped learning", we found 412,000 in January, 2016 which is an increase of about 200,000 in just under 2 years. In Google scholar, using the same terms they found 314 in June, 2014. We found 5440 hits which is an increase of over 5000 in 2 years. Therefore, there does appear to be an increase in interest in the concept of flipped learning at least.

As flipped learning, the type of learning that occurs within a flipped classroom, becomes part of the academic vernacular so does the need to develop a clear definition of flipped learning and an understanding of how it works or why it works based on theoretical frameworks. Thus, the goal of this paper is multi-fold, a) to provide a synthesis of the definitions of the concept of the flipped learning as used in the field, b) to review the various theoretical models that account for and explain learning in the flipped classroom and c} to synthesize current information about flipped learning into a potential framework for flipped learning. While we are far from fully understanding all of the areas in which flipped learning is successful or not successful, this model is a first step in developing a better understanding of the process.

2. WHAT IS FLIPPED LEARNING

Inverting the classroom so that the transmission of information (lecture) happens outside of class and the traditional out-of-class work is completed in class with the teacher is not a recent concept. The researchers often credited with first mentioning inverted learning, Lage, Platt and Treglia, published the paper "Inverting the Classroom: A Gateway to Creating an Inclusive Learning Environment" in 2000. In this article they explain that inverting the classroom is an approach that occurs when "events that have traditionally taken place inside the classroom now take place outside the classroom and vice versa." (2000). Lage, Platt and Treglia (2000) results indicated that both students' and teachers' perceptions of the new methodology were positive. Crouch and Mazur (2001) conducted a study where they investigated the concept of peer instruction that is in its essence similar to the flipped classroom in the sense that transmission of information occurs outside of the classroom while class time was devoted to conceptual questions and mini lectures which ideally would include higher order thinking and assimilation. Strayer (2007) published his dissertation entitled "The effects of the classroom flip on the learning environment: a comparison of learning activity in a traditional classroom and a flip classroom that used an intelligent tutoring system". This study examined students' comfort with learning in an inverted classroom. However, the term "flipped classroom" was not readily adopted till Bergman and Sams, two chemistry teachers, started flipping their classroom by providing the students with videos to watch at home and devoting class time to projects. Their book Flip your classroom: reach every student in every class every day (2012) outlines the concept of the flipped classroom and defines its key elements. From this, we can note that the development of flipped learning was organic and that the changes in the method, and therefore the definition, mirrors technological developments in the world at large. Technology and specifically social media has changed the way that information is transferred. Therefore, at one point flipping the classroom included reading and/or the dissemination of videotapes or even DVDs. However, now it is possible to access, edit and disseminate videos easily so flipped classrooms have adapted to match this technological transformation.

Flipped classrooms differ from traditional classes in many respects. Traditional classes as opposed to flipped classrooms, include lectures, and therefore transmission of information, in class (Talbert 2012). In this format, students often take notes during the lecture while in class. Outside of class, students complete assignments that are often targeted at assimilation of the information acquired during class time. This work is then submitted or assessed in class. In this approach, individuals work outside of class either alone or in groups but usually without the presence of an expert or a mentor.

The flipped classroom implies a reversal of the traditional class and relies on a different process. There are a number of definitions of flipped classrooms and they range from broad to specific depending on how the teacher uses the method. The broadest definition of flipped learning is one that proposes that assigning readings to give the students prior exposure to new material is a form of flipped learning. The narrowest definition, on the other hand, limits the concept of flipped learning to instances where educators use technology, especially videos, to transmit information outside of class. In the extant literature, the researchers who are often credited as the originators of the flipped learning concept, Lage, Platt and Treglia (2000), defined flipping (or inverting) the classroom as an instructional method in which "events that have traditionally taken place inside the classroom now take place outside the classroom and vice versa" (30-43). Interpretations of this definition can be quite general and thus can create the idea of an unstructured classroom design; however, using this definition as a starting point can provide teachers with a certain amount of flexibility as well as give them the freedom to employ flipped learning using various methods. One drawback when using this broad definition of flipped learning is that it can be difficult to assess effectiveness. Other researchers (Bishop and Vergler 2013, Gannod, 2008, Enfield 2013, Moroney 2013, Gaughan 2014) have defined flipped classrooms narrowly and include specific methods such as interactive group learning inside of the classroom and videos outside of the classroom. In more pedagogical vernacular, this definition means that the transmission of information takes place out of the classroom; whereas assimilation takes place in the classroom (Talbert 2012). The following table provides examples of definitions of flipped learning and key findings as provided in previous scholarly works.

Table 1. Definitions of Flipped learning.

Title	Author	Definition	Findings
Inverting the classroom: A gateway to creating an inclusive learning environment	Lage, Platt, and Treglia (2000)	"inverting the classroom means that events that have traditionally taken place inside the classroom now take place outside the classroom and vice versa" (30-43)	1. Students generally prefer the inverted classroom. 2. Students would prefer future classes in the inverted classroom format.
Using the inverted classroom to teach software engineering.	Gannod, Burge, and Helmick (2008)	"An inverted classroom is a teaching environment that mixes the use of technology with hands-on activities. In an inverted classroom, typical in-class lecture tie is replaced with laboratory and in-class activities. Outside class time, lectures are delivered over some other medium such as video on-demand" (777-786)	• Students perceive that outcome of the course is met. • Students view that some level of learning occurred.
The Flipped Classroom: A Survey of the Research	Bishop and Verleger (2013)	"We define the flipped classroom as an educational technique that consists of two parts: interactive group learning activities inside the classroom, and direct computer-based individual instruction outside the classroom. A graphic representation of this definition is shown in Figure 1. We re- strict this definition to exclude designs that do not employ videos as an outside of the classroom activity. While a broad conception of the flipped classroom may be useful, definitions that be- come too broad suggest that assigning reading outside of class and having discussions in class constitutes the flipped classroom. We reject these definitions."	Results of this survey show that most studies conducted to date explore student perceptions and use single-group study designs. Reports of student perceptions of the flipped classroom are somewhat mixed, but are generally positive overall. Students tend to prefer in-person lectures to video lectures, but prefer interactive classroom activities to lectures. Anecdotal evidence suggests that student learning is improved for the flipped compared to traditional classroom. However, there is very little work investigating student learning out- comes objectively.
Remixing chemistry class.	Bergman and Sams (2008).	students watch vodcasts or listen to podcasts and then complete activities in class (24-27)	just as effective as traditional classrooms quantitatively and perhaps more effective based on anecdotal results
Internet and the Inverted Classroom	Lage and Platt (2000)	"The classroom is designed to mirror the resources or experiences that traditionally take place in a lecture classroom, including online lectures and information about videotaped lectures" (11).	
How learning in an inverted classroom influences cooperation, innovation and task orientation.	Strayer (2012).	" relies on technology to introduce students to course content outside of the classroom so that students can engage that content at a deeper level inside the classroom" (171-193).	
The Flipped Classroom in World History	Gaughan (2014)	The Flipped Classroom is one in which lectures are presented as homework outside of class in online videos so that class time is reserved for engaging directly with the materials	Action research paper that showed both students and teachers indicated that they had a positive reaction to flipped learning
Seamless flipped learning: a mobile technology-enhanced flipped classroom with effective learning strategies	Hwang, Lai, and Wang (2015)	"the flipped classroom is a pedagogical approach which moves the learning contents taught by teachers' direct instruction to the time before class in order to increase the chances for the students and teacher to interact. Therefore, teachers would have more time to guide the learning activities and solve students' problems in order to promote the learning effects" (452).	
Flipping the classroom for English language learners to foster active learning	Hung (2015)	flip teaching can be conducted with many kinds of instructional videos, and other forms of pre-class assignments, such as reading quizzes or worksheets, are often presented together to help students better prepare for in-class participation (p. 82).	The main purpose for this study was to describe instructional design for flipped learning in the classroom. While the paper did include a research component, it was exploratory. The results were therefore not generalizable. The paper is significant in that the subject was language and not a STEM based subject.
The use of flipped classrooms in higher education: A scoping review	O'Flaherty and Phillips (2015)	content in advance (generally the pre-recorded lecture), educator awareness of students understanding, and higher-order learning during class time. Outcomes of implementing a successful flipped class approach should consider effective student learning that facilitates critical thinking, and importantly improves student engagement, both within and outside the class 9. 95).	This research was an analysis of the current research in flipped learning to understand the meaning of flipped learning and techniques used for flipped learning.

As we can see from this table, the research shows that flipped learning may yield positive results in terms of students' engagement (Farah, 2014; Enfield, 2013), and differentiation of learning (Enfield, 2013). As Bishop and Verleger (2013) suggested, the studies mostly focused on perceptions and feedback from students and teachers. To our knowledge, there has been little research that includes empirical data. This is uncommon. Indeed in a second- order meta-analysis, Tamim, Bernard, Borokhovski, Abrami, and Schmid's (2011) found that high caliber, detailed research evaluating the efficacy of specific methodologies and approaches of blended learning to be rare. For the purposes of this study, we mainly focus on the narrower definition of flipped learning, which includes recordings of either presentation software or lectures.

3. THEORETICAL BACKGROUND

Despite the increasing popularity of flipped learning, the concept itself as well as the methodologies utilized to achieve it have not yet been comprehensively examined in the existing body of research and neither have the theoretical underpinnings that could explain and justify the perceived success of this approach. The goal of this paper is to address this gap in the literature by presenting how learning theories connect with the concept of flipped learning and how components of these theories are operationalized.

3.1 Bloom's taxonomy

Bloom developed a concept of learning, which is often depicted as a pyramid with various levels of learning. This is commonly referred to as "Bloom's taxonomy". This framework can often be used as a lens through which to view the various stages of learning. The process of learning from a knowledge acquisition to critical thinking activities was amended by Lorin Anderson in the 1990's. This revised version of Bloom's Taxonomy is relevant to flipped learning in that the transmission of information, which is the basis for learning, is obtained independently and outside of class; while the assimilation of information, which requires greater critical reasoning occurs during class under the guidance of an instructor or mentor. The higher the tier portrayed on the pyramid, the more assimilation is required; whereas, the lower the level, the more transmission of information occurs somewhat independently, but not completely, of assimilation. The areas in the middle may require a more balanced or less skewed combination of the two. The notion of describing flipped learning in terms of assimilation and transmission was highlighted by Talbert (2012).

While Bloom's taxonomy is valuable at showing the stages of learning and the type of learning that occurs at each stage, it does not explain best practices in how to master each level in a given context. The benefit of flipped learning as it relates to Bloom's taxonomy is that students are actively helped supported during some of the activities that require higher order thinking. Other models and theories explain how learning occurs at the various stages as explained by Bloom's Taxonomy these include: Bloom's Mastery Learning, Cognitive Constructivism and Social Constructivism.

Indeed, most research on the flipped classroom employs group-based learning activities inside the classroom, based on student centered learning theories grounded in the works of Piaget (1967) and Vygotsky (1930-1934/1978). In addition, flipped learning as a pedagogical approach lends itself to the Mastery Model as outlined by Bloom (1968) and described by Block and Anderson (1975) which also shows some relation to the work of Skinner and operational conditioning.

3.2 Constructivism

Vygotsky viewed learning as a process that occurs when a learner is assisted by others who are more competent in the skills being learnt, and that learning is optimized by collaboration within the learner's zone of proximal development. Vygotsky (1978) defines the zone of proximal development (ZDP) as "the distance between the actual developmental level as determined by independent problem solving and the level of potential development as determined through problem solving under adult guidance, or in collaboration with more capable peers". In other words, learning occurs when a student works either with a more skilled adult or peer to solve problems that are just beyond her/his actual abilities. Hence, while using the flipped classroom technique, students are assigned problem-solving tasks where they need to utilize the information they learnt through watching the video outside of the classroom. To solve these tasks students either work individually or in groups under the supervision of the teacher.

Research shows that students learn best when taught according to their particular learning style that may be dependent, collaborative or independents. Piaget's theory of cognitive development is based on a belief that learners are like scientists trying to make sense of reality. Learners, in order to acquire new knowledge, are not directly presented with information they are supposed to immediately understand and use. Instead, learners must "construct" their own knowledge. They build their knowledge through experience. Experiences enable them to create schemas or mental models in their heads. These schemas are changed, enlarged, and made more sophisticated through two complementary processes namely assimilation and accommodation. According to the Piagetian cognitive constructivist theory, to reach a higher level of learning, students need to interact with peers with the main mechanism driving development being "cognitive conflict" to reach accommodation of knowledge.

These two key principles of cognitive constructivism are practiced in the flipped classroom. The first principle is that learning is active. Practically, prior to attending class, the teacher gives the students a video that introduces the information that needs to be learned. This information is introduced an aid to problem solving. It is a tool that furthers and facilitates.

Gannod (2008) conducted a study in which they investigated the use of the flipped classroom in a software engineering class. They made 65 podcasts available to students and they devoted class time to collaborative learning where students collaborated to create, analyze and evaluate software. They designed in-class activities that require students to work in pairs or in groups and to utilize the information gained from the video to solve real problems. Their methodology reflects the precepts of a Vygotskian approach to learning.

Lage, Platt and Treglia (2000) carried a study where they explored the use of the inverted classroom to teach economics. Lage, Platt and Treglia (2000) designed in class activities where students worked in groups under the supervision of the instructor to conduct economic experiments. During the activities, the students brought to the task their different understandings of the information presented, and worked together through continuous assimilation and accommodation of new information to reach an understanding of the information. The results of the study showed that students positively perceived the use of that methodology.

3.3 Mastery Learning

Benjamin Bloom popularized Mastery Learning in the 1960s. Instead of being a theory that supports the use of flipped learning in general, it highlights the importance of using flipped learning in a meaningful and structured manner. Using mastery learning, students learn at their own pace. Therefore learning is differentiated. Based on the tenets of Mastery Learning, all students are required to learn common, well-structured objectives. When a student does not master an objective, remediation is required. Bergman and Sams (2012) argue that Mastery Learning supports flipped learning because it provides instruction that is differentiated, asynchronous and student-centered; and it provides a context for remediation and efficient feedback. This aligns with flipped learning where students have the potential to learn in their own time with a certain amount of autonomy in regards to time management. Mason, Shuman and Cook (2013) used a semi-Mastery Learning model in their study of flipped learning in engineering courses. They used a mixture of project work, group work and quizzes during the class. While the study had elements of Piaget and Vygotsky, there were quizzes and elements of assessments which resembled Mastery Learning. They found that the students' performance overall did not change from traditional learning but that there were benefits to using flipped learning techniques in the classroom such as greater student autonomy and differentiated and active learning.

The concept of reinforcement as part of behaviorism and the ideas of operant conditioning, is related to Mastery Learning and the study of flipped learning in several different ways. For one, akin to mastery learning, students have a stimulus, making a good grade or obtaining knowledge, and based on the theory, they will continue to study until they have mastered the concept to an acceptable extent. Using the flipped classroom scenario, not only do the students need to study the materials (i.e. the videos), they need to be able to study in such a way as to prepare for the classroom activities. According to Skinner, in the initial phase students may be confused but over time they understand the concept or at least the process needed to understand the stimuli. Like mastery learning, a learner will produce a certain output, based on formative or summative assessments that will determine whether he needs to relearn or move on to another stage or topic. According, to Skinner after a period of time, students will be trained to respond appropriately if they want the intended reward or if they do not want the opposite – a bad grade, lack of understanding. So, while, the reinforcement theory may not be the main theory supporting the pedagogical underpinnings of flipped learning, it could explain the successful transition from traditional style learning environments to one that is supported by flipped classrooms; and also the conditioning-stimuli relationship of flipped learning and to some extent mastery learning.

4. A THEORETICAL FRAMEWORK FOR THE FLIPPED CLASSROOM

The theories mentioned explain aspects of flipped learning and could account for its perceived success as an instructional methodology. In this paper, we propose a possible theoretical framework that encapsulated the various aspects of the theories reviewed and how they are operationalized in flipped learning. indeed, though quantitative and rigorous qualitative data about the flipped classroom is limited, there is a consistent body of research that reports improvements in students' achievements as well as their perceptions of the learning environment, their engagement and their motivation while utilizing the flipped classroom. from our perspective, a source of confusion when trying to explain the effectiveness of flipped learning is if we view it as a didactic method that is separate from and independent of models and theories of learning, and that can account for learning in and of itself. We propose that the effectiveness of flipped learning as an instructional methodology and flipped learning as a process could be explained and accounted for through the juxtaposition and the dynamic interaction of different learning theories and models.

Figure 2 provides a visualization of the information provided in this article and is a synthesis of the way in which the theory and frameworks connect to flipped learning based on previous studies and theoretical underpinnings. In the middle of the image is the pyramid associated with Bloom's taxonomy. This version of Bloom's Taxonomy is a new version as developed by Anderson, et al (2001). Based on this version, the items listed in the taxonomy refer to the following:

1. remembering - retrieving, recognizing, and recalling relevant knowledge from long-term memory;
2. understanding - constructing meaning from oral, written, and graphic messages through interpreting, exemplifying, classifying, summarizing, inferring, comparing, and explaining;
3. applying - carrying out or using a procedure through executing, or implementing; analyzing - breaking material into constituent parts, determining how the parts relate to one another and to an overall structure or purpose through differentiating, organizing, and attributing;
4. evaluating - making judgments based on criteria and standards through checking and critiquing; creating - putting elements together to form a coherent or functional whole;
5. reorganizing elements into a new pattern or structure through generating, planning, or producing (p. 67-68).

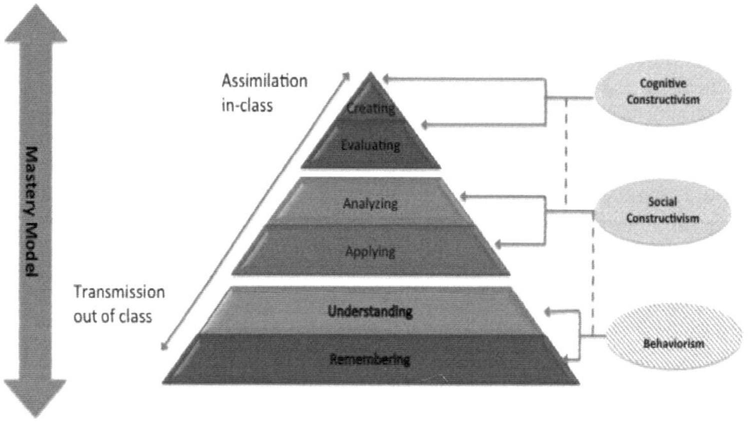

Figure 2. Synthesis of the models and theories associated with Flipped Learning.

When viewing flipped learning through Bloom's taxonomy, the skills highlighted at the base of the triangle (remembering and understanding) occur outside of class without teacher supervision. Students can watch videos as many times as needed to remember information and to understand concepts. The stimuli being the information that is needed to function in class appropriately; a reversal in the way students view learning and the actions of those participating in the learning environment and a change in the way students' approach a new learning environment learning (Skinner, 1974). During the beginning of adopting a flipped learning environment, this is especially significant. The middle levels of the pyramid – analyzing and applying – occur in class with the help of a teacher or peers and is more collaborative than the bottom levels. The top levels – evaluating and creating – while can still be collaborative they are moving toward student autonomy. They would still occur in class but as students master a concept, theoretically they should be able to complete tasks independently and accurately. Theoretically, at least, students can re-watch presentations as often as needed and at their own pace in order to master the first two levels. The top four levels will be mastered under the supervision of instructor with possible peer influence at varies times.

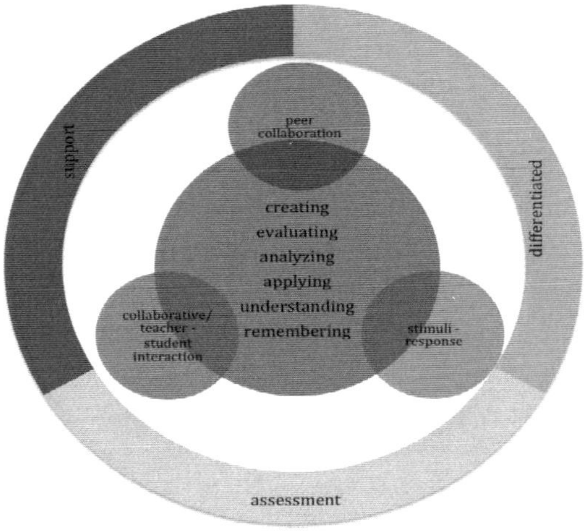

Figure 3. Synthesis of learning processes in flipped learning.

Figure 3 is an attempt to design a framework that has the potential to depict the dynamic nature of Flipped learning and to illustrate how the various learning theories can apply to different stages in the learning process. Much of this depends on the teacher, the students' needs and the content of the course being flipped. In this framework, flipped learning is viewed as a flexible concept where there is a certain amount of fluidity in the way theories can be utilized.

5. CONCLUSION

It is difficult to capture all of the methodologies incorporated into a flipped classroom context. There is a lot of freedom in the manner in which teachers present information and plan lessons, and students synthesize the content. This is both a benefit and a drawback to the field of flipped learning. It is a benefit because it provides a vehicle for differentiated teaching and learning. However, it is a drawback, because it is difficult to research which factors, it any, contribute to its effectiveness or lack thereof. In the future, research should be conducted into the connection between differentiated learning (DL) and flipped learning.

DL refers to the process of designing different instructional material to meet the needs of student with varying levels and abilities. DL involves offering individualized and meaning content through multiple modalities of instruction where students have flexibility to study at their own pace (Keefe, 2007). Flipped learning does not necessarily target differentiated learning. It is a tool that could be used for achieving differentiated instruction. A research study could look at the effectiveness of flipped learning in a classroom where students have mixed abilities. Students with lower abilities would be given support material such as instructional videos and recorded lectures that can be accessed outside the class in a flipped learning format. The goal of this support material is to help students achieve parity with the rest of the class. The performance of the students that were given the videos would be compared to the rest of the class.

Research into the fields of learning styles and personality types and their role in the way materials are presented and assimilated in a flipped learning scenario might be beneficial. In addition to differentiated learning, more research attention needs to be given to subjects outside of the STEM arena. This could possibly increase our understanding of how flipped learning could be used successfully across and within subject areas.

REFERENCES

Anderson, L.W., Krathwohl, D.R. and Bloom, B.S., 2001. A taxonomy for learning, teaching, and assessing: A revision of Bloom's taxonomy of educational objectives. Allyn & Bacon.

Bergmann, J. and Sams, A., 2009. Remixing Chemistry Class: Two Colorado Teachers Make Vodcasts of Their Lectures to Free Up Class Time for Hands-On Activities. Learning & Leading with Technology, 36(4), pp.22-27.

Bishop, J.L. and Verleger, M.A., 2013, June. The flipped classroom: A survey of the research. In ASEE National Conference Proceedings, Atlanta, GA (Vol. 30, No. 9).

Block, J.H. and Anderson, L.W., 1975. Mastery learning in classroom instruction. Macmillan Pub Co.

Bloom, B. (1968) 'Learning for Mastery', Evaluation Comment, 1(2), pp. 1–12.

Bloom, L. (1970) Language development: Form and function in emerging grammars. 4th ed. Cambridge, MA: M.I.T. Press.

Crouch, C.H. and Mazur, E., 2001. Peer instruction: Ten years of experience and results. American journal of physics, 69(9), pp.970-977.

Enfield, J., 2013. Looking at the impact of the flipped classroom model of instruction on undergraduate multimedia students

at CSUN. TechTrends, 57(6), pp.14-27.

Farah, M., 2014. The Impact of Using Flipped Classroom Instruction on the Writing Performance of Twelfth Grade Female Emirati Students in the Applied Technology High School (ATHS).

Hung, H.T., 2015. Flipping the classroom for English language learners to foster active learning. Computer Assisted Language Learning, 28(1), pp.81-96.

Hwang, G.J., Lai, C.L. and Wang, S.Y., 2015. Seamless flipped learning: a mobile technology-enhanced flipped classroom with effective learning strategies. Journal of Computers in Education, 2(4), pp.449-473.

Gaughan, J.E., 2014. The flipped classroom in world history. History Teacher, 47(2), pp.221-244.

Gannod, G.C., Burge, J.E. and Helmick, M.T., 2008, May. Using the inverted classroom to teach software engineering. In Proceedings of the 30th international conference on Software engineering (pp. 777-786). ACM.

Keefe, J. (2007). What is personalization? Phi Delta Kappan, 89(3), 217–223.

Lage, M.J., Platt, G.J. and Treglia, M., 2000. Inverting the classroom: A gateway to creating an inclusive learning environment. The Journal of Economic Education, 31(1), pp.30-43.

Lage, M.J. and Platt, G., 2000. The internet and the inverted classroom. The Journal of Economic Education, 31(1), pp.11-11.

Mason, G., Shuman, T.R. and Cook, K.E., 2013, June. Inverting (flipping) classrooms–Advantages and challenges. In Proceedings of the 120th ASEE annual conference and exposition, Atlanta.

Moroney, S., 2013. Flipped teaching in a college algebra classroom: An action research project.

O'Flaherty, J. and Phillips, C., 2015. The use of flipped classrooms in higher education: A scoping review. The Internet and Higher Education, 25, pp.85-95.

Paige, R., Hickok, E. and Patrick, 2004. Toward a new golden age of American education: how the internet, the law and today's students are revolutionizing expectations. National technology plan: US Department of Education, Washington D.C.

Shimamoto, D., 2012, April. Implementing a flipped classroom: An instructional module. TCC Conference.

Skinner, B.F.,1974. About behaviorism. New York: Knopf; [distributed by Random House].

Strayer, J.F., 2007. The effects of the classroom flip on the learning environment: A comparison of learning activity in a traditional classroom and a flip classroom that used an intelligent tutoring system (Doctoral dissertation, The Ohio State University).

Strayer, J.F., 2012. How learning in an inverted classroom influences cooperation, innovation and task orientation. Learning Environments Research, 15(2), pp.171-193.

Talbert, R., 2012. Inverted classroom. Colleagues, 9(1), p.7.

Tamim, R.M., Bernard, R.M., Borokhovski, E., Abrami, P.C., & Schmid, R.F. (2011). What forty years of research says about the impact of technology on learning. Review of Educational Research, 81(1), 4–28.

Vygotsky, L. S., 1978. Mind in society: The development of higher psychological processes (M. Cole, V. John-Steiner, S. Scribner & E. Souberman., Eds.) (A. R. Luria, M. Lopez-Morillas & M. Cole [with J. V. Wertsch], Trans.) Cambridge, Mass.: Harvard University Press. (Original manuscripts [ca. 1930-1934]).

Yarbro, J., Arfstrom, K.M., McKnight, K. and McKnight, P., 2014. Extension of a review of flipped learning.

THE TECHNOLOGY ACCEPTANCE OF MOBILE APPLICATIONS IN EDUCATION

Mark Anthony Camilleri[1] and Adriana Caterina Camilleri[2]
[1]*University of Malta, Department of Corporate Communication, Faculty of Media and Knowledge Sciences, Msida, MSD2080, Malta*
[2]*University of Bath, Department of Psychology, Claverton Down, Bath, BA2 7AY, United Kingdom*

ABSTRACT

This research explores the educators' attitudes and behavioural intention toward mobile applications. The methodology integrates measures from 'the pace of technological innovativeness' and the 'technology acceptance model' to understand the rationale for further investment in mobile learning (m-learning). A quantitative study was carried out amongst two hundred forty-one educators in small EU state. It has investigated the costs and benefits of using ubiquitous resources, including tablets for m-learning in schools. A principal component analysis has indicated that the educators were committed to using mobile technologies. In addition, a stepwise regression analysis has shown that the younger teachers were increasingly engaging in m-learning resources. In conclusion, this contribution puts forward key implications for both academia and practitioners.

KEYWORDS

Mobile, Mobile Learning, Technology Acceptance Model, Technology Innovation Principal Component Analysis, Stepwise Regression Analysis.

1. INTRODUCTION

Innovative technologies may have brought powerful, transformative tools which are improving on our quality of lives (Fullan, 2013; Prensky, 2005). Stakeholders in education are also promoting innovative pedagogical practices by using technology (Fullan, 2013); as students from a tender age are acquiring 'digital skills' and expertise in media and information communication technologies (ICT). Many pupils operate offline specialised software as well as online programmes on internet (Castaño-Muñoz, Duart & Sancho-Vinuesa, 2014; Tyner, 2014). ICT has improved their ways of accessing knowledge, researching, communicating, socialising and succeeding in all levels of education (Hoskins & Crick, 2010; Smith, Higgins, Wall & Miller, 2005). Nowadays, many children and teenagers can easily access a personal computer at home or at school. Many of them are also using their own wireless devices, including smart phones and tablets for many purposes (Sampson, Isaias, Ifenthaler, & Spector, 2012; Sharples, Arnedillo-Sánchez, Milrad & Vavoula, 2009). Hence, educators ought to respond to these new realities as they need to adapt their teaching designs and methodologies to better respond to today's students' abilities, interests and learning styles (Sánchez & Isaías, 2014).

The students' use of digital and mobile media during lessons is related to the teachers' confidence level in their digital competences (Bocconi, Kampylis & Punie, 2013). Inevitably, students are affected by the teachers' stance toward technologies in education. The pupils' motivation for learning may also be correlated to the access and availability of innovative learning resources, including mobile games in school environments (Sardone & Devlin-Scherer, 2010). The EU (2013) has underlined the importance of high access to ICT infrastructure at school; as its survey reported that between 20-25% of European students are taught by digitally competent teachers who have high access to ICT. Academic evidence also shows that increasing professional development opportunities for teachers is an efficient way of boosting technology acceptance in teaching and learning, since it helps build highly confident and supportive teachers (Sampson et al., 2012; Sharples et al., 2009).

The use of digital learning resources requires ongoing support – not only technical but also pedagogical (Fullan, 2013; EU, 2013). Ongoing training and continuous professional development ought to be provided by school staff and others to teachers of all disciplines, including subject-specific training on learning applications (Spector, Ifenthaler, Sampson & Isaías, 2016). Confident and supportive teachers are highly required to effectively use educational technologies including ubiquitous mobile applications to exploit their potential (Sánchez & Isaías, 2014; Martin & Ertzberger, 2013). In this light, this paper explores the educators' attitudes toward technology in education. It unfolds their motivations behind their use of mobile learning technologies (Sánchez & Isaías, 2014; Arrigo, Kukulska-Hulme, Arnedillo-Sánchez & Kismihok, 2013; Sardone & Devlin-Scherer, 2010).

1.1 Aims and Objectives

This paper makes use of previous tried and tested measures, namely; 'the pace of technological innovativeness' (De Smet, Bourgonjon, De Wever, Schellens & Valcke, 2012; Grewal, Mehta & Kardes, 2004); 'technology acceptance' (Cheon, Lee, Crooks & Song, 2012; Huang, Huang, Huang & Lin, 2012; Davis, 1989); and 'technology anxiety' (Celik & Yesilyurt, 2013; Camilleri & Camilleri, 2017); Meuter, Bitner, Ostrom & Brown, 2005) as it investigates the educators' attitudes for (or against) mobile learning resources.

This research was principally guided by the following research question: 'How do factors such as 'technology acceptance' (Davis, 1989); 'pace of technological innovativeness' (Grewal et al., 2004) and 'technology anxiety' (Meuter et al., 2005) affect the educators' attitudes towards the use of mobile learning resources in-class? Therefore, the intention of this project was to advance theory on the subject of technologies in education and to put forward the empirical findings in the field of 'mobile learning'. A quantitative study explored the educators' perceptions about the use and the ease of use of the latest mobile applications in a primary educational setting. Hence, a multivariate regression analysis has investigated the relationships between 'the pace of technological innovativeness', 'the perceived ease of use of technology' and 'the perceived usefulness of technology' as well as 'technology anxiety'. At the same time, this empirical study has considered whether socio-demographic variables affected these correlations. The over-arching aim of this research project was to identify and to analyse the determinants which explain why educators are (or are not) engaging themselves mobile-learning technologies. This research project was built on the foundation of the following research questions:

- What are the educator's attitudes toward mobile learning resources in education?
- Are they actively using (or avoiding) mobile learning resources including educational applications on tablets in their classrooms?

1.2 Research Setting

One of the priority areas for the first cycle of the strategic framework for education and training ('ET 2020') is the promotion of creativity and innovation through the use of new ICT tools and teacher training (EU, 2013). ICT transforms teaching and learning as it contributes to the acquisition of basic or key competences. In this day and age, it is imperative that students achieve digital fluency (Smith et al., 2005). Digital skills and ICT competences are a pre-requisite for employment, personal fulfilment, social inclusion and active citizenship in today's rapidly-changing world (Hoskins & Crick, 2010). In a sense, education institutions are there to help their students develop competences. From a tender age, schools teach their pupils to be analytical and reflexive. Students are taught how to work autonomously as well as collaboratively. They learn how to seek information and support as they make use of new resources and technologies (Fullan, 2013). National education policy makers have articulated specific policies to use ICT in teaching and learning (EU2013). These authorities have implemented support measures to increase the frequency of students' ICT-based activities for learning in the classroom.

The EU (2013) survey indicated that the schools that had specific policies about ICT integration in teaching and learning experienced the highest frequency of the use of digital learning resources (DLRs) and ICT learning based activities. Furthermore, the report suggested that these schools implemented support measures including teacher professional development and also sought the provision of ICT coordinators. Interestingly, students who attended schools with focused ICT policies were more engaged in DLRs when compared to other students who hailed from schools with no ICT policies or support measures. The European Union member state have set national strategies covering training measures for ICT in schools, digital / media literacy and e -skills development,training and research projects in e-learning, and research projects in e-inclusion (European Schoolnet, 2012b). There are central steering documents for all ICT learning objectives at secondary education level and for using a computer, using office applications, searching for information, and using multimedia at primary level (European Schoolnet, 2012). ICT is taught as a general tool for other subjects / or as a tool for specific tasks in other subjects. In addition, ICT is taught as a separate subject in secondary schools. Recommendations and support is provided to all primary and secondary schools in all ICT hardware areas, except for mobile devices and e-book readers, and for all ICT software categories.

According to official steering documents, both students and teachers at primary and secondary level are expected to use ICT in all subjects both in class and for complementary activities, except for in foreign languages at primary level where it is used only for complementary activities (European Schoolnet, 2012). There are no central recommendations on the use of ICT in student assessment. Public-private partnerships are increasingly promoting the use of ICT as they are encouraged to use digital technologies.

2. KEY CONCEPTS AND THE FORMULATION OF HYPOTHESES

Relevant literature suggest that educational institutions are inevitably influenced by the latest advances in technology on teaching and learning. Fullan (2013) held that educators should embrace technologies and apply them in meaningful ways to positively impact students. He went on to suggest that a "new pedagogy" of higher-order skills that focuses on the harnessing of fast and innovative technologies can bring about change in the right direction (for the delivery of student-centred education).

2.1 Pace of Technological Innovativeness

The educators' personal insights and perceptions of mobile learning resources may affect the frequency of how students' engage themselves in education. Garcia and Calantone (2002) maintained that the innovation process comprises the technological development of an invention combined with the market introduction of that invention to end users through adoption and diffusion. They claimed that the pace of technological innovativeness is 'iterative' as it involves continuous engagement with new emerging innovations. Therefore, the schools should remain up-to-date with the latest ICT infrastructure (EU, 2013; Greenhow & Robelia, 2009). Continuous professional development and ongoing training is a prerequisite for an effective and efficient use of ICT infrastructure and digital (and mobile) learning resources (Camilleri & Camilleri, 2016; Wastiau, Blamire, Kearney, Quittre, Van de Gaer & Monseur, 2013; Prensky, 2005). This leads to the first hypothesis:

i. There is a relationship between 'the pace of technological innovation' in schools and 'the technological acceptance' of educators.

2.2 The Technology Acceptance Model and Technological Anxiety

The technological acceptance model has often investigated the respondents' behavioural intention to use technology (Davis, 1989; Davis, Bagozzi & Warshaw, 1989). This purported model has explained the causal relationship(s) between the users' internal beliefs, attitudes, intentions and computer usage behaviours. In the past, the technological acceptance model sought to explain why people accepted or rejected a particular technology (Mac Callum & Jeffrey, 2014; Davis, 1989). Therefore, the technological acceptance model has been chosen for this research to find out why educators used (or avoided) mobile learning resources. Davis (1989) suggested that perceived usefulness is the degree to which a person believes that using a particular system would enhance his or her job performance. From the outset, the researchers presumed that the respondents would perceive both the usefulness and would probably indicate their ease of use of mobile learning resources in their classroom environments (Sánchez & Isaías, 2014; Arrigo et al., 2013).

Notwithstanding, Davis (1989) explained that the perceived ease of use (PEOU) was "the degree to which a person believes that using a particular system would be free of effort" (Davis, 1989, p. 320). Davis (1989) held that the usage of technology is influenced by its perceived ease of use. In this case, the researchers investigated whether the educators at St Clare's College were (or were not) proficient in the use of mobile learning technologies. Although potential users could believe that a given technology is useful, they may, at the same time be against (for some reason) its use in their classroom. They may perceive that there aren't sufficient performance benefits for using mobile learning technologies (Sampson et al., 2012; Meuter et al., 2005; Garcia & Calantone, 2002). This leads to the second and third hypotheses:

ii. There is a positive relationship between perceived usefulness and the perceived ease of use of digital learning resources. (This hypothesis investigates the technological acceptance model).

iii. This empirical study will also investigate the causal relationships (by using stepwise regression) between perceived usefulness, perceived ease of use, the pace of technological innovativeness and technological anxiety.

3. THE METHODOLOGY

This study has targeted all members of staff including heads, assistant heads, teachers and learning support assistants in eleven schools at St Clare's College in Malta, Europe. The survey's responses were presented as a five-point likert scaling mechanism. Their values ranged from 1 (strongly disagree) to 5 (strongly agree) with 3 signalling indecision. After filtering and eliminating the incomplete survey observations, a total of 241 valid responses were obtained. Reliability and appropriate validity tests have been carried out during the analytical process. Cronbach's alpha was calculated to test for the level of consistency among the items. There was an acceptable level of reliability for this study; as Alpha was always more than the 0.7 threshold.

3.1 The Measures

The researcher has adapted six items from the 'pace of technological innovation'; that intended to measure the educators' attitudes toward the unprecedented pace of technological advances in m-learning resources. Originally, this scale has reported a construct reliability of 0.97 (Grewal et al., 2004) and had used confirmatory factor analysis to provide evidence to support the scales' convergent and discriminant validities.

In previous studies, the technological acceptance model has played an important role in evaluating the users' perceptions on their ease of use, their perceived usefulness and behavioural intention toward technology. Davis's (1989) six items that represented 'perceived usefulness' attained a constructed reliability of 0.97, while the six items about 'perceived ease of use' had a reliability of 0.91. The technology acceptance measures were acceptable as their factor loadings were reported to be significant and there was evidence of discriminant validity for each construct (Davis, 1989).

Another four items that were used to measure the degree to which educators were apprehensive, or for some reason rejected the usage of mobile learning resources (Mac Callum & Jeffrey, 2014; Meuter et al., 2005). These items were also similar to the computer anxiety scale that were used by Celik & Yesilyurt (2013). Meuter et al. (2005) reported an alpha of 0.93 for these items. Their measurement model was acceptable as the factor loadings were significant and there was evidence of discriminant validity for each construct using different tests (confidence interval and variance extracted).

4. ANALYSIS

There were twenty one males (9%) and two hundred twenty females (91%) (n=241). Again, the respondents' 'age' varied, and this was evident in the standard deviation of 0.70. Respondents were also classified into five age groups (16-25; 26-35; 36-45; 46-55 and 56-65). The majority of the respondents were aged between 36 and 45 years of age (37%, n=89), followed by those aged between 26 and 35 years (26%, n=62). The designation / 'role' of the respondents taking part in this study consisted of heads (4.1%, n=10), assistant heads (5.4%, n=13), teachers (71.4%, n=172), instructors (5%, n=12), facilitators (7.9%, n=19) and kindergarten assistants (6.2%, n=15). All the respondents were full time educators and held an indefinite engagement contract with the Ministry of Education and Employment in Malta. The respondents' mean work experience within the education sector' was approximately fifteen years. The responses ranged from a minimum of a year to a maximum of thirty-one years of relevant industry experience. The majority of respondents indicated that they attended tertiary education (85.1%, n=205). Whereas, twenty-four respondents (9.9%) attended vocational institutions and twelve individuals (5%) indicated that they completed the secondary 'level of education'.

This study is consistent with the extant literature on the technology acceptance model' (Cheon et al., 2012; Huang et al., 2012; Davis, 1989; Davis et al., 1989) as there were high mean scores of near 4, which reflected the educators' stance on mobile learning resources. Moreover, the respondents have conveyed their strong agreement with the 'pace of technological innovativeness' (De Smet et al., 2012; Grewal et al., 2004). The educators suggested that learning technologies are changing fast, as the mean score was of 4.05 and there was a standard deviation of 0.47.

4.1 Data Reduction

The Kaiser Meyer Olkin (KMO) measure of sampling adequacy was acceptable at 0.9. Bartlett's test of sphericity also revealed sufficient correlation in the dataset to run a principal component analysis (PCA) since $p < 0.001$. The principal component analysis (PCA) has been chosen to obtain a factor solution of a smaller set of salient variables, from a much larger dataset. A varimax rotation method was used to spread the variability amongst the constructs. PCA was considered appropriate as there were variables exhibiting an underlying structure. Many variables shared close similarities as there were highly significant correlations. Therefore, PCA has identified the patterns within the data and expressed it by highlighting the relevant similarities (and differences) in each component. In the process, the data has been compressed as it was reduced in a number of dimensions without much loss of information. PCA has produced a table which illustrated the amount of variance in the original variables (with their respective initial eigenvalues) which were accounted for by each component. There was also a percentage of variance column which indicated the expressed ratio, as a percentage of the total variance. A brief description of the extracted factor components, together with their eigenvalue and their respective percentage of variance is provided hereunder in Table 1. With respect to scale reliability, all constructs were analysed for internal consistency by using Cronbach's alpha. The composite reliability's coefficient were well above the minimum acceptance value of 0.7 (Bagozzi, & Yi, 1988).

Table 1. The Extracted Factor Components.

Factor Component	Initial Eigenvalues	% of Variance	Extraction Sums of Squared Loadings	% of Variance	Rotation Sums of Squared Loadings	% of Variance
1 Perceived Usefulness of DLR	5.533	25.152	5.533	25.152	4.04	18.362
2 Pace of Technological Innovation	2.378	10.809	2.378	10.809	2.555	11.613
3 Technological Anxiety	1.846	8.391	1.846	8.391	2.27	10.319
4 Easy Interaction with DLR	1.662	7.553	1.662	7.553	1.711	7.776
5 Perceived Ease of Use of DLR	1.192	5.418	1.192	5.418	1.681	7.642
6 Effective DLR	1.119	5.085	1.119	5.085	1.473	6.695

The sum of the eigenvalues equalled the number of components. Only principal components with eigenvalues greater than 1 were extracted. The factors accounted for more than 62% variance before rotation. There were six extracted components from twenty-two variables. The factor components were labelled following a cross-examination of the variables with the higher loadings. Typically, the variables with the highest correlation scores had mostly contributed towards the make-up of the respective component. The underlying scope of combining the variables by using component analysis was to reduce the data and make it more adaptable for regression analysis.

4.2 Multivariate Regression

A stepwise procedure was purposely carried out to select the most relevant predictive variables in the regression models. The *p*-value was less than the 0.05 benchmark. There were adequate F-ratios, implying that the significant amounts of variation in regression were accounted for. More importantly, in the stepwise procedure the insignificant variables were excluded without appreciably increasing the residual sum of squares (Field, 2009). The regression models produced the regression coefficients which represented the strength and significance of the relationships. Moreover, the control variables, namely 'age' and 'gender' were also entered into the equations.

Initially, the first factor component; namely, perceived usefulness was inserted as the outcome variable. All the other five factor components as well as the variables of "age" and "gender" were inserted as independent variables in the stepwise regression equation. The results indicated that there was a positive and significant relationship between perceived usefulness of the digital learning resources and the respondents' age where Spearman's rank correlation coefficient was 0.265 (Spearman's rho). This relationship was significant at ($p < 0.05$). It transpired that the 'perceived usefulness' was dependent on the respondents' age ($F = 10.457$). Two regression equations were inconclusive when the factor components; namely, 'pace of technological innovation' and 'easy interaction' with DLRs were inserted as the dependent variables and all the other factor components were entered as independent variables (along with the 'age' and 'gender' variables).

Afterwards, the factor component; namely, 'technological anxiety' was inserted as the dependent variable and all the other five factor components were considered as possible antecedents (in the stepwise regression equation) the results indicated that there was a positive and significant relationship between 'technological anxiety' in using digital learning resources and 'age' where Spearman's rho was 0.217. This relationship was very significant at ($p < 0.01$) and $F = 6.872$. Again, the stepwise regression indicated a positive and significant relationship between 'perceived ease of use of DLR' and the 'gender' variable. In this case, Spearman's rho was 0.191. This relationship was significant at ($p < 0.05$) and the analysis of the variance; the F statistic was 5.274. When the factor component, 'effective use of DLR' was inserted as a dependent variable in the regression equation, the stepwise regression indicated that the 'age' variable was its antecedent. There was a positive and highly significant relationship ($p > 0.001$). Spearman's rho was 0.293. This equation shows that that an effective use of digital learning resources was dependent on the respondents' age ($F = 13.084$).

In conclusion, the stepwise regression analysis indicated that this study's hypotheses were all negative as there was no relationship between perceived usefulness and the perceived ease of use for mobile learning resources. Moreover, there was no positive and significant relationship between perceived usefulness, perceived ease of use, the pace of technological innovativeness and technological anxiety. Nevertheless, this empirical study revealed that the acceptance of mobile learning resources in education was affected by gender and the age of respondents.

5. DISCUSSION, CONCLUSIONS & FUTURE RESEARCH

This empirical study has applied previously tried and tested measures from the 'pace of technological innovativeness'; 'technology acceptance' and 'technology anxiety' as it revealed the educators' attitudes and perceptions toward mobile learning resources. Moreover, it investigated whether socio-demographic variables affected the educators' perceived ease of use and the usefulness of mobile technologies in classroom activities. The quantitative results have indicated that there was a positive and highly significant relationship between the effective use of mobile resources and the respondents' age. In addition, there were significant relationships between the perceived usefulness of the digital learning resources and the respondents' age; between 'technological anxiety' in using digital learning resources and 'age' and between perceived ease of use and gender.

This study has shown that educators were aware that they ought to adapt their educational methodologies to today's realities. Evidently, they were already using digitally-mediated resources in their lessons. However, the educators also indicated that they were not extremely confident on how to use certain technologies in their lessons. The results suggest that teachers may require continuous professional development and training in this regard. The researcher believes that there is scope for educators to consider the results of this research, as ongoing investments in digital infrastructures will often result in improved engagement levels by teachers and students (Wastiau et al., 2013; Perrotta, 2013; Sampson, Isaias, Ifenthaler, & Spector, 2012; Sharples, Arnedillo-Sánchez, Milrad & Vavoula, 2009; Prensky, 2005).

Although the number of survey participants was sufficient in drawing conclusions about the educators' attitudes on the use of mobile learning resources in small EU country; this study is not amenable in drawing general conclusions in other contexts. The findings of this study ought to be supported by further research on mobile learning resources, including game-based learning and digital stories in other contexts. Perhaps, further research can specifically investigate the motivational appeal of mobile games in supporting educational outcomes. Moreover, there is scope in analysing the designs of electronic games and digital stories in terms of their complexities and sophistication levels. There may be diverse motivations in favour or against mobile learning among different demographics. In addition, the researcher believes that there is scope in undertaking face to face interviews with educational leaders including heads and assistant heads, as they may raise different concerns. There can be different digital literacies across other schools.

ACKNOWLEDGEMENTS

We thank the Ministry of Education and Employment (in Malta) and the Principal at St Clare's College who allowed us to disseminate the survey questionnaire among the primary and secondary schools' educators.

REFERENCES

Arrigo, M., Kukulska-Hulme, A., Arnedillo-Sánchez, I. and Kismihok, G., 2013. Meta-analyses from a collaborative project in mobile lifelong learning. *British Educational Research Journal*, Vol. 39, No 2, pp.222-247.

Bagozzi, R. P. and Yi, Y. 1988. On the evaluation of structural equation models. *Journal of the academy of marketing science*, Vol. 16, No. 1, 74-94.

Bocconi, S., Kampylis, P. and Punie, Y., 2013. Framing ICT-enabled Innovation for Learning: the case of one-to-one learning initiatives in Europe. *European Journal of Education*, Vol. 48, pp. 113–130.

Camilleri, M.A. and Camilleri, A.C., 2017. Digital Learning Resources and Ubiquitous Technologies in Education. *Technology, Knowledge and Learning*, Vol. 22, No. 1, pp. 65-82. http://link.springer.com.ejournals.um.edu.mt/article/10.1007/s10758-016-9287-7

Celik, V. and Yesilyurt, E., 2013. Attitudes to technology, perceived computer self-efficacy and computer anxiety as predictors of computer supported education. *Computers & Education*, Vol. 60 No. 1, pp. 148-158.

Cheon, J., Lee, S., Crooks, S. M., and Song, J., 2012. An investigation of mobile learning readiness in higher education based on the theory of planned behavior. *Computers & Education*, Vol. 59, No. 3, pp. 1054-1064.

Davis, F.D., 1989. Perceived usefulness, perceived ease of use, and user acceptance of information technology. *MIS quarterly*, pp. 319-340.

Davis, F.D., Bagozzi, R.P. and Warshaw, P.R., 1989. User acceptance of computer technology: a comparison of two theoretical models. *Management science*, Vol. 35, No. 8, pp. 982-1003.

De Smet, C., Bourgonjon, J., De Wever, B., Schellens, T. and Valcke, M., 2012. Researching instructional use and the technology acceptation of learning management systems by secondary school teachers. *Computers & Education*, Vol. 58, pp. 688–696.

EU, 2013. *Survey of schools: ICT in Education, Digital Agenda for Europe*. Publications Office of the European Union, Luxembourg.

European Schoolnet, 2012. Survey of Schools: ICT in Education. Country Profile Malta. Available from: https://ec.europa.eu/digital-agenda/sites/digital-agenda/files/Malta%20country%20profile.pdf [Accessed 15th June 2014].

Field, A., 2009. *Discovering statistics using SPSS*. Sage publications, London, UK.

Fullan, M., 2013. *Stratosphere: Integrating technology, pedagogy, and change knowledge*. Pearson, Don Mills, Canada.

Garcia, R. and Calantone, R., 2002. A critical look at technological innovation typology and innovativeness terminology: a literature review. *Journal of product innovation management*, Vol. 19, No. 2, pp. 110-132.

Greenhow, C., and Robelia, B., 2009. Old communication, new literacies: Social network sites as social learning resources. *Journal of Computer-Mediated Communication*, Vol. 14, No. 4, pp. 1130-1161.

Grewal, R., Mehta, R. and Kardes, F. R., 2004. The timing of repeat purchases of consumer durable goods: The role of functional bases of consumer attitudes. *Journal of Marketing Research*, Vol. 41, No. 1, pp. 101-115.

Hoskins, B. and Crick, R.D., 2010. Competences for learning to learn and active citizenship: different currencies or two sides of the same coin? *European Journal of Education*, Vol. 45, No. 1, pp. 121-137.

Huang, Y. M., Huang, Y. M., Huang, S. H. and Lin, Y. T., 2012. A ubiquitous English vocabulary learning system: Evidence of active/passive attitudes vs. usefulness/ease-of-use. *Computers & Education*, Vol. 58, No. 1, pp. 273-282.

Mac Callum, K. and Jeffrey, L., 2014. Comparing the role of ICT literacy and anxiety in the adoption of mobile learning. *Computers in Human Behavior*, Vol. 39, pp.8-19.

Meuter, M. L., Bitner, M. J., Ostrom, A. L. and Brown, S. W., 2005. Choosing among alternative service delivery modes: An investigation of customer trial of self-service technologies. *Journal of Marketing*, Vol. 69, No. 2, pp. 61-83.

Prensky, M., 2005. Computer games and learning: Digital game-based learning. *Handbook of computer game studies*, Vol. 18, pp. 97-122.

Sánchez, I. A. and Isaías, P. 2014. Proceedings of the International Conference on Mobile Learning 2014.(10th, Madrid, Spain, February 28-March 2, 2014). *International Association for Development of the Information Society*.

Sardone, N. B., and Devlin-Scherer, R. 2010. Teacher candidate responses to digital games: 21st-century skills development. *Journal of Research on Technology in Education*, Vol. 42, No. 4, pp. 409-425.

Sampson, D. G., Isaias, P., Ifenthaler, D. and Spector, M. (Eds.). 2012. *Ubiquitous and mobile learning in the digital age*. Springer Science & Business Media, New York, USA.

Sharples, M., Arnedillo-Sánchez, I., Milrad, M. and Vavoula, G. 2009. Mobile learning. In *Technology-enhanced learning* (pp. 233-249). Springer Netherlands.

Smith, H. J., Higgins, S., Wall, K. and Miller, J., 2005. Interactive whiteboards: boon or bandwagon? A critical review of the literature. *Journal of Computer Assisted Learning*, Vol. 21, No. 2, pp. 91-101.

Spector, J. M., Ifenthaler, D., Sampson, D. G. and Isaías, P. 2016. A Synthesizing Look Forward in Teaching, Learning, and Educational Leadership in the Digital Age. In *Competencies in Teaching, Learning and Educational Leadership in the Digital Age* (pp. 345-354). Springer International Publishing.

Wastiau, P., Blamire, R., Kearney, C., Quittre, V., Van de Gaer, E. and Monseur, C., 2013. The Use of ICT in Education: a survey of schools in Europe. *European Journal of Education*, Vol. 48, pp. 11–27. doi: 10.1111/ejed.12020

ENGAGING CHILDREN IN DIABETES EDUCATION THROUGH MOBILE GAMES

Nilufar Baghaei[1], John Casey[1], David Nandigam[1], Abdolhossein Sarrafzadeh[1] and Ralph Maddison[2]
[1]*Unitec Institute of Technology, Private Bag 92025, Victoria Street West, Auckland 1142, New Zealand*
[2]*National Institute for Health Innovation, The University of Auckland, Auckland PO 92019, 1142, New Zealand*

ABSTRACT

Traditional methods for diabetic education rely heavily on written materials and there is only a limited amount of resources targeted at educating diabetic children. Mobile games can be effective, evidence-based, and motivating tools for the promotion of children's health. In our earlier work, we proposed a novel approach for designing computer games aimed for educating children with diabetes and applied our design strategy to a mobile Android game (Mario Brothers). In this paper, we report the findings of a preliminary evaluation study ($n = 12$) conducted over 1 week. The initial results showed that the children found the game engaging and improved their knowledge of healthy diet and lifestyle.

KEYWORDS

Games, diabetes, game design, evaluation, self-management, mobile health.

1. INTRODUCTION

Addressing diabetes is a priority for several major reasons: (1) the number of people diagnosed with diabetes is increasing (estimated to be over 240,000 New Zealanders[1]); (2) the prevalence is increasing rapidly (between 5-10% each year since 2005); (3) it is the major preventable cause of costly and debilitating renal failure, lower limb amputation, and avoidable blindness; and (4) it is a major contributor to inequalities in life expectancy (Ministry of Health, 2008).

Children with diabetes in New Zealand currently receive medical care from a physician-coordinated team of nurses, dieticians, and health psychologists with a special interest in diabetes. This approach is resource-intensive and potentially could benefit from an inexpensive, popular new mode of delivering diabetes health-related education. Existing research evidence supports the use of videogames to promote health-related behaviors. A randomised controlled trial, which provided health behavior information and support in the form of a videogame, helped children aged 10–12 years consume more fruits and vegetables (Baranowski et al., 2011). A systematic review of interactive multimedia interventions to educate children about their health demonstrated potential to improve children's health-related self-efficacy, which could in turn enable them to become more competent on complex topics such as dietary behaviour change discussions (Raaff et al., 2014).

Playing games with mobile devices has become increasingly popular both in the development of games and in the field of research. The use of smartphones and tablet computers may offer opportunities to engage young people during inactive times between visits to the healthcare professionals, tests, or treatments by providing interactive health education modules (Greysen et al., 2014). Mobile technologies offer the potential for a new phase in the evolution of technology-enhanced learning. As the current research points out (e.g. Chai et al., 2014), meaningful learning could take place when learners are engaged in activities that allow for experimentation, conversation, collaboration, and reflection. Using mobile games for exploring new ways of learning has been shown to be very promising. Mobile gaming could be very well used in creating

---

[1]New Zealand Ministry of Health, http://www.health.govt.nz/your-health/conditions-and-treatments/diseases-and-illnesses/diabetes, Accessed in July 2016

authentic and engaging activities that combine teaching and gaming (Lieberman, 2012). Informal learning coupled with games can provide a foundation for innovation when applied to more formal learning situations.

Driven by the initiative of the Adult & Pediatric Diabetes Psychology Service of New Zealand, research has been undertaken to design and develop proactive mechanisms for diabetes education. To enhance children's learning about their condition, we chose to focus on exploiting interactive features of computer games to deliver education knowledge through immersive and situational learning. As a result, we embarked on developing a novel game design for teaching children how to manage their diabetes. We then applied the design ideas to an open source 2D game (Mario Brothers), developed a mobile version of the game and proposed several heuristics designed for subjective evaluation of educational mobile games (Chen, 2011; Baghaei, 2016). In this paper, we report the results of a pilot study conducted with 12 children to determine the effects of playing the mobile game 1) on engaging children and 2) on enhancing their knowledge of healthy diet and lifestyle. We hypothesize that game-based support will enhance the diabetes health-related knowledge, which in turn can stimulate and facilitate the conversation of the children with health-care providers about their self-management practices.

The rest of the paper is structured as follows. Section 2 explains the research question and the main idea of our research. The discussion of the modified mobile Mario Brothers game is outlined in Section 3. Section 4 describes the study and reports our findings. Finally, Section 5 concludes the paper and highlights future research opportunities.

2. DESIGN OF MOBILE GAMES FOR DIABETES EDUCATION

2.1 Research Questions

The main aim of this project is to investigate how we can effectively embed diabetes knowledge in a computer game to engage children for immersive learning. Two research questions are, therefore, investigated: 1) will engagement with the mobile game result in gaining greater knowledge of healthy diet and lifestyle? 2) how engaged are the participants with the game? We hypothesised that the participants will enjoy playing the game and that game-based support will enhance the diabetes health-related knowledge, which in turn can stimulate and facilitate the conversation of the children with health-care providers about their self-management practices.

2.2 Design Strategies

To address these questions, the very nature of computer games needs to be carefully examined. The key concept that is frequently utilized to explain the level of engagement in a computer game is that of "flow", first introduced by (Csikszentmihalyi, 1990). Many researcher consider flow as the state of intensive involvement. It is widely believed that flow is the key to the success of an educational game. According to Malone (1982), several conditions are likely to induce the flow state. Among them, a few conditions are of particular importance for designing diabetes education games (Chen, 2011):

C1. The activities in a game should be structured so that the level of difficulty of the game can be adjusted to match children's diabetes knowledge.

C2. The activities in a game should provide concrete feedback to children so that they can tell how well they perform and perhaps what they need to do to perform better. In particular, the performance of the game should be closely related to children's skill of managing their diabetic condition.

C3. The activities in a game should present a variety of challenges such that children can obtain increasingly complex information about different aspects of managing their diabetic condition.

It can be argued based on Malone's conditions that, instead of aiming for a gaming experience that superficially conceal the educational purpose behind fun activities, a careful design of the structure of the game is highly desirable. Specifically, the game structure should contribute to the flow and subsequently the creation of an active learning environment.

Among all types of games, it appears that simulation and role play games are most likely to satisfy these requirements. Simulation and role play games are the most popular types of games. In fact, learning through direct experience, which is enabled by simulation and role play, has been consistently demonstrated to be more effective and enjoyable than learning through "information communicated as facts". Guided by Malone's conditions, efforts have been made to compare and select suitable games as the basis for our quest towards tackling the research question. Many open-source games were studied in respect to their educational value. The Mario Brothers game was finally selected for our game design since it enjoys a good match with the three conditions (i.e. C1, C2, and C3). The Mario Brothers game is open source and has long been considered as an engaging game for children thanks to its structured design with varied levels of difficulties. Thus, condition C1 is satisfied. The game has built-in feedback mechanisms that allow children to explore various game-play strategies through proactive interaction within a simulated environment. It hereby satisfies condition C2. In addition, the Mario Brothers game presents a variety of challenges through its stage-based design. It is easy to embed increasingly complex knowledge about living with diabetes at different game-playing stages. Thus the game agrees well with condition C3 and is suitable for providing an enduring and fun-filled learning experience.

All these reasons confirm the suitability of the Mario Brothers game for our research. Although our implementation of the education features was based on this game, we believe that the design strategies as explained below are generic enough to be applied to more education games. It is worthwhile to mention that these strategies can be considered as natural consequences of Malone's conditions.

- The first strategy is what we call the *Structure Enhancement* (*SE*). This means that the inclusion of education features should enhance rather than weaken the game structure. For example, adding education features to a game should contribute to the creations of a series of fine-grained difficulty levels so that children can gain new knowledge gradually as they progress from one level to another.
- The second strategy is the so-called *Feedback Enhancement (FE)*. Namely education features should embody themselves in the form of knowledge-rich visual feedbacks. The triggering of these feedbacks is likely to be situational and is subject to certain properties of the game character. Feedbacks can assume various forms, with message boxes, and on-screen performance indicators being a few examples.
- The third strategy is termed the *Challenge Enhancement* (*CE*). According to this strategy, education features in a game should bring more challenges to be faced by children while they play the game. This is because challenge encourages proactive knowledge discovery and therefore enhances engaged learning. We found that one good approach is to consider a stage-based game design. In this way, simple education features will be embedded in early stages of a game. On the other hand, complex features will be reserved for later stages of the game to facilitate progressive learning.

The three design strategies above have been applied to modify the Mario Brothers game, described further in the next Section. There are perhaps many other game design strategies that could be explored when designing education games. For example, a good education game should enhance the reward provided to children when a learning target embedded in a challenging task has been accomplished. This and other possible design strategies will be investigated in our future research.

3. GAME MODIFICATION FOR DIABETES EDUCATION

Driven by the three design strategies, namely *SE*, *FE*, and *CE*, modifications have been made to incorporate educational features into the mobile Mario Brothers game (see Figure 1). In line with the fundamental principles of role play games, the main character of the game, named Mario, is assumed to have type I diabetes. The health problems faced by Mario become the health problems to be solved by the game player. The ultimate goal of the game is to save a princess who is locked in a castle. To achieve this goal, Mario needs to manage his diabetes and maintain a healthy condition while fighting against a variety of evil guards during multiple stages of the game.

It is expected that, as children progress through stages of the game, they will gradually learn the skills to remain healthy by eating healthy food, having regular exercise, and injecting suitable amount of insulin when needed. *SE*, *FE*, and *CE* have been extensively utilized to support effective learning in the game. Feedback is given both in textual format (e.g. "*Mario's blood sugar level is well below the normal range he needs to eat something!!*") and visual format, i.e. blood sugar level changing colour from green to orange (warning) or red (critical). Below we discuss some representative examples of using the proposed strategies.

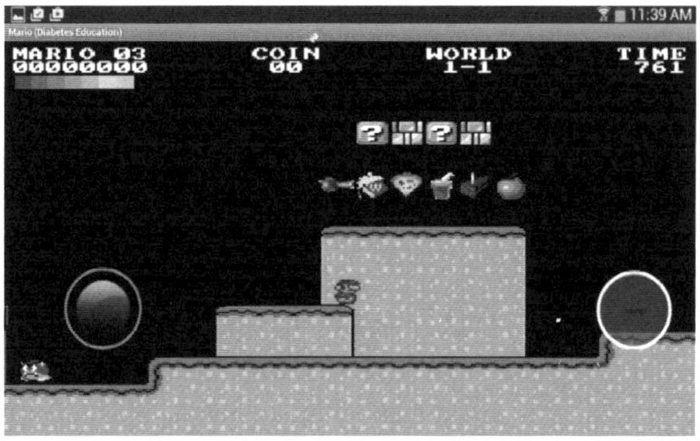

Figure 1. The screenshot of the Android mobile version - Diabetic Mario should maintain his blood sugar level (shown at the top) while trying to save the princess.

Example 1: Managing Mario's healthy condition, especially his blood sugar level, is designed as a main challenge at every stage of the game. If Mario's blood sugar level goes outside a healthy region, children's effort to rescue the princess will fail. To emphasize the importance of the blood sugar level, an indicator is placed at the top left corner of the game screen. In line with *FE*, the indicator as shown in Figure 1 is designed to change its colour whenever Mario's blood sugar level goes up or drops down. The way that the blood sugar level changes is determined by many factors, including playing time, the amount of exercises Mario had such as walking and jumping, and any food consumed by Mario.

Example 2: The modified Mario Brothers game is designed to help children learn the right skills to cope with their diabetic condition. As illustrated in Figure 1, choices regarding food consumption or insulin injection will pop up occasionally when Mario's blood sugar level deviates to a certain degree from the healthy level. According to *SE*, the options essentially represent fine-grained challenges since children need to make right choices through eating healthy food or injecting suitable amount of insulin in order to continue playing the game. The choice is to be made based on Mario's health condition and the progress of the game. The level of difficulty is adjusted to match the player's knowledge.

For the purpose of behavioural analysis, children need to login with their user name in order to play the game. Password is not required as this might pose problem to some children, especially those at very young age. Many game-playing activities, such as the amount of food consumed, the amount of insulin injection, and the amount of exercises, will be recorded in the system log. The log will help us find out whether children's skill of managing blood sugar levels will improve after playing the game for some time.

4. PRELIMINARY EVALUATION

A pre-post pilot study was conducted with the modified mobile version of Mario Brothers in 2015. Eligible participants were 12 children aged 9-13 years (6 females, 6 males), recruited from the greater Auckland area through community advertisements, schools and word of mouth. For the purpose of this study, participants were not required to have diabetes mellitus, nor had to have any particular experience playing video games of any time. The study was approved by the University of Auckland Human Participants Ethics Committee (Ref 013217). Participation in the study was entirely voluntary. Interested participants were given a participant information sheet to read, and completed written informed consent at baseline data collection.

Assessments were conducted at baseline and one-week after (post-intervention). At each time point, participants filled out a health-related questionnaire concerning their diet, physical activity, and lifestyle choices. Following the baseline assessment, participants were loaned a Samsung tablet for one week so they could play the mobile game in their free time if/when they wanted to. For the purpose of this study, participants were required to login with a unique user ID. The game automatically logged all the interactions, including when and for how long they played each time, which choices they made, how much feedback they received etc. At the end of the week, we collected the tablets and asked them to fill out the health-related questionnaire again, followed by a survey with closed and open questions about what they thought of the game.

4.1 Evaluation Metrics

The main objectives of this study were to determine the effect of playing the mobile game on enhancing children's knowledge of healthy diet and lifestyle. We also wanted to know whether children found the game engaging over the period of one week. Thus, the change of users' knowledge of healthy diet and lifestyle as well as their engagement with the game were our dependent variables.

To measure lifestyle knowledge enhancement, we used the health knowledge questionnaire developed by Saksvig and colleagues (2005) , based on previous work from the CATCH Health Behaviors Program (Edmundson, 1996) and the Kahnawake Schools Diabetes Prevention Program (Macaulay, 1997). The questionnaire aims to measure change in diet and physical activity psychosocial constructs in children over time. We used a set of questions measuring health-related knowledge (i.e. diet, physical activity, and diabetes) and adjusted the wording of some items to reflect the New Zealand context (e.g. for the originally developed item "Do people in Sandy Lake get more exercise or physical activity today than they did 30 years ago", Sandy Lake was replaced by Auckland).

The questionnaire consisted of 21 items about diet and exercise, each with four answer options and took approximately 10 minutes to complete. A sample question was:

Which one is the healthiest choice for supper (tick one only)?

1) lamb meat and macaroni soup, baked crumpet, water

2) hot dogs, french fries, jelly, fizzy or soft drink (e.g. Coke, Sprite, Fanta)

3) 2 minute noodles, chips, fruit juice

4) I don't know

To measure engagement, we analysed the number of times they played the game over the course of one week, amount of time they spent per session, average number of feedback messages they received etc. The acceptability/perceptions of the game questionnaire was developed by the research team for the purpose of this pilot study. Both questionnaires/surveys were pilot-tested in a small sample (n = 2) of children of the same age as those to be recruited to ensure reading comprehension of the items. Additionally, a research assistant was in place during the completion of the questionnaires, should reading or vocabulary explanations be necessary.

4.2 Results

We analysed the interaction logs recorded on each tablet during the 7-day period participants played the game (Table 1). On average, our participants played the modified Mario Bros game for 22.2 times over the 1-week period, spent 12.3 minutes in average on each session and were shown 38.6 feedback messages (box textual and visual). Out of all participants, two completed all seven levels of the game and the rest completed at least up to level 4. See Table 1 for more details.

Table 1. Analysis of User Interaction Logs.

Users ID	Number of sessions	Total number of feedback provided (textual & visual)	Average number of feedback shown per session
11	24	555	23.125
10	22	774	35.18
6	25	868	34.72
3	21	330	15.71
5	52	4355	83.75
7	42	3468	82.57
8	5	160	32
13	9	295	32.77
14	24	529	22.04
15	16	962	60.12
16	9	217	24.11
17	17	307	18.06
Average	22.2	1068.33	38.68

The analysis of the Health Knowledge Questionnaire (Table 2) shows that the confidence of the participants increased from pre to post event with respect to selecting healthy eating choices (pre = 66% to post = 77%) and initiating regular exercise habits (pre = 62% to post = 66%). The average score on the post-health questionnaire was higher than the pre-test score for all categories. More studies are needed to examine the effect of playing the game on children's knowledge and confidence over a longer period of time.

Table 2. Pre and Post study statistics.

	Average		**s.d.**	
	Pre-test	**Post-test**	**Pre-test**	**Post-test**
Questions related to Healthy food choices	66%	77%	24%	16%
Questions related to Exercise	62%	66%	22%	32%
Overall	65%	73%	12%	13%

Overall, the game was viewed as a good and fun experience by the players. Subjective evaluation of the data showed that the participants enjoyed playing the game. They also believed that it would have added educational value, as it involved players in problem-solving and decision-making, by requiring them to balance food and exercise to keep Mario's blood sugar level (displayed throughout the game) within the optimal levels.

5. CONCLUSIONS & FUTURE WORK

This work aimed to exploit the popularity of mobile games in an attempt to impact diabetes health-related knowledge of children. We proposed and described the design, implementation and preliminary evaluation of Diabetic Mario Bros, a mobile game intended to engage and motivate children to adopt a healthy lifestyle, which would enable them to take increasing control of their condition.

The contributions of this work were: 1) proposing a novel game design for teaching children how to manage diabetes 2) applying the proposed design to an open source 2D game and developing a mobile version 3) evaluating the effect of playing the game on enhancing children's knowledge of healthy diet and lifestyle and 4) analysing the participants' interaction logged over a period of one week. The results showed that the participants enjoyed playing the game. Interacting with the game for a week also enhanced children's diabetes health-related knowledge, which in turn can stimulate and facilitate the conversation of the children with health-care providers about their self-management practices. However, there were a few limitations in terms of players' competence and health background. The current version of the game does not take the history of the player into account and all users are presented with the same challenges regardless of their gaming experience.

The core research effort going forward will focus on effects on engagement and health knowledge changes as a result of personalisation technology in computer games. Personalising the game according to players' preferences and abilities can sustain their engagement in the long-term and encourage them to use and explore all features supported by the system. In addition, for the purpose of this study, participants were not required to have diabetes mellitus, nor had to have any particular experience playing video games of any time. For the next evaluation study, we will be recruiting children with type I diabetes.

We will also further analyse the player interaction data logged on each tablet, such as number and nature of the daily sessions over the course of the week to see whether food items they picked changed as they kept playing the game. Some of the food options the participants were presented with were: APPLE, BANANA, MEAT, PIZZA, CARROT, MILKSHAKE and CAKE. We would like to investigate the number of times a healthy food choice was made after blood sugar level jumped up and compare that with the number of sessions each user played the game and the number of textual and visual feedback messages they received. Our hypothesis is that the more they played, the healthier food choices they made. Full analysis of the interaction data will also allow us to think in terms of what motivates a participant to play a health educational mobile game and how that motivation can be sustained over time. We believe our research paves the way for the systematic design and development of full-fledged computer games dedicated to diabetes education in the future.

REFERENCES

Baghaei, N., Nandigam, D., Casey, J., Direito, A., & Maddison, R.: *Diabetic Mario: Designing and Evaluating Mobile Games for Diabetes Education.* Games for Health Journal: Research, Development, and Clinical Applications (Vol. 5(4)), pp.270-278 (2016)

Baranowski, T., Baranowski, J., Thompson, D., Buday, R., Jago, R., Griffith, M. J., ... & Watson, K. B. *Video game play, child diet, and physical activity behavior change: A randomized clinical trial.* American journal of preventive medicine, 40(1), 33-38 (2011).

Chai CS, Koh E, Lim CP, Tsai CC. *Deepening ICT integration through multilevel design of technological pedagogical content knowledge.* J Computer Education 1:1–17 (2014)

Chen, G., Baghaei, N., Sarrafzadeh, H., Manford, C., Marshall, S., & Court, G.: *Designing Games to Educate Diabetic Children.* 23rd Australian Computer-Human Interaction Conference (OzCHI), Canberra, Australia (2011)

Csikszentmihalyi, M.: Flow: *The Psychology of Optimal Experience.* New York: Harper & Row, (1990).

Edmundson E, Parcel GS, Feldman HA, et al. *The effects of the child and adolescent trial for cardiovascular health upon psychosocial determinants of diet and physical activity behavior.* Prev Med; 25:442–454 (1996)

Greysen, S. R., Khanna, R. R., Jacolbia, R., Lee, H. M., & Auerbach, A. D.: *Tablet computers for hospitalized patients: A pilot study to improve inpatient engagement.* Journal of Hospital Medicine, 9(6), 396-399 (2014)

Lieberman DA. *Digital games for health behavior change: Research, design, and future directions.* In: eHealth Applications: Promising Strategies for Behavior Change. Noar SM, Harrington NG (eds.). New York: Routledge; pp. 110–127 (2012)

Macaulay AC, Paradis G, Potvin L, et al. *The Kahnawake Schools Diabetes Prevention Project: Intervention, evaluation, and baseline results of a diabetes primary prevention program with a native community in Canada.* Prev Med; 26:779–790 (1997)

Malone, T.T.W.: *Heuristics for designing enjoyable user interfaces: Lessons from computer games.* Human Factors in Computer Systems, 63–68 (1982)

Ministry of Health: *Diabetes and Cardiovascular Disease Quality Improvement Plan.* In. Wellington: Ministry of Health; (2008).

Raaff, C., Glazebrook, C., & Wharrad, H.: *A systematic review of interactive multimedia interventions to promote children's communication with health professionals: implications for communicating with overweight children.* BMC medical informatics and decision making, 14(1), 8. (2014)

Saksvig BI, Gittelsohn J, Harris SB, et al. *A pilot schoolbased healthy eating and physical activity intervention improves diet, food knowledge, and self-efficacy for native Canadian children.* J Nutr, 135:2392–2398 (2005)

A MOBILE APPLICATION FOR USER REGULATED SELF-ASSESSMENTS

Fotis Lazarinis[1], Vassilios S. Verykios[1] and Chris Panagiotakopoulos[2]
[1]*School of Science & Technology, Hellenic Open University, Patras, Greece*
[2]*Department of Primary Education, University of Patras, Greece*

ABSTRACT

In this paper we present a mobile application for self-assessment. The work describes the main features of the application and focuses on its acceptance by students and the increase on their learning, through its usage in real testing settings. The application supports the retrieval of questions based on a number of criteria and it was evaluated with the aid of students who self-assessed their knowledge prior to in-class pencil and paper tests. An improvement in the performance of students who actively engaged with the system has been observed.

KEYWORDS

Assessment, mobile learning, self-assessment, adaptation.

1. INTRODUCTION

Mobile devices have significantly changed in recent years. While their primary purpose was to enable users to communicate through voice, their functions have considerably expanded, to simulate a resourceful personal computer. New applications are constantly being developed, giving the user personalized access to various data. Education is a field which could greatly benefit via this technology. Collaboration, personalized learning, peer-assessment, learning in context and all these novel ideas which have been proposed in the literature could more easily be realized by the utilization of a personal mobile device.

In this work, we focus on self-assessment through the utilization of a mobile application. Students are able to adjust the assessment data to prepare for the actual exams. They can define the topics and the difficulty level of the testing material and they get detailed explanations based on their answers to True/False, multiple choice and fill-in-the gap questions. The application has been implemented as an android application and utilized in real classes. The evaluation showed that the application is useful and students advanced their understanding on the selected topics. The main focus of the work is to discuss the effect in learning by using such a mobile application for exam preparation.

The paper is organized as follows: a literature review is provided in section 2, then in section 3 the system is described and in section 4 the evaluation results are presented. Conclusions and recommendations for future expansions are made in the final section.

2. LITERATURE REVIEW

Assessment plays an important part of every educational activity (Biggs, 1998; Gipps, 1999; Harlen, 2007). Several forms of assessment have been proposed. Fetterman et al. (1996) discuss the importance of self-assessment in knowledge. Self-assessment techniques have been applied in large scale in MOOCs and has been proved beneficial (Kulkarni et al., 2013). Formative assessment refers to assessment that is specifically intended to generate feedback on performance to improve and accelerate learning (Sadler, 1998). Tools for self-regulating the assessment process have been already proposed (Nicol & Macfarlane-Dick, 2006). Castle and McGuire (2010) conducted a study concerning student self-assessment of learning at an online university and suggested a positive impact on self-assessment to student learning. Self-assessment in secondary education students showed an improvement in performance and also improved their ability to self-assess their performance over time (Butler and Lee, 2010). With the improvement of technology and the ability to carry a personal computer anywhere and whenever, a number of systems have been proposed in order to take advantage of these technologies in assessment.

Hwang et al. (2011) proposed a formative assessment-based approach for improving the learning achievements of students in a mobile learning environment. Their experiments showed that their proposed approach promotes students' learning interest and attitude and improves their learning achievement. A formative assessment-based approach for improving the learning achievements of students in a mobile learning environment has been implemented. The researchers combined digital learning resources and real-world learning contexts to improve the understanding of students.

Lalos et al. (2009) developed a version of the "snakes and ladders" game for portable devices. They used a combination of location detection techniques, m-learning, m-assessment and learning standards to support the learning process of young children. Zhu et al. (2010) used a novel mobile telephone food application that will provide an accurate account of daily food and nutrient intake. They collected and evaluated dietary information reducing in that way the burden of more classical approaches for dietary assessment. This is an example of one of many practical aspects of mobile phones in various forms of assessment in a broader sense.

The effects of using vocabulary learning programs in mobile phones on students' English vocabulary learning have been investigated in (Başoğlu and Akdemir, 2010). The results of this study indicated that using mobile phones as a vocabulary learning tool is more effective than one of the traditional vocabulary learning tools.

In a more recent study, Bogdanović et al. (2014) showed that the integration of the mobile quiz application into Moodle improves students' results and increases satisfaction and motivation for using mobile devices in their learning process. Jacobs et al. (2015) developed an app which provides an individual student with summary feedback from tutors and provisional/final marks for all their assignments. The app is available on desktop and mobile devices. The aim of their work was to make feedback more accessible, and thus to engage students more actively in the process and this will have a beneficial impact on their learning.

Our work focuses on self-regulating formative assessments and we aim to make the process of self-assessment more accessible and adaptable to the students' goals. The system described below provides a summary of the process to make individual students aware of their true knowledge.

3. DESCRIPTION OF THE SYSTEM

mSAT (mobile Self-Assessment Tool) is an android app with the aim to help users to prepare for their exams through the execution of preparatory tests. This work is a new implementation for mobile devices of one of our older works presented in (Lazarinis et al., 2015). As in our older work, the main goal of the current work is to provide a flexible environment for self-assessment, where the test participants can regulate the testing process based on their current goals. However, the new design grants the users the freedom to test their knowledge anywhere and whenever they need to. Further, the system is enriched with more focused feedback per item and suggestions for further studying based on the performance of a student.

Each mobile app has a layered architecture, which implements the user experience, the business logic and the data. The data play a crucial point in this application as the testing material should be readily accessible once they are created or updated. Limitations arising from the features of the mobile device running the application (e.g., the characteristics of memory, storage, processor speed etc.) should not challenge the features of the application.

The application was developed in Android Studio with the SDK Android, using different libraries in order to extend the services with features such as cloud database. The selected cloud platform was the Parse Server at Parse.com in which a database was created. The main entities of our application are:

- Users: where the details of the registered users of the application are stored. It is used for the login and the authentication process.

• Topics: the details of the topics of the testing items.

• Question Items: contains the text, the type, the choices and the correct answer(s) of the testing items. These are managed centrally by a single administrator in the first version of the system, but adding more users with administrative rights is a straightforward approach.

• User Results: where the results for each attempt are stored.

Users can use the system either as registered users or as guests (see Figure 1 – images have been edited to present the messages in English). This flexibility was granted in order to increase the utilization of the application, as students could be discouraged to use the application if more information on their behalf is needed. The older experiences with the Web based version of the system, showed that many students were reluctant to register, due to lack of technical ability or techno anxiety or due to unwillingness to be engaged in such a process. Therefore, we preferred to offer both options with the goal to gradually persuade them to register through their involvement with the tool in order to benefit from the additional features, such as comparison to older attempts, etc.

Figure 1. Initial Screen.

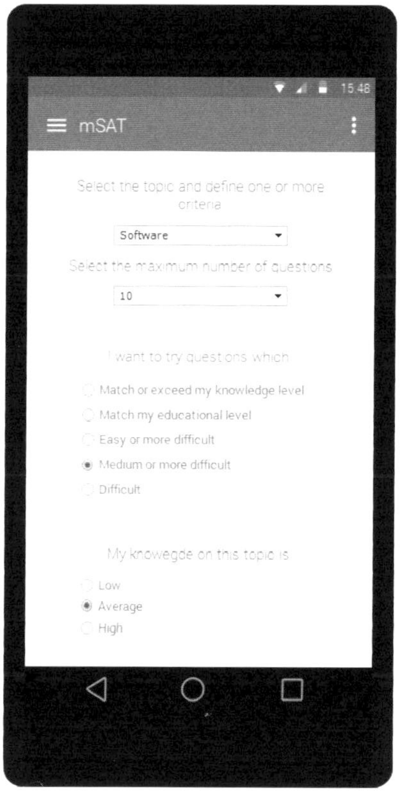

Figure 2. Self-assessment criteria.

The system is designed to be a flexible self-assessment tool, where users are able to regulate the testing process by defining their knowledge and their goals (see Figure 2):

i. Selecting the assessment topics to be tested on.

ii. Describing their knowledge level and/or the level of completed education on the selected topics.

iii. Defining the characteristics (difficulty, type, number etc.) of the testing items they wish to attempt.

Simply put, the application logic is that administrators define and update the topic hierarchy; educators enrich the item bank with questions of various topics, difficulty and education level and students fulfill their assessment goals by selecting the most appropriate items to be tested on.

Test participants select testing items by applying one of the following strategies:

i. The level of difficulty and/or the appropriate educational level of the testing items: Questions are classified as easy, medium or difficult, and learners can select assessment items based on their difficulty. They can select questions that match or pass or are below a specific level of difficulty, e.g., "show questions that are above average difficulty".

ii. The learners' knowledge level: students can select questions that match or are above or below their knowledge level. Easy, medium and difficult questions correspond to low, good and high knowledge level. So students who, for example, have a "good" knowledge of a topic, they can define rules like "show questions greater or equal to my knowledge level". In that case, the tool retrieves testing items with a high difficulty.

iii. The learners' educational level: this possibility supports the selection of questions based on the educational level they correspond to. Users are able to instruct the system "retrieve testing item that match their level of education".

Alternatively students may ask the tool to decide on the arrangement of testing items based on the user provided data of registered users. The application retrieves items that correspond to the student's educational level, on a specific topic. The questions are grouped by subtopic and by their level of complexity.

In the next step, the list of questions matching the criteria is presented and students can select anyone of the list to answer. The retrieved testing items are clustered by the subtopic they relate to. If a student has defined the maximum number of questions to attempt, and there are remaining questions in a subtopic, these are grouped at the end of the list of questions under a title called "More questions".

Administrators and educators log in through a Web interface and update the question database. They define the text of the question, the possible answers, the correct one(s), the difficulty level and the educational level. They match each question to a broad topic or a narrow subtopic. In any case the question is automatically assigned to the topics in the higher level of the hierarchy. This supports more clustering alternatives which could eventually improve the self-testing process.

Once a student completes the self-evaluation of her/his knowledge, the tool estimates the knowledge level and presents statistics per topic. For registered users, these statistics are stored in the database to be utilized in future assessments for this user. The new level of knowledge is based on the average score on each topic. Scores are normalized based on their question weights. A mark below 50% results to "low" understanding while good knowledge means a score between 50% and 75%. A result greater than these limits, leads to high knowledge level. Further, statistics per topic and subtopic are presented to students who are informed about their weaknesses with the encouragement to study the relevant materials for the topics with low performance.

4. EVALUATION

mSAT is designed to be a flexible tool which can be used even between classes to help students assess their understanding using a multicriteria question retrieval approach. The main purpose of the current study is to discuss the results of an evaluation experiment with the aim to understand whether the tool has an impact to the learning of students. An evaluation experiment was carried out with the aid of 87 students of the first grade of a Greek senior high school.

The research goals of the experiment were:

(i) to measure the potential improvement on the performance of the learners in regular in-class assessments, *and*

(ii) to understand if the mobile version of the tool prompts users to be more engaged in the process of evaluating their understanding.

The trials run between September and December 2016. Students (aged 15 to 16) were randomly divided into two groups of 44 (Group A) and 43 students (Group B). During this period three paper & pencil in-class tests have been planned for both students groups. The in-class tests concerned basic algorithmic skills and Scratch programming questions. Group A (experimental group) had the ability to utilize the android application for one day prior to each test, while Group B (control group) did not have access to the application. The questions loaded in the application concerned the same topics but they were not same as those asked in the summative tests. Moreover, we only included a few representative questions of varying difficulty for each subtopic. We primarily needed to make the students aware of their true knowledge per subtopic and topic they worked on and not to simply give them the opportunity to practice extensively on questions which resemble the actual testing items.

Prior to the experimental setting, we administered the same paper & pencil test to both groups to understand whether there are significant differences in the distribution of knowledgeable students. The t-test run with the scores of the two groups showed no significant difference in the results. The two groups of students had statistically equivalent abilities before learning the subject unit. This outcome was expected as both groups were randomly created and consisted of an enlarged number of students.

Table 1 shows the results of the first in-class paper & pencil test. Group A had an average of approximately 64.55% and Group B an average of 62.69%. The distribution of the results are comparatively similar and again the t-test showed no significant difference. Admittedly, these first results were discouraging. However, we looked closer to the individual results and we compared them to the results of the pre-experiment test and also to the utilization of the application among students. Through this comparison, it was made obvious that only 12 students of Group A used the application, which is about 25% of the student population of the experimental group. Furthermore, only 4 of them actually retrieved questions with a difficulty level higher than their knowledge level, as it was provided to the tool by them prior to the testing. These students received some alarming statistics at the end of the evaluation and as they informed us in the focused personal interviews, they had to re-study for the exam. Thus they had actually an improvement on the actual summative test. The other 8 students, either tried easy questions or quitted the application early or had already a high knowledge level, so they received no worrying results.

Table 1. Scores of the student groups in the first in-class paper & pencil test.

Score	Group A	Group B
0-50%	9	8
50%-75%	27	30
75%-100%	8	5

This qualitative analysis of the individual results showed some improvement to some students and these participants actually "spread the word" to their peers. So, in the second phase of the experiment, 33 students used the mobile application and we measured an improvement in the scores. The average score of Group A increased to almost 67%, while the average score of the Group B increased by approximately 1%, i.e. to 63.4%. The t-test showed that the two averages are different (t-value=2.56677 at $p < .05$). The greatest difference was in the middle class where the averages score was 68.24% for Group A and 63.4% for Group B. All the students of Group A of this class have used the application to practice and to study again some of the learning materials.

Table 2. Scores of the student groups in the second in-class paper & pencil test.

Score	Group A	Group B
0-50%	8	5
50%-75%	25	30
75%-100%	11	8

The last in-class test, showed again an improvement to the performance of the students of Group A, who used the application. The marks of Group A in the individual classes have been increased to almost reach the upper limit of each class which was not the case in Group B. By this trial, several students of Group B wanted to try this application as well, especially students who performed worse than expected in the previous two tests.

Table 3. Scores of the student groups in the third in-class paper & pencil test.

Score	Group A	Group B
0-50%	7	6
50%-75%	24	27
75%-100%	13	10

Based on the statistics, the comparison of the individual cases, and the opinions of the students during the focused interviews, we have strong indications that the application helped the students to get a better mark and prompted users to be more engaged in the process of evaluating their understanding. Further, students found the application easy to use and they liked the fact that it supports various options. In the next round of evaluations we will look closer on the specific adaptive options offered by the tool with respect to their utilization by the students and the opinions of the students. That way the default options of the system could be better customized to more effectively guide the student.

5. CONCLUSION

In this paper we briefly presented the characteristics of a mobile tool for self-assessments and we focused on understanding its overall pedagogical value in real learning settings. The experimental group has shown an increase in the utilization of the application between the trials and an increase on the average marks. A pre-experiment test was administered to ensure that the random distribution of the student population did not lead to groups with uneven distribution of knowledgeable students. Through focused interviews, students shared their opinions which were quite positive towards the tool.

In this version of the system the focus was on the acceptance by the students and the pedagogical gains. Several aspects of the tool need to be tested. For example, the importance and the extension of the criteria for customizing the assessment process is a very significant research direction. In the current experimentation we worked with senior high school students and therefore all the material was related to this educational level. Would such a system be acceptable to tertiary education students or for vocational training? This is another research path. The feedback needs to be examined. Has it been used properly or did the students find it helpful? Implementation issues could also be explored. Would the response be acceptable in case the database increases significantly?

All things considered, this tool has been proved to have a practical value and if its database is enriched with more topics it could become a very useful teaching assistant.

ACKNOWLEDGEMENT

This work has been partially supported by a grant from Stavros Niarchos Foundation (SNF).

REFERENCES

Başoğlu, E. B. and Akdemir O. (2010). A comparison of undergraduate students' english vocabulary learning: using mobile phones and flash cards. *TOJET: The Turkish Online Journal of Educational Technology* Vol. 9 No 3

Biggs J. (1998) Assessment and classroom learning: A role for formative assessment? *Assessment in Education: Principles, Policy and Practice* 5(1): 103–110

Bogdanović, Z., Barać, D., Jovanić, B., Popović, S., and Radenković, B., (2014) Evaluation of mobile assessment in a learning management system, *British Journal of Educational Technology*, Vol. 45, No 2. pp. 231–244

Butler, Y. G., and Lee J. (2010). The effects of self-assessment among young learners of English. *Language Testing*, 27(1), 5–31.

Castle S., and McGuire, C. (2010). An Analysis of Student Self-Assessment of Online, Blended, and Face-to-Face Learning Environments: Implications for Sustainable Education Delivery. International Education Studies,3 (3), p. 36-40.

Fetterman, D. M., Kaftarian, S. J., & Wandersman,A.(Eds.). (1996). *Empowerment evaluation: Knowledge and tools for self-assessment and accountability*. Thousand Oaks, CA: Sage.

Gipps, C. V. (1999). Socio-cultural aspects of assessment. In P.D. Pearson & A. Iran-Nejad (Eds.), *Review of Research in Education*, Vol. 24, pp. 355-392.

Harlen, W. (2007). *Assessment of learning*. Sage Publications Ltd, London.

Hwang, G.-J., Chang, H.-F. (2011). A formative assessment-based mobile learning approach to improving the learning attitudes and achievements of students. *Computers & Education*, 56, pp. 1023–1031.

Jacobs, C., Wilson, M. and Barker, C. (2015) Using the latest developments in mobile technology to improve students' engagement with assessment feedback, *International Conference on Interactive Mobile Communication Technologies and Learning (IMCL).*

Kulkarni, C., Koh, P. W., Le, H., Chia, D., Papadopoulos, K., Cheng, J., Koller, D., & Klemmer, S.R. (2013). Peer and self-assessment in massive online classes. *ACM Transactions on Computer-Human Interactions, 9*(4) Article 39.

Lalos, P., Lazarinis, F. and Kanellopoulos, D. (2009). E-snakes and ladders: a hypermedia educational environment for portable devices. *IJMLO* 3(2), pp. 107-127

Lazarinis, F., Verykios, V.S. and Panagiotakopoulos C. 2015. An Adaptive Web Tool for Self-assessment using Lightweight User Profiles. *7th International Conference on Computer Supported Education (CSEDU)*, Lisbon, Portugal, pp. 14-23.

Nicol, D., Macfarlane-Dick, D. (2006). Formative assessment and self-egulated learning: a model and seven principles of good feedback practice. *Studies in Higher Education*, 31(2), pp. 199–218.

Sadler, D. R. (1989). Formative assessment and the design of instructional systems. *Instructional Science*, 18, 119–144.

Zhu, F., Bosch, M., Woo, I., Kim, S., Boushey, C., Ebert, D., and Delp, E. (2010). The Use of Mobile Devices in Aiding Dietary Assessment and Evaluation, *IEEE J Sel Top Signal Process*, 4(4): 756–766.

ACCEPTANCE OF MOBILE LEARNING AT SMES OF THE SERVICE SECTOR

Marc Beutner and Frederike Anna Rüscher
University Paderborn, Chair Business and Human Resource Education II
Warburger Str. 100, 33098 Paderborn, Germany

ABSTRACT

Mobile Learning (mLearning) is becoming popular in several parts of education. The increasing availability of mobile technology and devices is an important fact, which fosters this trend. However, even if it attracts more and more attention at huge enterprises it is not clear what small and medium enterprises (SMEs) think about Mobile Learning. Moreover, in a modern society, the Service Sector increases as well and here Mobile Learning could be a helpful concept to cope with rapid change and innovation on information. The texts provides results of an acceptance study with regard to Mobile Learning at SMEs in the Service Sector. This is related to advantages and disadvantages which companies expect. This qualitative interview study gathered information form 14 SMEs in Germany. As a basis for a successful implementation of mLearning in companies of the Service Sector the acceptance by decision makers and users is crucial. The results show that acceptance already exists but that there are a lot of challenges and requirements as well.

KEYWORDS

Mobile Learning, Acceptance, Service Sector, SME.

1. APPROACHING MOBILE LEARNING

Very early, already in 2002, Keegan anticipated that "mobile learning is a harbinger of the future of learning" (Keegan 2002, 9). Nowadays, almost nobody in highly developed countries of Europe can image a world without smartphones, tablets, laptops, personal digital assistants (PDAs) and other mobile devices with hybrid functions and assess to the internet (see already similar ideas several years ago by INQA 2007).

In 2016, such devices are already located in almost all establishments, administrations, and private households in Germany. In addition to that, the speed of mobile devices is increasing as well as their availability (see e.g. Beutner / Pechuel 2012a). This means that since the early beginnings of Mobile Learning the experience and expertise in use of these devices increased, too (see already Traxler 2009).

But, the fact that mobile devices are currently available does not mean the acceptance of these technologies for learning processes is already established. To get acceptance it needs to have a conceptual basis to get credibility.

To address Mobile Learning in an adequate way a definition is needed. Scholars like Chinnery define mLearning just as a subset of eLearning. Most of the definitions since 2000 look at the specifics of mLearning and focusing on mobile technologies (see Clarke and Flaherty 2002 or see Quinn 2000).

Geddes (2004, 214) points out, "mLearning is the acquisition of any knowledge and skill through using mobile technology, anywhere, anytime, that results in an alteration in behaviour". In 2005 O´Malley et al. defined mobile learning as learning which takes place at no fixed, predetermined location when a learner takes advantages from learning by using mobile technologies (see O´Malley et al. 2005).

Since the beginnings of Mobile Learning (mLearning) there were several discussions about this topic. At the beginning of the millennium we had several studies about the crucial aspects of mLearning (see e.g. Freimuth 2002, Kynäslathis 2003, Reys 2004, Kinshuk / Goh 2004). In 2012 Beutner / Pechuel put these aspects together and included the ideas of Stone 2010 (see Beutner / Pechuel 2012a and Beutner / Pechuel 2012b) and could identify:

• Efficiency: through learning opportunities at different locations
• Personal sphere: by learning in the personal environment of the learners
• Interaction connection: between learners as well as between students and teachers and also to available databases
• Context sensitivity: the ability to analyze information environment of the learner (situated learning)
• Content should exist on both stationary and mobile platforms
• Convenience
• Expediency
• Immediacy
• Support at critical moments of need (see as well Beutner 2014)

Mobile Learning can be used in different approaches. With focus on portable learning often already existing pedagogical solutions of eLearning are just miniaturized and provided on mobile devices (see e.g. Traxler 2009, 12) sometimes for new target groups (see Beutner / Teine 2016). If mobile technologies are only used to demonstrate the feasibility of technology and possible pedagogical opportunities it will be a very general way of using Mobile Learning (see e.g. Traxler 2009, 12). Some Mobile Learning developments are created to enhance the social exchange and support collaborative learning (see e.g. Traxler 2009, 12). Some are especially focusing productivity and efficiency in learning (see e.g. Traxler 2009, 12) and some are using the real advantages of mobile situations, were the user is in an real environment for example in an enterprise, a museum etc. and can get situated learning which could not exist otherwise (see e.g. Traxler 2009, 12, see Beutner 2016, see Beutner / Teine / Gebbe / Fortmann 2016).

To make mLearning and the framing elements more explicit and to enhance the rational analysis of mobile education Marguerite L. Koole provided a frame model of Mobile Learning which addresses three core perspectives the device itself (D) the learner (L) and the social aspects (S) (see. Koole 2009).

Since the early days of mLearning there is already a strong discussion on its acceptance. With regard to Motiwalli 2007 Wang /Wu / Wang state in research on acceptance of Mobile Learning "Despite the tremendous growth and potential of the mobile devices and networks, wireless e-learning and m-learning are still in their infancy or embryonic stage" (Wang /Wu / Wang 2009 and see as well Motiwalla, 2007).

Concerning acceptance there are several approaches. The TAM model for example focusses on the technical acceptance and is often used in its original way or its modifications to measure the usability of a tool. In addition to these approaches it is also important to get qualitative insights into the field. Nevertheless, there is currently a lack of research concerning qualitative information on acceptance and experiences in different fields of economy and their specific focus on mLearning.

Already in 2009 Kukulska-Hulme et al. provided an idea of the European perspective of mLearning and addresses here parts of the Service Sector as well (see. Kukulska-Hulme et al. 2009).

Taking all these parts of the scientific discussion into account, we designed an Acceptance study for Mobile Learning activities in the Service Sector. In modern societies, the Service Sector is becoming more and more important (see Eichengreen / Gutpa 2013) as Kim stated already 10 years ago (see Kim 2006). But, there is a huge diversity concerning the services. For example the department of innovation, industry, science and research of Australia described this diversity of services with regard to different activities:

• "delivering bricks to delivering a violin concerto
• designing a floral arrangement to designing a pub
• advising on investments to advising on health
• preparing a banquet to preparing a construction site
• driving a taxi to driving a nail
• fixing roof tiles to fixing a heart valve."

(Australian Government - Department of innovation, industry, science and research 2009. 5)

In Service Sectors like the Banking Sector the importance of Mobile Learning is already recognized and first implementations are currently running (see Beutner 2016.)

2. DESIGN OF THE SME ACCEPTANCE STUDY

Studies often focus big companies due to the fact, that they often have more resources for Mobile Learning than smaller ones with less staff members and less capital. There is a lack of research concerning what happens in small and medium sized enterprises (SMEs) in the field modern mobile technologies.

These ideas and discussions lead to the aim of our study. This text and the study behind it are designed to reflect on and understand the position of mLearning in the Service Sector and especially at SMEs. A core objective of our research is to gather and provide ideas what persons in this sector think about mLearning in general. We gather their experiences and attitudes. It is important to get an idea about the advantages and disadvantages which they see in mLearning in this specific field. We addressed staff members and owners of companies at 14 SMEs in the middle of Germany in the region of Paderborn. This is an area of 250.000 people living in it and its surrounding smaller cities and villages. Moreover, it also includes a more rural environment where also about 100.000 people are situated. All of the addressed interview partners are decision makers or they are responsible for training programmes or act as a trainer. To get information about their acceptance of mLearning concerning their educational measures or programmes we developed and pretested a short questionnaire to structure the interviews. The interviews were conducted in a half-structured way. The respondents had always the opportunity to provide additional information and had several parts where they could talk in a narrative way about the topic (see Flick 1998; Strauss / Corbin 1998). All of them got the same introduction with as short explanation why we are focusing on Mobile Learning and what is a sort of general understanding.

After a general introduction and a welcome to the interview, we gathered information on age, about the function in the company, about the branch within the Service Sector etc. In the core part of the interviews, we looked at their experiences with mLearning and their ideas about its use. We led them define the term mLearning to come to a concreate idea of what they are focusing when they were talking about the topic. We asked for the mobile devices used in their company and how they have used Mobile Learning so far. Moreover, we asked in which ways the staff members are currently using their devices. To get a more detailed insight we asked about the requirements for the use of mLearning in their company and about advantages and disadvantages the participants could describe. With regard to the future, we also asked them to tell us their ideas about how mLearning could look like in 5 years with regard to their own company.

We conducted our interviews as telephone interviews and were immediately documented via text-recordings after each call and structured via argumentation tables. To get deeper insight and more interpretation opportunities in a structured way, we used content analysis. This was the basis to analyze and categorize the data. In order to assure trustworthiness the interviews were conducted by an interviewer group, which was right small, so that we could ensure that all participants had a similar interview structure and the same information. The core aim was here to create credibility and validity. Moreover, it was important to secure of the identity of all our interviewees. Validity is existing in our study because all categories emerged from the data of the interviews. In addition to that, they are also consistent with the understandings of the participants. To ensure this we did random checks at the participants. The average duration of each telephone interview was about 10 minutes. The team conducted the interviews after first informative telephone contacts to ensure that the randomly selected persons are informed and available. The interviews with all SMEs were conducted in in first two weeks of December 2016.

3. AN INSIGHT IN THE CORE RESULTS

At first, the core results will be described, following a further analysis of the findings to give an overall insight of the core results of the acceptance study.

92.86% of the participants are aware of the term mLearning and are able to describe the core aspects of mLearning. 7.14% do know what mLearning entails, but were not able to define the term.

85.71% of the participants are using mobile devices in their company. Nearly all of the participants who use mobile devices in their company stated that they use smartphones and laptops (91.67%). Tablets were mentioned nearly as often with 83.33% of those who use mobile devices in their company. 7.14% of the participants who use mobile devices in their company stated that they use PDAs/Organiser as well as smartphones, tablets and laptops.

57.14% of the participants are using mLearning in their company. 14.29% of the participants stated at first that they are not using mLearning, but adjusted that thought after hearing some examples for mLearning. 42.86% stated that they are not using Mobile Learning in their company. As a reason for not using mLearning one participant argued that in their company there are no limitations if a staff member wants to use their own tablet, but they still prefer the traditional learning path, and named seminar rooms equipped with computers as one of their ways to provide further education. Another participant stated that they are probably not familiar enough with that kind of learning tool. Another participant pointed out that they probably fulfil the requirements, but further education is provided externally. Another participant named as a reason for not using mLearning the preference of using traditional learning tools, like books, which provide more safety, trust and is most relevant for source work. The other half of participants who do not use mLearning stated that in their company there is no need nor demand for mLearning so far. On the other hand, the participants who are using mLearning in their company stated different reasons for using mLearning. One reason for 50% of the participants who use mLearning is the element of research. Further reasons for the participants who are using mLearning are:

- usage for further education on a train or plane (12.5%),
- refreshment of knowledge (12.5%), for further education on different topics (12.5%),
- learning portals (37.5%),
- e-seminars (25%)

and more specific:

- instructor led training, self-based online training and massive open online courses (for customers and staff members) (12.5%),
- for staff member training on their soft skills (12.5%),
- tutorials on the homepage for customers (12.5%),
- YouTube channel with learning videos for customers (12.5%).

4. ADVANTAGES AND PROBLEMS OF MOBILE LEARNING

The question “Under which circumstances could you imagine using Mobile Learning in your company?” was answered by 71.43% of the participants. The other 28.57% referred to their answer on the question before. 30% stated that they cannot imagine using mLearning in their company at the moment. One of the 30% stated that their company is too small and a direct personal communication is most of the times easier and that mLearning is only applicable for customer trainings or information at the moment. The latter was an argument of another participant as well. Another 20% could imagine using mLearning, but only when the topic is more familiar and the circumstances are adjusted. One participant stated that for the placement of organisational, formative and simple content they could imagine using mLearning in their company. Another participant stated that for staff members who are away on business a lot mLearning would be an advantage. Another participant stated that it depends on the topic and on the reliability of the content. Another one stated that they use mLearning for further education of their staff members.

21.43% do not see any advantages in the usage of Mobile Learning. 78.57% see advantages in the usage of Mobile Learning. Same numbers are applicable for the disadvantages in the usage of Mobile Learning. The following table shows the arguments for and against the usage of Mobile Learning mentioned by the participants. The items which were mentioned with a higher frequency are at the top followed by the items which were mentioned less frequently.

Table 1. SMEs on the advantages and disadvantages of the usage of mLearning in their companies.

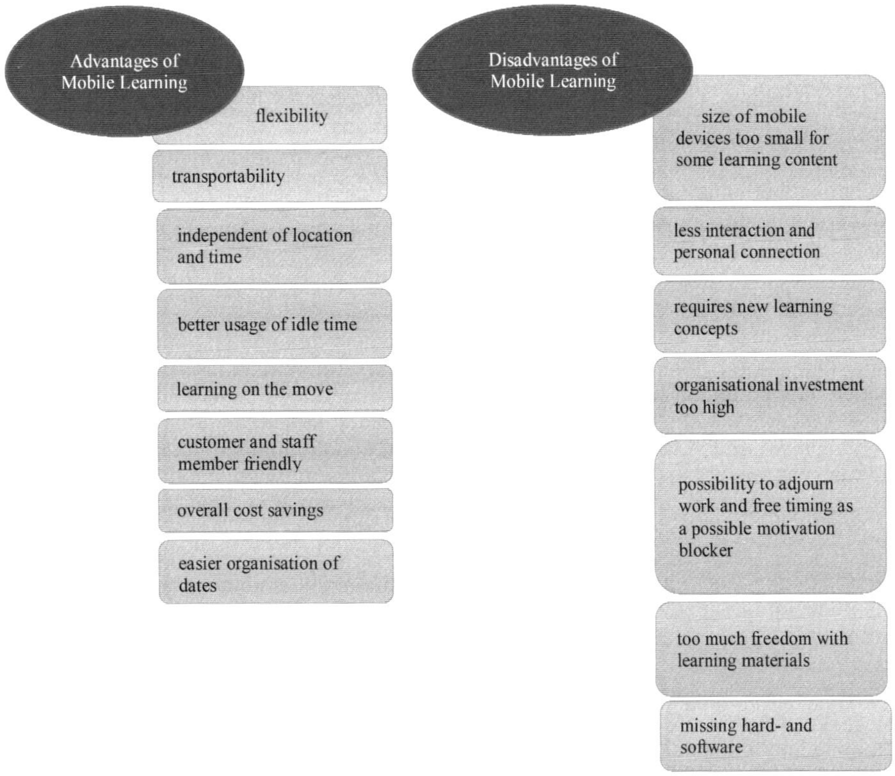

5. FUTURE CHALLENGES AND CHANCES OF MOBILE LEARNING

Mobile Learning is a supplementary tool to traditional learning rather than as replacement of it. This is becoming more and more important for the future. Regarding the development of mLearning in the next five years especially in the participants´ companies, most participants (92.86%) think that the usage of mLearning will increase due to the advantages mentioned before. Furthermore, some participants (28.57%) argued that mLearning will be used as an addition to the common learning tools and integrated in the Blended Learning Scenario as the range of mLearning tools will increase in the future. Most of the participants think that mLearning will increase, but have no plans to integrate it in their daily work at this point (28.57%). One participant argued that they have and will integrate mLearning in their company, but not so much for staff members as for customers. Another participant mentioned that the staff members have to accustom themselves to the new learning environment, but in the end, the staff members and the company will benefit from it. After presenting these initial findings follows now a further analysis of the data. The high number of participants who did know what Mobile Learning means shows that the term Mobile Learning is increasing in the consciousness of SMEs at least in the service sector.

A lot of SMEs already use mobile devices in their companies which are mostly smartphones, laptops and tablets. This indicates that there already exists the technical basis to use Mobile Learning.

Mobile Learning is indeed known, but not as much used or integrated in the SMEs daily work and learning methods. Nevertheless, a lot of SMEs still prefer the traditional learning methods due to the fact that mLearning is still very new and unknown to them. A common answer was that there is no need nor demand for mLearning in their company, which indicates that there have not given mLearning that much thought and that mLearning is not as integrated as other learning methods so far.

The SMEs who are using mLearning have indicated their individual benefit in using mLearning and are already profiting from the advantages of mLearning. Which indicates that mLearning is already a part of some SMEs and that mLearning is able to foster further education in the setting of a company. The fact that some SMEs do not want to use mLearning in their companies shows that they do not see the advantages of Mobile Learning for their company, nonetheless this does not mean that they think mLearning is not usable in general, it just does not fit in their company's thinking. Moreover, it shows that there is still scepticism towards mLearning this means that there are still barriers that Mobile Learning has to overcome to be used by the majority of the companies. The advantages and disadvantages the SMEs reasoned with show that, too.

The advantages mentioned by the SMEs show that they identified the main aspects of mLearning and are already profiting from them. Such as flexibility, transportability, independency of location and time. Furthermore, SMEs indicated that idle time is better used as learning on the move is possible, it is customer and staff member friendly, there can be overall cost savings and an easier organisation of dates is possible. All these advantages show that mLearning comprises the possibility to stay ahead of the digital change, which also concerns the current learning methods.

The disadvantages show a curtain hesitance towards mLearning, regarding the ability to deliver the wanted outcomes or to provide the wanted learning material. The argument that the mobile devices are too small for some learning content shows that some SMEs are unfamiliar with mLearning, because depending on the learning content a smartphone, tablet or laptop is used to provide the learning material or tool which provide different sizes of screens. Moreover, it seems that SMEs are afraid of losing control over the learning process and development of their staff members when implementing mLearning. SMEs prefer the personal interaction. These arguments indicate that there is a resistance in changing a running system to a new unknown approach. The argument that the hard- and software is missing is a weak one due to the fact, that the private devices of the staff members can be integrated in the process. It indicates that mLearning is still growing and that it will take a great effort to integrate it as a future common approach in SMEs. Most of these arguments against using mLearning are due to the fact that mLearning is still in its infancy and has to develop further to improve the way SMEs are thinking about mLearning which also show the answers to the question about the future of mLearning as a part of the future of their company.

Most of the participating SMEs think that mLearning will play some part in the future of the company, but are not sure on how to integrate or implement it in their company which indicates the need of further guidance for SMEs regarding the implementation of mLearning as to the fact that especially SMEs can profit from the individual learning material mLearning can provide. Furthermore, it shows that mLearning is seen as a future way to provide further education. As some SMEs already identified, mLearning is meant as an addition to further education and is not supposed to replace all other approaches this can be counted as a first accomplishment of mLearning developers. The comment that one company will use mLearning more for their customers than for their staff members indicates that there are quite different aspects of a company's targets. They might see the advantages of mLearning for their customers, but not for their staff members. Probably because they see mLearning in different dimensions and not so much as an overall approach for further education. Overall the disadvantages and vague answers to how the SMEs see the development of mLearning in the next five years in their companies indicate that mLearning is already seen as a possible way to provide further education, but show the range of uncertainties when thinking about implementing mLearning in their company.

The results of the acceptance study indicate that depending on the branch of the company the level of importance and open mindedness towards mLearning might differ. For example, a company which is providing software solutions to their customers is already familiar with the technical environment and is more open minded towards new innovative learning methods such as mLearning than a company which is delivering goods for the last twenty years.

6. CONCLUSION

To sum up, the core results of the acceptance study with SMEs in the service sector show that Mobile Learning is already known, but not (yet) integrated in all of the SMEs. The SMEs identified the advantages, however are uncertain about the disadvantages and therefor hesitate to implement mLearning in their company. These results call for further implementation strategies and development for mLearning.

Undoubtedly the design, the structure and the quality of Mobile Learning is an important part of the future of the Service Sector as well. In our study it becomes clear that the companies recognise that Mobile Learning is a growing challenge and that the topic and its implementations are also effecting SMEs. Even when participants admit to not knowing exactly what happens in the field of Mobile Learning they see that simple implementations are already possible and also more challenging implementations could wait in the future. They are not looking exactly at the specifics of the Service Sector but often use very general argumentations. However, due to the fact that Mobile Learning is a young development this does not really surprise. The chances focus on a collaboration and individual aspect while the challenges seen by our respondents seem to be more company related and organisational aspects. The lack of adequate software does not focus the market but the situation at the companies, where often such resources have not been available, yet.

It is an important fact that the companies seem to be demand driven in their actions because several persons stated that there is currently no demand for mobile approaches concerning learning processes. With demands the usually focus on the end-user - the learner. No company focussed neither directly on market needs nor on internal company needs or stakeholder demands and behaviours.

Nevertheless, at the same time 78.57% of the participants see advantages in Mobile Learning and can explain in which ways mLearning could be useful and how it could be integrated in specific parts of training. Currently they are aware that mLearning exists. But, in most cases the interviewees had only a vague idea what it could look like. Our study highlights the concerns of SME owners and staff with regard to Mobile Learning. It seems that they are searching for good solutions and technical equipment as well as pedagogical opportunities to deal with these new challenges. Providing and finding information quickly is an important aspect in the Service Sector and maybe a combination of learning and information tools could address the real needs of the companies and the staff members in this field. The integration in existing training programmes takes time and resources and especially cost related resources are an important factor for SMEs and influences their way of dealing with the topic.

On the whole, the acceptance of mLearning is already to find in the Service Sector at SMEs but the implementation will be a challenge for several years. The use of mLearning in an educational environment is often said to have a very positive effect on the learning experience. Currently, the requirements of Mobile Learning are not very clear to the Service Sector. The sector is open to innovation in this area and to new future ways but at the same time the companies want to gather more information, like to learn from proposals and model implementations. Mobile Learning is a young topic that will continue to gain popularity. And this popularity is based on convenience. This will be the challenge and the work programme for the future.

REFERENCES

Australian Government - Department of innovation, industry, science and research (2009): Overview of structural change. Industry Brief 2007–08. Industry and Small Business Policy Division. Department of innovation, industry, science and research. July 2009. On the internet: https://industry.gov.au/industry/OtherReportsandStudies/Documents/ServicesSectorOverviewStructuralChange.pdf, date: 14.12.2016.

Beutner (2016): NetEnquiry. Innovative Ansätze zum m-Learning für Aus- und Weiterbildung. Paderborn 2016.

Beutner, M. (2014): Mobile Learning in der betrieblichen Aus- und Weiterbildung – Konzepte, Akzeptanz und Einstellungen in Ausbildungs- und Personalabteilungen. 7.50.100. Zweitdruck. 718 GdW-Ph 117-AL umbruch1, S. 99-116.

Beutner, M. / Pechuel, R. (2012a): Acceptance, Chances, and Problems of Mobile Learning in Vocational Education in Enterprises. Helsinki 2012. On the Internet: http://ceur-ws.org/Vol-955/papers/paper_37.pdf. Date: 26.06.2014.

Beutner, M. / Pechuel, R. (2012b): mLearning. Akzeptanz von Mobile Learning. Chancen und Probleme in der betrieblichen Bildung. In: Siepmann, F. /Müller, P. (Hrsg.): Jahrbuch eLearning und Wissensmanagement 2013. Die Zukunft der Bildung und die Rolle der digitalen Medien. Albstedt 2012, S. 30-34.

Beutner, M. / Teine, M. (2016): Conceptualizing an M-Learning System for Seniors. In: IADIS – International association for development of the information society: Sánchez, I. A. / Isaías, P. (2016): Proceedings of the 12th International Conference mobile learning 2016. April 9th to 11th 2016. Vilamoura, Portugal 2016, S. 85-88.

Beutner, M. / Teine, M. / Gebbe, M. / Fortmann, L. M. (2016): NetEnquiry - A competitive Mobile Learning Approach for the Banking Sector. In: IADIS – International association for development of the information society: Sánchez, I. A. / Isaías, P. (2016): Proceedings of the 12th International Conference mobile learning 2016. April 9th to 11th 2016. Vilamoura, Portugal 2016, S. 11-18.

Chinnery, G. M. (2006). Going to the MALL: mobile assisted language learning. Language Learning and Technology, 10 (1), 9–16, Retrieved June 18, 2011, from. http://llt.msu.edu/vol10num1/emerging/default.html, date: 14.12.2016.

Clarke, I., III, / Flaherty, T. B. (2002). Mlearning: using wireless technology to enhance marketing education. Marketing Education Review, 12. (3), 67–76.

Eichengreen, B. / Gutpa, P. (2013): The two waves of service-sector growth. In: Oxford Economic Papers. Vol. 65, No. 1, 2013, 96-123.

Flick, U. (1998): An introduction to qualitative research. London: Sage.

Freimuth, N. / Meier, R. / Reichwald, R. (2002): Die mobile Ökonomie – Definition und Spezifika. In: Reichwald, R. (Hrsg.): Mobile Kommunikation. Wertschöpfung, Technologien. Wiesbaden 2002, pp. 3- 16.

Geddes, S. J. (2004): Mobile learning in the 21st century: benefit for learners. Knowledge Tree e-journal: An ejournal of flexible learning in VET, Vol. 30 No.3, pp. 214-28.

INQA – Initiative Neue Qualität der Arbeit – Krauss-Hoffmann, P. / Kuszpa, M. A. / Sieland-Bortz, M. (2007): Mobile Learning. Grundlagen und Perspektiven. Dortmund / Dresden / Berlin 2007.

Keegan, D. (2002). The future of learning: From eLearning to mLearning, ZIFF papiere 119. Retrieved from ERIC ED472435 database. On the internet: http://www.fernuni-hagen.de/ZIFF , date: 01.05.2016.

Kim, H.-J. (2006): The Shift to the Service Economy: Causes and Effects. Institute for Monetary and Economic Research. The Bank of Korea. 2006. 7. 7. On the internet: https://faculty.washington.edu/karyiu/confer/seoul06/papers/kim_hj.pdf, date: 14.12.2016.

Kinshuk, M. / Goh, T. (2004): Getting Ready For Mobile Learning. ED- Media, pp. 56 - 63. Lugano 2004.

Koole, M. L. (2009): A Model for Framing Mobile Learning. In: Ally, M. (Ed.): Mobile Learning. Transforming the Delivery of Education and Training. Edmonton 2009, 25-49.

Kukulska-Hulme, A. / Sharples, M. / Milrad, M. / Arnedillo-Sanchez, I. / Vavoula, G. (2009): Innovation in Mobile Learning: A European Perspective. In: International Journal of Mobile and Blended Learning (IJMBL). 2009. On the internet: http://www.igi-global.com/article/innovation-mobile-learning/2755, date: 01.12.2016.

Kynäslahti, H. (2003): In Search of Elements of Mobility in the Context of Education. In: Mobile Learning (eds. H. Kynäslahti & P. Seppälä) pp. 41–48. IT Press, Helsinki.

Motiwalla, L. F. (2007). Mobile learning: a framework and evaluation. Computers & Education, Vol. 49, No. 3, 581–596.

O´Malley, C. / Vavoula, G. (Glew, J. / Taylor, J. / Sharples, M. / Lefrere, P. / Lonsdale, P. / Naismith, L. / Waycott, J. (2005): Guidelines for learning/teaching/tutoring in a mobile environment. Public deliverable from the MOBILearn project (D.4.1). 2005. On the internet: https://hal.archives-ouvertes.fr/hal-00696244/document, date: 14.12.2016.

Quinn, C. (2000). M-learning: Mobile, Wireless and In-Your-Pocket Learning. Line Zine.

Rey, A. (2004): Mobiles CSCL in der universitären Lehre. Best Practices und kritische Erfolgsfaktoren. Winterthur 2004.

Stone, T. (2010): Enterprise Mobile Learning and Development. Enterprise Mobile Learning and Development Rochester/ Surrey /Toronto / New Dehli.

Strauss, A. / Corbin, J. (1998): Basics of qualitative research: Techniques and procedures for developing grounded theory. 2nd ed. Thousand Oaks, CA: Sage.

Traxler, J. (2009): Current state of Mobile Learning. In: Ally, M. (Ed.): Mobile Learning. Transforming the Delivery of Education and Training. Edmonton 2009, 9-24.

Wang, Y.-S. / Wu, M.-C. / Wang, H.-Y. (2009): Investigating the determinants and age and gender differences in the acceptance of mobile learning. In: British Journal of Educational Technology, Vol. 40, No. 1, 2009, 92–118.

Short Papers

POSSIBLE POTENTIAL OF FACEBOOK TO ENHANCE LEARNERS' MOTIVATION IN MOBILE LEARNING ENVIRONMENT

Mehwish Raza
Alpen – Adria University of Klagenfurt
15 - Sterneckstraße, 9020 Klagenfurt, Austria

ABSTRACT

Facebook is world's leading social network, 29% of its active members represent Pakistan. This study utilized Facebook for teachers' in-service training. Thirty teachers from different parts of Pakistan took part in this training that lasted for ten weeks. The researcher tested the impact of three independent variables namely: social interactions, quality of experiences and behavior on learners' motivation (dependent variable). The hypothesis of this study propose a positive impact of independent variables on the dependent variable, the research was able to prove the hypothesis.

KEYWORDS

Facebook, Pakistan, motivation, social interaction, experiences, behavior.

1. INTRODUCTION

A phenomenal growth in use of social media has surged globally irrespective of cultural and geographic boundaries. Social media are a collection of Internet websites, services, and practices that support digital interaction, collaboration, community building, and sharing across stakeholders (Special, & Li-Barber, 2012). With over 1.79 billion monthly active users, Facebook has been ranked as number one world's most popular social networking site in the year 2016 (GSMS, 2016). The service allows users to create: a unique profile; closed/ open groups; pages of common interests; and events. In addition to regular multimedia features Facebook borrows the best aspects of other popular services and integrate them to create a central hub for example: voice and video calling, instant embedded articles, and Facebook live video for all (Hew, 2011).

Facebook has been rapidly embraced by all aspects of life such as e-commerce, entertainment, and education etc. Billions of users release, critique, reshape and re-imagine opinions and personal preferences to influence vital dynamics in different fields of life (Friesen & Lowe, 2012; Chen, 2014). It can be downloaded on smart phones in form of an inbuilt mobile application that integrates device features to launch mobile Facbeook (m-Facebok) on users' cell phones providing them a much quicker and easier access to the social media service. 90 % of active users access their accounts via mobile phones (Facebook, 2016).

1.1 Facebook in Pakistan

With 3G and 4G LTE cellular technology available in Pakistan, the local society has witnessed new levels of Internet penetration. Low-cost Chinese version of smart phones has taken over the market making it possible for a family with a monthly income of $300 and above to afford smart phones (Chinese version). According to a survey Pakistan penetrates 29% of the total active Facebook user accounts and 63% of these users are between ages 20 – 30 years (Qureshi, U. 2016).

1.2 Educational Advantages of Facebook

m-Facebook offers an autonomous and interactive information space to users to generate and exchange new ideas (Chen, 2014). It offers a potential a low-budget mobile learning environment that most learners and tutors are already familiar with and understand its possible potential for prompt interaction and providing a sense of self-direction (Chen, 2014: p.14; Hew, 2011). Extant literature acknowledges the ease of use of m-Facebook because it facilitates users to find opportunities for learning while keeping alongside their digital social activity (Chen, 2014).

1.3 Significance of the study

Most prior researches examine the use of m-Facebook in context of higher education and report possible limitations. In addition to the factor of distraction, Friesen and Lowe (2012) question the possibility of experiencing low motivation and distractive attitudes of learners when and if it is used only for an educational purpose (p. 49). There is limited research available that explores learners' motivation levels during a professional development program especially in context of Pakistan. Through this study the researcher aims to fill this void in the current research in the field of m-Facebook.

1.4 Research Motivation

This study describes lessons learnt from a small scale ten weeks long online teachers' in-service education and training (INSET) program 'Teaching with Digital Technologies' which was conceived as a low-budget alternate to high-cost face-to-face INSET method. The total cost of this training project accounted up to $ 95. All participants represent a large network of private schools spread across Pakistan; the researcher does not disclose the name of school network to maintain privacy.

1.5 Research Model

The educational value of m-Facebook remains dependent on learners' motivation level (Manca & Ranieri, 2013) which plays a significant role in information seeking behavior (Hew, 2011). Educators and researchers make substantial efforts to find interventions which can sustain or promote learners' motivation in m- learning expeditions. Figure 1 explains the hypothesis for this study.

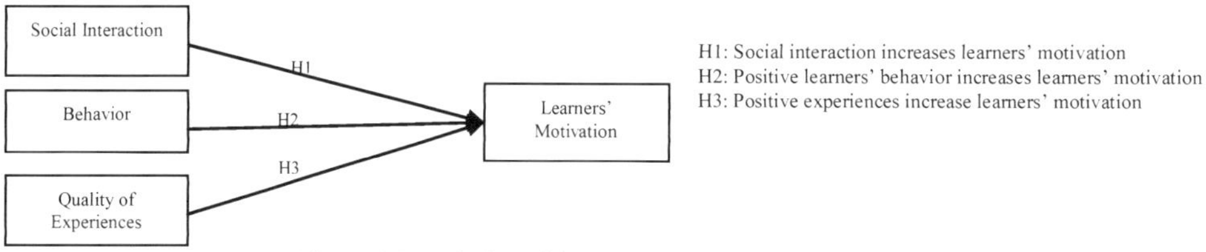

Figure 1. Description of the proposed hypothesis for this study.

It is necessary to explain how the three independent variables are perceived for this research.

1- Social Interaction: In this study social interaction is determined by level of communication between learners and tutor as well as among learners in order to exchange ideas. An interactive learning process enhances self-reflection and motivates learners to achieve higher learning outcomes (Mifsud, 2002, Barker et al., 2005). Parsons et al. (2009) argue that interactive learning creates lasting understanding of the subject matter for all contributors or group members.

2- Behavior: The manner in which learners conduct themselves in the online learning environment refers to their behavior (Li, 2009). In this study, behavior refers to the ability of learners to utilize the provided freedom to express their thoughts, generating productive dialogue with peers, meeting deadlines and self-regulating their learning.

3- Quality of Experience: The overall quality of satisfaction refers to the quality of experience. Course content is vital to define learners' satisfaction. Relevance, utility for self efficacy and diversity of experience may enhance the total learning quality (Chen, 2014). The quality of learners' experiences influences their motivation; relevant experiences tend to enhance learners' motivation towards learning (Qureshi, U. 2016).

1.6 Research Questions

During the course of research the researcher addressed the following questions:

1- Do positive social interactions enhance learners' motivation for engaging in learning activities (H1)?
2- Does a self-regulatory behavior indicated by learners impact their motivation level (H2)?
3- Does a diverse, autonomous and relevant experience positively impact learning outcomes (H3)?

2. RESEARCH METHODOLOGY

2.1 Research Sample

Thirty respondents from different primary school branches of one of the largest private school networks in Pakistan participated in this study. All participants were selected by their school head teachers.

2.2 Research Instrument

Data were collected using three questionnaires; commenced before, during and after the training had started. The first questionnaire was used to collect learners' demographic data and to establish their digital context. The second questionnaire had four parts; Use of Social Media, Social Interaction, Quality of Experience, and Behavior. Responses were collected on 5 point Likert's scale with 5 as 'very frequent' and 1 as 'never'. The third questionnaire was commenced after the project was over and focused mainly on learners' motivation levels during the course of training. Responses were collected on 5 point Likert's scale with 5 as 'very frequent' and 1 as 'never'. The researcher used IBM SPSS statistical software package version 19.0 (SPSS, 2010) for data analysis. A pilot study was conducted with 8 respondents that are not a part of the sampled respondents.

3. RESULTS

A total of 30 teachers (response rate = 100%) completed the pre-training questionnaire. With exception of one, all respondents (n = 29, 96.6%) had an active Facebook account. The one without an account was prepared to create in order to participate in the training program. Most respondents (n = 25, 83.3%) were females and their average age was 33.6 years. 50% respondents reported to be able to proficiently navigate through different options given by m-Facebook such as: uploading and downloading media resources, commenting on news threads, and tagging other members in a group activity.

The second questionnaire consisted of 26 items in 4 subscales namely: 1) Use of social media; 2) Social interaction; 3) Quality of experience; and 4) Behavior. The purpose was to measure learners' motivation level by applying a 5-point symmetrical Likert scale. Table 1 provides an overview of mean value for each item and Table 2 summarizes statistics used to define learners' motivation level.

Table 1. Descriptive data for Questionnaire 2.

Use of Social Media	Mean
You are a member of more than one knowledge development group on FB.	3
It is easy to learn using FB from your mobile phone.	4
You have to think a lot before you communicate with your peers during a learning expedition on FB.	3
You check the group activity more than five times a day.	5
You think about the previous online activity and anticipate next activity in the group.	4
You think your online activity consumes a lot of time due to participation in this training.	4
Information is duplicated in the group due to several responses on one post.	4
Social Interaction	
Response to questions is faster on mobile phone compared to using FB on computer.	5
The group offer channels of frequent communication which tutor and peers.	4
Increased interaction frustrates you.	4
Increased interaction helps you in thinking about your own experiences.	4
FB helped you in making stronger relationship with peers and tutor.	5

You feel a social responsibility to meet deadlines. You feel a social pressure in presenting quality work. Thoughts, opinions and digital behavior of your peers influence your decisions in the course of learning.	2 4 3
Quality of Experience	
Learning, sharing of opinion and receiving feedback is faster. Mobile phone features help you to upload, download media files to the group. Feature of 'notification' helps you stay connected to the on-going learning expedition. The feature of 'notification' reminds you to complete learning tasks. You can access course content from anywhere at any time. Hyperlinked information is easier to access from Facebook. Embedded media files make resource access easier. I was able to link learning to prior experiences in my professional life.	4 5 5 4 5 3 2 4
Behavior	
You set your learning goals. You are able to meet your learning objective in all tasks. You look forward to view work of your peers. A look back on your activity in the group enables you to reflect on your actions.	5 3 4 4

Table 2. Descriptive data for learners' motivation levels.

Attributes for learners' motivation	Mean	SD
Interactions stirred critical thinking about different aspects of training contents.	4	0.896
The interactive nature of learning environment gave me many opportunities for problem-solving.	4	0.945
I was able to make suitable decisions for problem solving during the training period.	4	0.845
Participating in discussions enabled me to question my pre-determined beliefs about classroom teaching.	3	1.025
Interactions with peers helped me in staying focused and attentive.	5	1.033
I was able to set appropriate goals for my learning.	3	0.956
I was able to achieve my learning goals.	3	0.754
I did not need any reminders to complete due assignments.	4	0.858
I enjoyed the sense of control throughout the training period.	4	0.921
I can say that I was regulating my learning independently.	4	0.965

The data can be classified as approximately normal because the quantile pairs fell nearly on a straight line in a P-P plot conducted by the researcher to assess data normality. The researcher used multiple regression analysis to test the significance of three independent variables (social interaction, quality of experience, and behavior) on underlying dependent variable (motivation) by using Variance Inflation Factor (VIF). As shown from the table 3, the tolerance (T) and VIF values of all independent variables were within the range.

Table 3. Collinearity Statistics.

Independent variable [a]	Tolerance	VIF
Social Interaction	.309	2.491
Quality of Experience	.395	2.687
Behavior	.276	2.854
Durbin-Watson	1.972	

[a] Dependent variable: Learners' motivation T > .2 and VIF < 4

Reliability of each variable was calculated using Cronbach's alpha. The commonly acceptable level for all four variables was > 0.70. In terms of the correlations between variables, Social interaction ($r=.92$, $p<.001$) has the highest value, Quality of experience ($r = .88$) and Behavior ($r = .87$) take second and third place respectively. Table 4 outlines the reliability of all four variables.

Table 4. Descriptive statistics: Correlation and reliability among variables (n = 30).

Variable	Mean	SD	(1)	(2)	(3)	(4)	(5)
Use of Social Media	4	0.88	(.84)				
Social interaction	3.8	0.98	.68	(.92)			
Quality of experience	4	0.84	.70	.65	(.88)		
Behavior	4	0.96	.69	.60	.70	(.87)	
Learners' motivation	3.8	0.92	.65	.70	.72	.69	(.85)

3.1 Hypothesis testing

The researcher identified three essential elements as independent variables and carried out multiple regression analysis to test the hypotheses using SPSS. Table 5 shows the results of the regression analysis. All independent variables are considered to have significant relationships with learners' motivation with p-values <.05. Hypothesis 1 examined the influence of the social interaction on learners' motivation in mobile Facebook learning environment. It is supported, with p-values less than .0 and is significant. Hypothesis 2 examined the relationship between the positive experience benefit and learners' motivation in learning (β=1.71 , p<.01). Behavior gained during the learning expedition has positively significant effect on motivation in learning (β=.185 , p<.05). Therefore, Hypothesis 3 is also supported.

Table 5. Regression analysis.

Independent variable	B	Beta (β)	t-value
(constant)	.156		.532
Social interactions	.182	.160	2.015*
Positive experiences	.110	.171	2.148**
Behavior	.173	.186	2.806*
R	.805a		
R Square	.665		
Adjusted R Square	.661		

	Sum of Squares	Df	Mean Square	F
Regression	156.701	5	39.875	144.759***
Residual	28.373	117	.237	
Total	185.175	128		

* p < .05, ** p < .01, *** p < .001

4. DISCUSSION

The purpose of this study was to examine the impact of social integration, quality of experiences and behavior depicted by learners on their motivation. Analysis of results support findings of previous studies and establishes a positive relation of all three independent variables with learners' motivation (Chen, 2014). The adjusted R square suggests that 66% of learners' motivation during this training can be explained by these three variables (F = 144.759, p < .001). The model generated from the multiple regression analysis has a reasonable level of acceptance in the selected independent variables. The model can be presented in form of prediction formula as follows:

$LM^{*} = SI^{**} \times w1 + QE^{***} \times w2 + B^{****} \times w3 + C$ where C is constant; and w1, w2, w3, w4 are empirically determined weights.

4.1 Social interaction and learners' motivation

Social interaction is determined by the interpersonal behavior, relationships, exchange of ideas, and thoughts between individuals who are connected through a digital medium (Hew, 2011; Rovai et al., 2003). Prior research has placed interactions at the core of factors influencing motivation (Manca, S., & Ranieri, M., 2013; Sun & Bhattacherjee, 2014), this study also narrates this finding. Learners reported that engagement in interactions helped them to formulate their opinions, challenge pre-set ideas, and evaluate theirs and others responses/answers to enhance their understanding.

4.2 Quality of experiences and learners' motivation

Learners' experiences develop their behavior towards a set task; a diverse and relevant experience to learners that boosts their meta-cognitive ability, engages them in positive social activity, and provides opportunities to them for self-regulation (Raza, in press). Through this study the researcher is able to associate aspects of social media (notifications, prompt response rate, ease of access of resources) with quality of experiences gained by learners. Nikou and Bouwman (2014) associated quality of experiences with learners' social and digital contexts. This research explains learners' ability to handle resources with ease, links they develop with prior experiences and autonomy as positive experience factors that increases learners' satisfaction and motivation.

4.3 Learners' behavior and motivation

Learners' autonomy during learning expeditions defines their behavior (Sun & Bhattacherjee, 2014; Riendl et al. 2014). Most prior studies report the impact of learners' motivation on their learning behavior however this study reports that learners' behaviors during learning mobile Facebook learning expedition have significant impact on their motivation. Every individual has an internal guidance system that organizes priorities and informs the mechanism of learning that enables learners to derive their motivation levels. Through this study the research defines positive behavior with the ability to define learning goals, attempt to achieve those in a given time frame without external reminders (Questionnaire 2). When learners are able to self-regulate their learning they are more likely to show higher levels of motivation (Sun & Bhattacherjee, 2014).

5. CONCLUSION

Learners' motivation is the most vital factor for learning success. This research focuses on examining how the world's leading social media service benefits improving learners' motivation levels. Facebook offers a great potential to answer most commonly identified shortcomings in success of distance learning. The social interactivity, ease of use, positive experiences offered to learners can help motivate learners to be more regular, attentive, and dedicated to learning. Facebook for mobile phones is a relatively new tool for instructional purposes in Pakistan but it offers great potential due to high penetration level in Pakitsani society, learners' ability to fully operate the service, and ease of use for educational purposes. Similar studies could be conducted to examine the effects of Facebook in different learning settings exploring the relationship between different learning styles and the successful educational use of mobile Facebook.

REFERENCES

Chen, Y. (2014). The effect of using a Facebook group as a learning management system. Computers in Education Journal, 5(4), 42-53.

Facebook (2016). Company info. Retrieved from http://newsroom.fb.com/company-info/

Friesen, N., & Lowe, S. (2012). The questionable promise of social media for education: Connective learning and the commercial imperative. Journal of Computer Assisted Learning, 28, 83-194. doi:10.1111/j.1365-2729.2011.00426.x

Hew, K.F. (2011). Students' and teachers' use of Facebook. Computers in Human Behaviour. Article available at doi:10.1016/j.chb.2010.11.020.

Kirschner, P. A., & Karpinski, A. C. (2010). Facebook and academic performance. Computers in Human Behavior, 26, 1237–1245.

Li, H. (2009). Correlation between achievement and behavior. Asian Social Science. 5(4). 3 – 9.

Manca, S., & Ranieri, M. (2013). Is it a tool suitable for learning? A critical review of the literature on Facebook as a technology-enhanced learning environment. Journal of Computer Assisted Learning, 29(6), 487–504.

Nikou, S., & Bouwman, H. (2014). Ubiquitous use of mobile social network services. Telematics and Informatics, 31(3), 422-433. https://dx.doi.org/10.1016/j.tele.2013.11.002

Qureshi, U. (2016). Facebook and eCommerce: A new beginning. Computers in Human Behaviour. doi:10.1035/j.chb.2010.11.020.

Special, W. P., & Li-Barber, K. T. (2012). Self-disclosure and student satisfaction with Facebook. Computers in Human Behavior, 28(2), 624–630

Sun, Y., & Bhattacherjee, A. (2014). Looking inside the "black box: Technological effects on IT usage. Journal of Computer Information Systems, 54(2), 1-15

D-MOVE: A MOBILE COMMUNICATION BASED DELPHI FOR DIGITAL NATIVES TO SUPPORT EMBEDDED RESEARCH

Otto Petrovic
Professor, Dr.
Institute for Information Science and Information Systems, Karl-Franzens-University of Graz
Universitaetsstrasse 15 G/3, AT-8010 Graz, Austria

ABSTRACT

Digital Natives are raised with computers and the Internet, which are a familiar part of their daily life. To gain insights into their attitude and behavior, methods and media for empirical research face new challenges like gamification, context oriented embedded research, integration of multiple data sources, and the increased importance of personal data. The paper presents and evaluates a method based on Delphi technique, which integrates multimedia data capturing in the field with multi-round face-to-face discussions. As the front end, a very fast and fuzzy platform was implemented, which is currently being used by over 100 million Digital Natives. It allows teaching the participants to use embedded research and to understand the impact of self-monitoring for health and fitness on business models, which was one central aim of the supported course. Additionally, it is used to gain insights into Digital Natives' attitude and behavior.

KEYWORDS

Delphi technique, embedded research, self-monitoring, teaching Digital Natives, innovative mobile learning.

1. CHALLENGES IN GAINING INSIGHTS INTO DIGITAL NATIVES' ATTITUDE AND BEHAVIOR

1.1 The Nature of Digital Natives

Table 1. Challenges for media and methods to gain insights into Digital Natives' attitude and behavior.

From	To
Boring	Gamification, Surveytainment, Visual presentation of questions and answers
Slow going	Fast, fuzzy
Questionnaire based research	Context oriented embedded research (use of smartphones)
Question-based	Quests, small tasks, experimental design
'Make' in data gaining	'Buy' and integration of many data sources
Anonymous research	Increased importance of personal data

Digital Natives' mother tongue is the digital language of computers and the Internet (Jones 2011). They are born after 1980, raised with digital technologies and have a high affinity to them. They are used to obtaining information quickly, have a high amount of ad-hoc-communication, work and communicate in form of multitasking and use mostly interactive digital media.

Traditional media and methods of empirical research used to gain insights into Digital Natives' attitude and behavior encounter some special challenges (Hagenhoff 2015) as shown in Table 1. These challenges call for new methods in empirical research and in the use of digital media, a major element of Digital Natives' daily life.

1.2 The Delphi Method as an Approach to gain Insights into Digital Natives

The traditional Delphi method as a means of empirical research gained popularity back in 1948 due to its use by the RAND Corporation for military related questions (Häder/Häder 2000). Linstone/Turoff (1975) defined this method as: „Delphi may be characterized as a method for structuring a group communication process so that the process is effective in allowing a group of individuals, as a whole, to deal with a complex problem.“ The main steps are: Formulation of theses about current or future issues, obtaining experts' opinions, aggregating these opinions and presenting them to the expert and finally, starting a second round to obtain consent/dissent about these issues.

A systematic literature review carried out by the authors (see also: de Loë 2016) shows that advanced Delphi methods are modified regarding the type of media used (from paper and pen to digital media), amount of channels used to send out invitations to participate (also email, social media, Lee & McLoughlin, C. 2010, Tapscott & Williams 2008), form of data collected (quantitative and qualitative), types of answers (e.g. multiple choice, comments, upload of pictures and videos, voice annotations), and presentation of results (e.g. graphical, pictures, videos).

Based on the learnings of these innovative forms of Delphi method, the authors designed D-Move Delphi as a first prototype of a Delphi method and communication tool with the aim to fulfill the requirements of Digital Natives as much as possible. An important requirement was the ability to use different front ends like Facebook, WhatsApp, or Snapchat, which are widely used by a certain group of Digital Natives, while D-Move's backend with its storing and sharing functionalities and the implemented Delphi procedures could remain constant (see Petrovic 2016 for an example of a different front end).

2. D-MOVE AS A MOBILE COMMUNICATION BASED DELPHI

To meet the challenges described in chapter 1 the D-Move Delphi offers five central characteristics:

- **The use of a familiar media**. D-Move Delphi uses as front end a communication infrastructure, namely Snapchat, which is very familiar for Digital Natives. As an image messaging and multimedia mobile application, launched mid 2011, it was used by 120 million people by the end of 2015. More than 10 billion videos are viewed daily via Snapchat on smartphones in 2016. 52% of the user base is 16 to 24 years and another 32% between 25 and 34 years old. Thus, it is a real Digital Natives' media and much 'younger' than e.g. Facebook.
- **Fast, fuzzy, and based on gamification**. An annotated picture or video shared in Snapchat with peers disappears after viewing. No archive or communications thread remains. Only with a special feature, the messages can be displayed for an entire day before disappearing. With the use of filters, pictures and videos can be modified and geo-tagged by using gestures. For the purpose of empirical research, D-Move Delphi allows the storing of contributions of each participant in the backend of the application to discuss and interpret them during the face-to-face meetings.
- **Context oriented embedded research.** Because Snapchat is a smartphone-only application, Digital Natives can use it directly in the context of the Delphi thesis. For instance, if a thesis is related to a certain communication pattern, the Digital Native films its real behavior, makes some annotations and shares it with peers. It is no longer necessary to reflect on one's own attitude or behavior in a certain situation while filling out a questionnaire, which has often raised problems such as bias, incomplete memory or behavior based on tacit knowledge.
- **Integration of many data sources.** While using Snapchat the main data sources are pictures and videos of personal behavior combined with annotations. These data are enriched with traditional sources like scientific publications, statistics or databases in preparing and running the face-to-face discussion between the different Delphi rounds to obtain consent and/or to find out theses with a strong dissent between the participants.
- **Increased importance of personal data.** The smartphone is the most personal device a Digital Native owns. D-Move Delphi is used to capture personal impressions of issues raised in the Delphi's theses. Proposed arguments and contributions during the face-to-face rounds can be assigned to a certain participant, which also highlights the known advantages and disadvantages of non-anonymous empirical research.

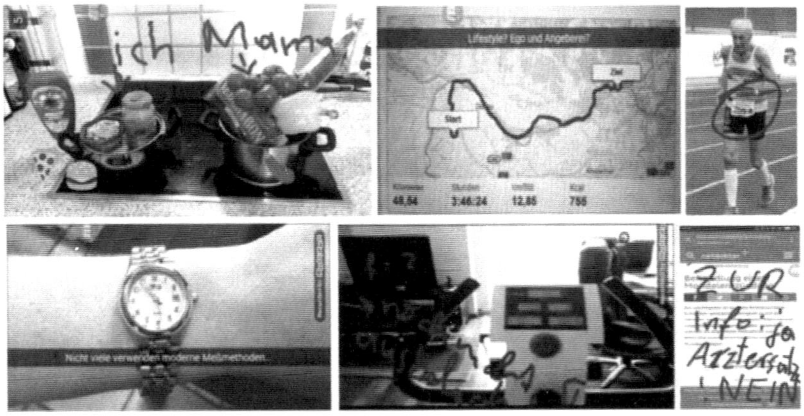

Figure 1. Example of contributions in the first round of D-Move Delphi to be discussed in the face-to-face meetings.

Figure 2 displays the Delphi method used to implement D-Move Delphi and gain insights into Digital Natives' attitude and behavior towards 'Self-monitoring in Health and Fitness'. First, the Delphi Method used was presented to the 24 participants of a master course in Information Systems. The technology-, social-, privacy- and business-related issues of self-monitoring as a major trend in information systems - based on the Internet of Things - were discussed. Examples of smartwatches and wristband sensors, wearable sensors and monitoring patches, brain-computer interfaces, neuro-sensing and emotion-mapping (Swan 2013) were presented together with relevant backend platforms like Strava, Nike+, and Runtastic. The main issue raised in the course and in the Delphi's theses was the impact of self-monitoring on business models, e.g. on the value proposition provided, attributes of goods and services and how they are produced as well as the revenue model.

In a pre-test the correct interpretation of the formulated thesis as well as the usability and stability of the D-Move Delphi application was tested by ten participants in their role as Delphi experts. After the refinement of the Delphi thesis and optimization of usability aspects, the first Delphi round was started with twelve Digital Natives as experts. They captured real world examples of using self-monitoring in health and fitness in the form of pictures and videos, annotated them and shared their findings using the functionalities of D-Move Delphi. Between the field periods the participants analyzed, presented, and discussed their results in face-to-face meetings to identify issues with high consent or dissent as a foundation for the next field round. In the first step, basic assumptions were discussed by the participants regarding their own behavior with the use of more open questions. Subsequently, results were aggregated to eight theses in the form of closed questions. In a second Delphi round, 17 Digital Natives captured more real world examples in their role as experts, annotated them in coherence with the presented thesis and shared them. In the face-to-face session that followed, the experts discussed topics with high amount of dissent to elaborate on its causes and to gain consent. The final step was the presentation of the Delphi results by each group and a written final report.

3. EXAMPLE RESULTS OF D-MOVE DELPHI FOR THE ISSUE OF SELF-MONITORING

This section puts forward some example results of the D-Move Delphi concerning the self-monitoring thesis. Two of the Delphi theses lead to the most homogeneous results. The first thesis posits that for Digital Natives health and fitness is a much more important part of their lifestyle than it was for their parent's generation (mode = 5 on a 5-point Likert scale, 5 meaning strong consent, standard deviation = 1.750). The second thesis claims that Digital Natives like to get immediate feedback by self-monitoring apps about their lifestyle and be rewarded for appropriate behavior much more than their parents' generation (mode = 5, standard deviation = 0.728). This consent corresponds to D-Move Delphi results using other front ends than Snapchat (Petrovic 2017), showing that Digital Natives believe that they use app-based fitness programs more than older generations and share the results more frequently than their parents. Digital Natives also believe the trend of health & fitness to have gained importance across all generations, particularly in regards to awareness and personal responsibility for one's own health. Participants think that this is not a question of generations but much more of social stratum and education. Another important finding is that the authorities setting the standards differ greatly between Digital Natives and their parents' generation. Digital Natives adapt themselves more to their peers using social media and self-monitoring technologies, whereas their parents' generation is strongly oriented on standards set by traditional authorities like the World Health Organization. Those results from D-Move Delphi evidently show that there already exists an on-going social impact of self-monitoring in an important field like health and fitness. Thus, a main characteristic of a disruptive innovation (Christensen, C. 1995) can be identified.

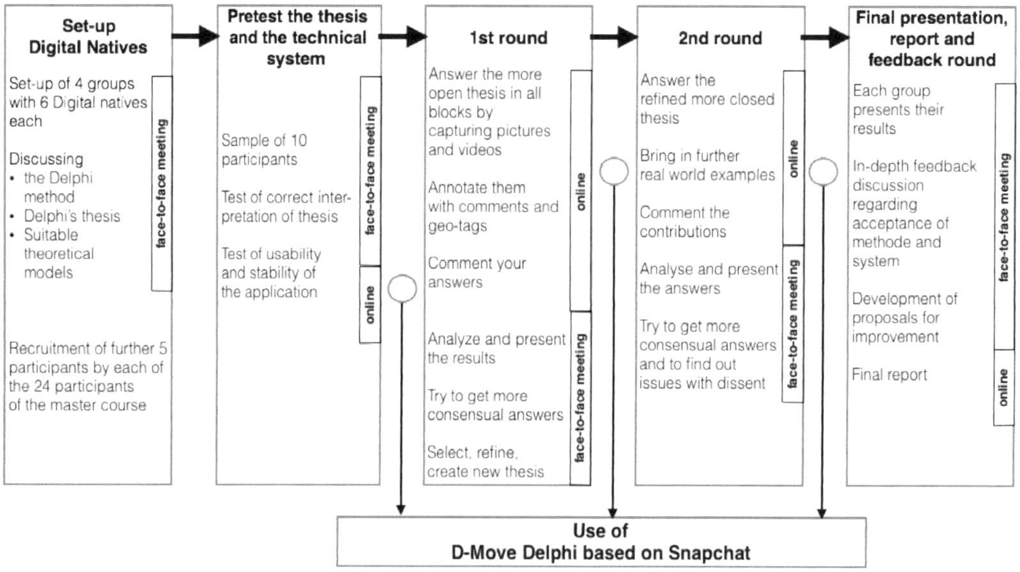

Figure 2. Method used by D-Move Delphi to gain insights into Digital Natives.

4. CONCLUSION AND NEXT RESEARCH STEPS

After finishing the D-Move Delphi using Snapchat as the front end, an in-depth group discussion with the participants identified starting points for improving the method and the software used. The results show that compared to Delphi methods based on traditional paper-based or online questionnaires the issues presented in Table 1 were addressed to a satisfying extent. Due to the visual presentation of questions and answers, the gamification aspect was supported and Snapchat as the used front end was perceived as fast and fuzzy. The feasibility of context oriented embedded research was experienced as a main advantage of D-Move Delphi. In particular, the implementation of different data sources including personal data can be viewed as an advantage of the method used. Simultaneously, privacy issues were heavily discussed, despite the fact that personal information is necessary to obtain high involvement and engagement.

The central finding is that the method used, as shown in Figure 2, is suitable for gaining insights into Digital Natives attitude and behavior, but Snapchat as the used front end was not. The participants described it as confusing, unfamiliar, and childish. They criticized the low perceived usability, the low dissemination among their peers, and the central characteristic of Snapchat, namely the disappearing of content after viewing. They stated that they would much more prefer WhatsApp and Facebook as the front end to D-Move.

We have learned that the term 'Digital Natives' is much too broad and that it ought to be divided into different subgroups, especially in regards to the communication tools used. While email is the main communication tool for Digital Immigrants, made up of people aged 35 and above, Facebook is familiar to both mature Digital Natives and Digital Immigrants. The participants of the Delphi stated that they prefer WhatsApp or partly Facebook – but not Snapchat. By looking at Snapchat's user base of more than 120 Million worldwide, it can be concluded that it mainly consists of people in the age group below the average age of master course participants.

In further research we will continue to refine the method and back end functionalities used in D-Move Delphi, but they will remain largely unchanged. Depending on the exact age group we will adapt the front end, using everything from traditional online questionnaires enriched with pictures and videos to Facebook, WhatsApp and Snapchat. The central challenge is to fulfill all requirements shown in Table 1 independently from the preferred front end of a group of Digital Natives to support embedded research and capture real world experiences. After this improvement D-Move Delphi will be used to gain insights into Digital Natives on a regular basis and can be further evaluated.

ACKNOWLEDGEMENT

This article is based on the results of the master thesis of Naida Hamzic, which was submitted to the author in 2016. Her valuable work is kindly acknowledged.

REFERENCES

Christensen, C. 1995. Disruptive Technologies Catching the Wave. Harvard Business Review, January– February p. 43-53.

Hagenhoff, W. 2015. Der und „Das" Befragte: Inwieweit findet Marktforschung künftig ohne Befragte statt?, in: Keller, B. et al.: Zukunft der Marktforschung. Wiesbaden: Springer Fachmedien.

Häder, M./Häder, S. 2000. Die Delphi-Technik in den Sozialwissenschaften. Methodische Forschungen und innovative Anwendungen. Wiesbaden: Westdeutscher Verlag.

Jones, C. 2011. The Net Generation and Digital Natives: Implications for Higher Education. The Open University, Walton Hall, Milton Keynes.

Lee, M. J. W./McLoughlin, C. 2010. Web 2.0-Based E-Learning: Applying Social Informatics for Tertiary Teaching. Hershey.

Linstone, H. A./Turoff, M. 1975. The Delphi method: Techniques and applications. Reading, Massachus- etts: Addison-Wesley Publishing Company.

Loë, R. C.et al. 2016. Advancing the State of Policy Delphi Practice: A Systematic Review Evaluating Methodological Evolution, Innovation, and Opportunities, in: Technological Forecasting and Social Change, vol. 104, p. 78-88.

Petrovic, O. 2016. Design, Development and Evaluation of a Field Learning Video Blog, in: Proceedings of the 12th International Conference on Mobile Learning, Vilamoura, Algarve, Portugal, p. 51-58.

Petrovic, O, 2017. Internet of Things as Disruptive Innovation for the Advertising Eco System, in: Commercial Communication, in print.

Swan, M. 2013. Sensor Mania! The Internet of Things, Wearable Computing, Objective Metrics, and the Quantified Self 2.0: Journal of Sensor and Actuator Networks, p. 217-253.

Tapscott, D./Williams, A. D. 2008. Wikinomics, How Mass Collaboration Changes Everything. New York.

SMALL PRIVATE ONLINE RESEARCH: A PROPOSAL FOR A NUMERICAL METHODS COURSE BASED ON TECHNOLOGY USE AND BLENDED LEARNING

Francisco Javier Delgado Cepeda
Tecnologico de Monterrey, campus Estado de Mexico
Carretera a Lago de Guadalupe km. 3.5, Atizapán, Estado de Mexico, CP. 52926, Mexico

ABSTRACT

This work presents a proposed model in blended learning for a numerical methods course evolved from traditional teaching into a research lab in scientific visualization. The blended learning approach sets a differentiated and flexible scheme based on a mobile setup and face to face sessions centered on a net of research challenges. Model is presented being supported by previous research works about its performance in terms of effective evaluation and skill development.

KEYWORDS

Blended, MOOR, Engineering, Mathematics, Research.

1. INTRODUCTION

Education is changing in an irreversible way due to technology, while digital natives' generation is pushing education into the technological arena. Nevertheless last concept is questioned and technology is not guiding completely learning processes, there is a challenge demand for science and engineering education for the next decades in terms of availability and quality standards in math, science, and engineering. Despite, deep differences in the incoming levels of technical skills for engineering programs' students will require optimal and differentiated schemes of instruction.

Laurillard (2005, 2008) has appointed that mobile technologies could enhancing the professional learning of disciplines under adequate contextual designs. That is particularly true for engineering education, which continuously involves new technologies as professional software to simulate, plan or calculate scientific and engineering processes. Today, this skill development is frequent in the university courses, promoting computer lab components together with the theoretical concepts. In addition, informational technology has gained terrain in education by proposing advanced and flexible scenarios to support the face to face sessions as a blended approach now centered on advanced learning activities. In terms of demand, Massive Open Online Courses (MOOC) and Research (MOOR) are being imposed as possible models of large scale instruction at the university (Gleeson, 2014). Nevertheless, other models have bet to lower scale instruction (Goral, 2014) as Small Private Online Courses (SPOC).

This work proposes a blended scenario for the Numerical methods course based on Challenge Based Learning (CBL) resting on mobile technology as support to introduce or reach in the face to face sessions, learning processes more elaborated oriented to the professional or research competencies development. The aim is set the concept and methodology of a Small Private Online Research (SPOR), whose justification was reached in a previous research work based on a first year of implementation (Delgado, 2016b). Last work exhibit the possibility to blend the basic knowledge content as online study together with oriented research face to face sessions in terms of the individual performance tracking for each student. The proposal moves the instruction on research based activities while the basic content is mainly covered online. The second section depicts the Numerical methods course as key in engineering education to support the orientation of the proposal. Third section presents the learning approach as is currently being applied in the course and its current outcomes based on an initial deployment to support its viability. Fourth section includes the conclusions.

2. NUMERICAL METHODS AS PROMOTOR OF HIGH LEVEL SKILLS

Numerical Methods courses are mandatory in the engineering programs at the university. This course is normally located after theoretical math and science courses, bringing the opportunity to review and to apply concepts since the numerical perspective of Calculus as well as to analyze more complex problems than those reached by analytical methods, connecting deeper math and science with engineering. For this reason, the traditional teaching has evolved with the spread of computer systems, demanding a transition from a Numerical Analysis course into a Computer Simulation one, moving to students into the professional practice. Numerical methods is a key course to align Higher Education with STEM prerogatives, in addition, it promotes scientific skills in the university engineers education.

Several years ago, an improvement was generated in the course by the inclusion of projects development related to scientific visualization in a curriculum integration context (Delgado and Martínez, 2011). To support this challenge, the author began to introduce complementary technologies in the course in addition to those oriented to develop the planned course skills (Excel, Mathematica, Phyton, etc.). As a result, since 2011, consolidated technologies and some additional emerging technologies let to reach a mobile learning approach in the course (Delgado, 2013). Through time towards, a blended scheme was constructed reaching compatibility between mobile resources and CBL orientation for the course (Delgado, 2016a). Blended learning has demonstrated its supposed efficacy there (Lothridge et al, 2013) through of modern and affordable technologies as Blackboard, Weebly, Socrative, Classmarker, Jotform and You Tube to round the blended strategy covering efficiently Flexibility, Evaluation, Learning styles inclusion, Scaffolding, Screencasting, Reporting and Feedback (Delgado, 2016b), which currently are supporting the basic knowledge acquisition (before given in the face to face sessions), not only as supplement (Wood et al, 2004).

3. SMALL PRIVATE ONLINE RESEARCH APPROACH

The last changes and requirements in the Numerical methods course have boosted the learning evolution into more flexible activities now reached through a blended scheme. Defining alternative paths to teach, to develop skills and to construct engineering competencies, a scaffold teaching strategy has been realized. In parallel, more complex, intensive and integrated research scenarios were introduced as guidelines and goals for the course.

Massive Open Online Research (MOOR) is conceptualized basically as a reduced MOOC with emphasis on research. Goals and recipients are different, MOOR's are oriented to work together in teams to solve a practical problem, thus working on targeted research projects under the guidance of a researcher (Hosler, 2014). Nevertheless, a better approach in Numerical methods course should consider the programmed inclusion of several course topics in the research in order to cover the contents, together with a more dynamic movement on short problems. Other version of MOOC's is a Small Private Online Course (SPOC), defined as an online course based only on a segment of the university. Then, being based on blended learning, this approach focuses on local requirements, including some face to face interactions (Goral, 2014). For these reasons, the ad hoc proposal for the Numerical methods course was labelled as Small Private Online Research (SPOR), being allocated on a selected segment of university and oriented to multidisciplinary research (Numerical methods course involves students of Chemical, Mechanical, Mechatronics, Electronics, Industrial and Biotechnological Engineering programs).

3.1 SPOR structure

Based on the analysis developed by Delgado (2016a), the new interactions emerging behind of the mobile approach for the course and the effective outcomes of blended activities included as individual and predictive evaluations of individual performance, a parallel instruction scheme is understood in the SPOR approach. By replacing the basic contents coverage in the face to face sessions with a series of research problems as guidelines (covering the basic contents in their development) and moving that basic coverage into a pure mobile learning strategy, the SPOR skeleton was stated. Thus, each student selects their resource learnings, pace and evaluation route in a flexible version for the course through resources as: a) daily screencasting series in a You Tube channel, b) extended repositories including simulations and programming codes,

c) theoretical reviews through an interactive e-Book for the course, d) individual homework (no mandatory, but alternative) and d) formative and summative evaluations alternated and being reached with Socrative and Classmarker tools. In parallel, in the face to face sessions, the teacher presents and develops in teams, scientific and engineering problems requiring numeric simulation and computer visualization. The connection between two knowledge layers is reached by integrated activities derived from the individual learning in the screencasting and in the basic evaluation. Thus teamwork activities are little projects or developments at the end of each knowledge unit and co-evaluated with periodic exams. Figure 1 shows a global scheme about the SPOR strategy, showing the basic exams (allowed to be presented in more than one time) at the end of each unit and the three component exam for each term including (only in necessary cases) this basic evaluation together with topics related to teamwork and research projects. Each semester includes three of these terms or segments (Delgado, 2016b).

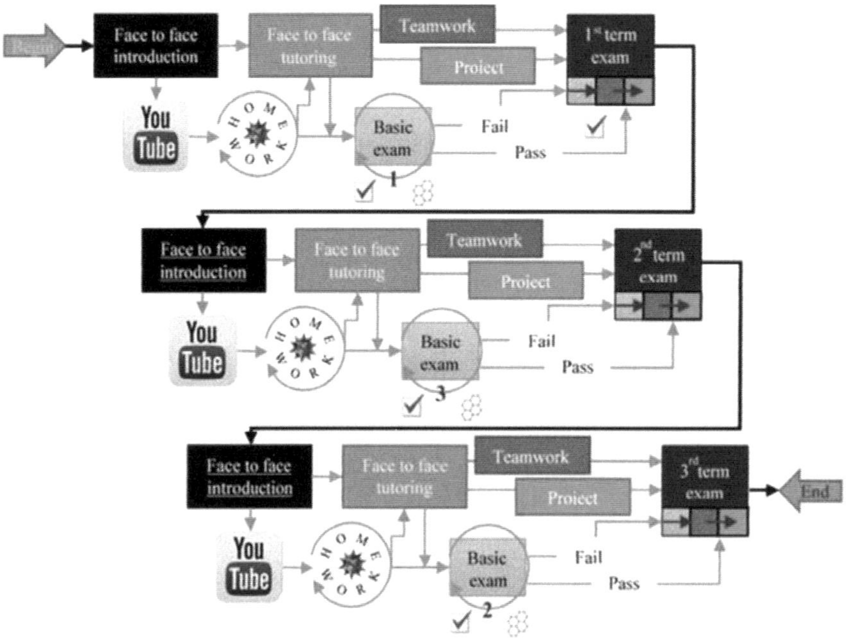

Figure 1. Main course activities and their chronology in the SPOR approach (Delgado, 2016b).

3.2 SPOR viability

One of the main concerns in online learning is related with the grade discrimination between individual and team evaluation components. This issue has been focused in a wider open way for the Numerical methods course. A CBL course develops skills and competencies as goal, so a stronger system of evaluation should be developed to reflect realistically this pretension. The SPOR approach has been validated by comparing individual and team performance of several dimensions: knowledge, skills, and competencies (Delgado, 2016b). In the analysis, the learning model shows a good discrimination for good and low performance students, in particular for the online evaluation. To summarize the outcomes reported there, the Figure 2 plots for the students in the first two years of implementation (2014-2015), the ratio between the averages of individual and teamwork grades (I/T x 100) -those associated with individual and team homework or exams- versus the average of teamwork grades for each one. The color of each dot correspond to the final grade in the course (Dark gray: <70, fail; Medium gray: between 70 and 85; Light gray: >85) and its radius was settled as the average number of times each individual Basics Exams was presented by the student through the overall course. In the course, 70 is the threshold to pass. First note the teamwork well performance. Then Figure 2 shows that individual activities discriminates very well to the good and satisfactory students (correspondingly located next to the dotted vertical line where team and individual effort is comparable). For unsatisfactory students, discrimination still works except for some few cases not properly allocated (those students next to the dotted vertical line). The number of applications in the individual Basic Exams is not correlated with their average (R^2=0.02), so this aspect of flexibility in the course do not give or remove advantage.

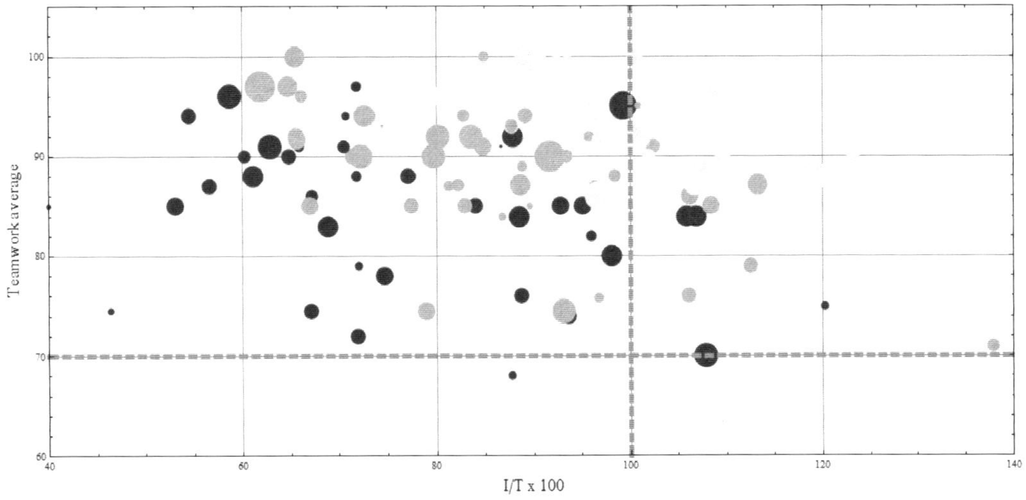

Figure 2. Scatter graph for individual performance outcomes in the SPOR approach implementation.

This scheme doesn't show an increasing in the grades corresponding to the basic knowledge segments, instead a deep development in solving applied problem skills. For the middle level students, a deep interpretation about the course final goal is still open in terms of the model to construct a global grade in it. Additional research in SPOR evaluation is still in order.

4. RESEARCH PROJECTS IN THE COURSE

Research projects using CBL strategy are based on short simulation and visualization tasks for science and engineering in each one of the three periods in the course term. The net of projects used in the first year of deployment for the SPOR approach is depicted in the Table 1. The projects are related to Mechanics, Cellular Automata rules, Heat diffusion, Electromagnetism, Lighting, Chaos, Complex kinematics and Bacteria growing models. Each project reviews several numerical methods included and developed in the online activities. The projects promote innovation and specialized research in the group of students. Teams of utmost four students are created in each period to develop the teamwork activities. The net of projects enhances and extends skills and competencies because each one summarizes previous knowledge into visual applications. In the SPOR scheme, basic knowledge and research problem solving become complementary.

Table 2. Net of projects and relation with the five units of the original course contents.

Projects	Non-linear equations	Derivatives and Integrals	Equations system	Interpolation and Approximation	Differential equations
Mechanics	X	X	X		X
Kinematics	X	X			X
Lighting	X	X		X	
Chaos	X	X	X		X
Heat diffusion	X	X	X	X	
Electromagnetism	X	X		X	
Cellular automata	X		X		X
Bacteria growing	X		X		X

5. CONCLUSION

Renewed schemes of instruction and education should be running to get a better approach in terms of effective promotion and flexible strategy. Blended schemes as the depicted here should be experimented and improved currently to be disposable for new generations. In a few years, several courses should be evolved into MOOC, MOOR or SPOR schemes, changing the traditional higher education as it has been known.

Skills and professional competences require a continuous practice and several steps before to be owned, superseding any course extent. Traditional evaluation is limited to the contents dominion, with uncertainty and not at the skilled level that each student need. The evaluation goes beyond the content knowledge, in the arena of skills and of competences development, there is a really complex task for teachers (Schwartz, 2014).

ACKNOWLEDGEMENT

Support through NOVUS initiative is acknowledged to Tecnológico de Monterrey.

REFERENCES

Delgado, F. and Martínez, S., 2011. Curricular changes generated due to employment of technology in the teaching of Numerical Methods. *Proceedings of XXXVIII ANFEI conference*, Querétaro, México.

Delgado, F., 2013. A numerical methods course based on b-learning: integrated learning design and follow up. *Int. J. of Mobile and Blended Learning*, vol. 5, no. 1, pp. 39-57.

Delgado, F., 2016. Follow-Up of a Numerical Methods Course Using m-learning to Propose the Evolution to Research Based Learning. *Proceedings eLmL 2016*, Mestre, Italy.

Delgado, F., 2016. Evolving a Numerical Methods Course into an Approach Based on Flexibility and Research Skill Development. *Proceedings of EduTeach 2016*, Toronto, Canada, pp. 58-65.

Gleeson, T. (2014). Co-Teaching a Blended Class across Universities. Inside Higher Ed. Retrieved from: http://www.insidehighered.com/blogs/higher-ed-beta/co-teaching-blended-class-across-universities

Goral, T., 2014. SPOC's may provide what MOOC's can't. *University business*. Retrieved from http://www.universitybusiness.com/article/spocs-may-provide-what-moocs-can%E2%80%99t

Hosler, A., 2014. Massive Open Online Research: The MOOC Evolves into the MOOR. *Emerging EdTech*. Retrieved from http://www.emergingedtech.com/2014/01/massive-open-online-research-the-mooc-evolves-into-the-moor

Laurillard, D., 2005. E-Learning in Higher Education. In P. Ashwin (Ed.), *Changing Higher Education: The Development of Learning and Teaching*. London, RoutledgeFalmer.

Laurillard, D., 2008. *Digital technologies and their role in achieving our ambitions for education*. Professorial lecture. London, England.

Lothridge, K., Fox, J. and Fynan, E., 2013. Blended learning: efficient, timely, and cost effective. *Journal for Forensic Sciences*, vol. 45, no. 4, pp. 407-416.

Schwartz, K., 2014. More Progressive Ways to Measure Deeper Levels of Learning. *Mind/Shift*. Retrieved from http://blogs.kqed.org/mindshift/2014/04/more-progressive-ways-to-measure-deeper-level-of-learning/

Wood, R., Baker, J. and Hopper, D., 2004. Hybrid structures: Faculty use and perception of web based courseware as a supplement to face-to-face instruction. *The Internet & Higher Education*, vol. 7, no. 4, pp. 281-297.

EXPERIMENTING WITH SUPPORT OF MOBILE TOUCH DEVICES FOR PUPILS WITH SPECIAL EDUCATIONAL NEEDS

Mgr. Vojtěch Gybas, Doc. Ing. Kateřina Kostolányová, Ph.D. and Mgr. Libor Klubal
University of Ostrava, Pedagogical Faculty, Department of Information and Communication Technologies
Fráni Šrámka 3, Ostrava, Mariánské Hory, 70900, Czech Republic

ABSTRACT

The aim of this paper is to describe one of the learning option for pupils with special educational needs with the support of ICT in the educational area Man and Nature, „a basic knowledge of chemistry." Form of experimental teaching is not commonly used in elementary school special education. With the support of ICT, specifically the iPad, we can try a simple experiment as a demonstration of unusual subject matter: the solubility of the substances, the density of matter, detailed structure of the fabric surface. Perception of microscopic object details is very difficult and sometimes impossible for pupils with special educational needs. Working with a microscope is very difficult because of various pupils affection, such as fine motor skills disorder, visual disturbances and so on. But if we use an iPad and an appropriate application, we can do experiments very effectively also in a special elementary school. iPad, in connection with Magniscope appropriate tool, is a great tool to capture any detail that a student with moderate mental disorder cannot notice Pupils can „experiment" on their own, they can create screens. These screens can be used in the creation of interactive books in Book Creator - add their descriptions, reviews and previews.

KEYWORDS

Pupils with special educational needs, ICT, iPad, experiment, Magniscope, Book Creator.

1. INTRODUCTION

ICT has been a part of education for many years - a computer, interactive whiteboard, laptop. However, cell touch technology - tablets are increasingly involved in students´ education. Tablet allows greater flexibility to pupils with special educational needs, „it requires less burden on graphomotorics control and facilitates visual and sensory Learning." (Flewitt, Kučírková, Messer, 2014), while „it significantly increasing attention at work." (Epps, online, 2016) . Fine motor skills difficulty is usually the most frequent manifestation of pupil´s moderate mental disability. Therefore, the tablets can be a very effective tool in teaching. In such a situation the teacher is able to work in a completely different way. New way. He can create experiments with students, he can use a different form of writing notes of relevant phenomena in the form of video recording, photography, writing on the virtual keyboard. This would be impossible by using a computer and a standard keyboard and using conventional paper materials would be unrealistic from the learner's point of view. *„ With its variety of input and output methods, the tablet provides easy access to a variety of users. For students with motor skills impairments, the touch screen is easier to use because they do not need to control their finger as precisely as with keyboards or other writing utensils. Tablets are also used to contribute to the development of these skills"* (Johnson, 2013, online). While other technology solutions exist, none is as easy to use as a tablet."

2. FORMS OF TEACHING

According to Muller, Valenta (2013), the most often forms of pupil´s work in special elementary school are characterized into four groups. These forms of work are complemented by our own knowledge from experience: **frontal work** - in a special elementary school it is highly recommended to use it with other forms of teaching. Frontal form is suitable in familiarizing students with the desktop application. We want to introduce one content to all pupils at the same time. **Group work** – all students work together on one output, each student meets one part that he can handle, the output is common. **Individual work** - this is the main approach to pupils in special elementary schools. The teacher works with each student individually, during certain time unit, with a predetermined aim. **Individualized work** – *„since it is very demanding for a pupil´s inner motivation, leisure skills and self-control ability, it is used sporadically in special elementary schools."* (Müller, Valenta, 2013, p. 388). *„Technology allows teachers to devote to all pupils at the same time, and concurrently plan lessons for individual students with diverse educational needs. Pupils can work individually on pre-prepared materials, or directly in an electronic environment, if a school allows that."* (Adamus, 2015, p. 9). In their own pace, there is a predetermined learning aim for the moment.

3. MOBILE TOUCH TECHNOLOGIES

Many researchers suggest that especially tablets are very useful. Eg. in the partial research Gybas, Kostolányová (2016) in Mobile touch screen devices as compensation for the teaching materials at a special primary school: special education teachers in the Czech Republic use tablets and applications as one of the most common forms of compensation for missing teaching materials, most often in the educational area Man and Nature.

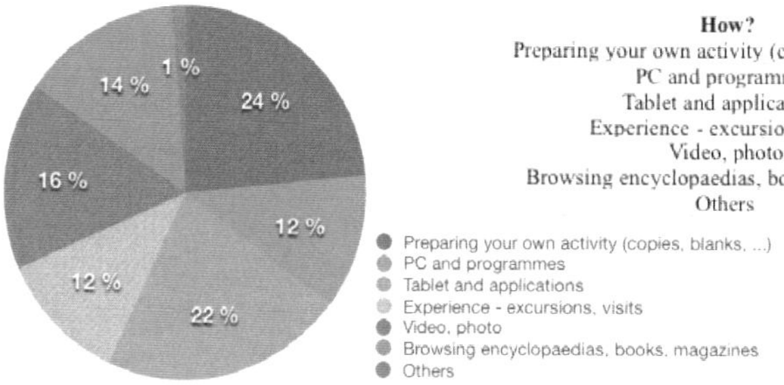

How?	Respondents
Preparing your own activity (copies, blanks, ...)	110
PC and programmes	54
Tablet and applications	102
Experience - excursions, visits	54
Video, photo	76
Browsing encyclopaedias, books, magazines	66
Others	6

Figure 1. Compensation of learning material - the most often used form?

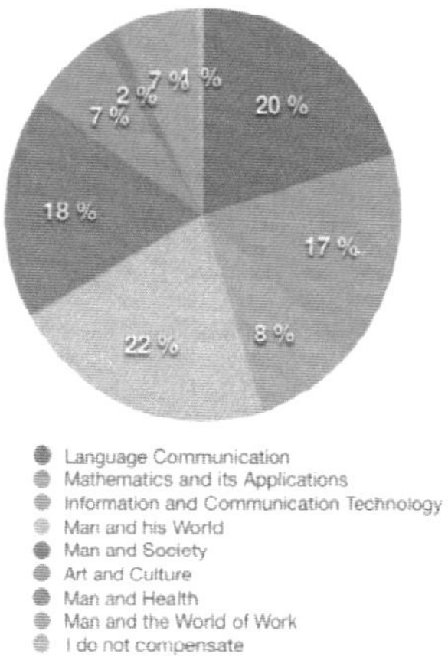

Score	Respondents
Language Communication	78
Mathematics and its Applications	64
Information and Communication Technology	32
Man and his World	84
Man and Society	68
Art and Culture	26
Man and Health	6
Man and the World of Work	26
I do not compensate	2

Figure 2. Compensation of learning material - what kind of educational field the most often?

The principle of the criteria above is confirmed by words of teachers from the state of Virginia, USA, where in 2010 there was the first pilot project with the introduction of the iPad into teaching in primary schools. As reported in Digital Directions (online, 2016): English teacher Erin Upton tries to personalize reading assignments based on proficiency, and uses a feature of the iPad to help highlight key vocabulary words for students. Math teacher Amreen Alvi has found some apps to help students understand Fractions and decimals, and Also has the students off the open worksheets Blackboard Inc. classroom-management site and complete theme with a stylus pen During a classroom exercise. Remember that *„learning process is successful when you involve all the senses in the learning process, as far as possible, especially when we are active ourselves.* " (Pipeková, Vítkov, 2001, p. 25). Holler (1996) states that a learning brain retains 10% of what we read; 20% of what we hear; 30% of what we see; 50% of what we hear and see; 70% of what we say, and 90% of what we do. iPads can support the claim. It's very important in special elementary schools. Allen (2016) states in his study that, digital technology affords a unique advantage and opportunity for customization that traditional paper material cannot provide. Apps can either be "closed" or „open": both are interactive, but only the latter allows the user to change or modify content. Flewitt et all. states, however, one of the key features of the tablets on which apps are used is their touch-screen; thus, touch, gesture, and pointing can be supported by the use of tablet hardware (Flewitt et al., 2014) and the apps used to support learning could be designed to enhance this type of sensory interaction to a greater extent than possible with traditional print medium embedded. MacDonald, Hill (2014) state that in particular, these devices can be categorised based on their primary use as augmentative and alternative communication (AAC), access equipment, environmental control units (ECU), assistive listening devices (ALD), visual aids and mobility and positioning technologies (eg, wheelchairs) and thus further determined as low-tech or high- tech gadgets according to the degree of electronic and computer components incorporated within the device.

4. EXPERIMENT IN A SPECIAL ELEMENTARY SCHOOL EDUCATION

Experiment, as a method of natural science research, may be highly beneficial in a special elementary school, but only if the teacher keeps certain rules. As it is indicated by Malčík, Mechlová (2014), the principle, for teaching the science subjects in general, is experimentation, which is based on effects research and patterns detection or verification of what students already know from the theory. Unfortunately, the intellectual capacity of pupils in special elementary school does not allow to base on a pupil's theoretical knowledge. Yet we can use experiment as a method of science research teaching, but we must adapt the process to the pupils. According to the Framework educational program for the field of education, in special elementary schools (hereinafter FEP ZSS), the basic knowledge of chemistry is learning content as well as. Bilek, Tobořiková (2010) report that digital technology has become an organic part of teaching chemistry as one of the natural sciences and enables discovery of new knowledge and principles. The experiment, in simpler form, can be an excellent tool to teach the curriculum, to introduce the phenomena to students, within their intellectual abilities. For pupils in special elementary schools, it is very important to re-fix the curriculum and try to keep memories. Redman, Jakab, Carlin (2014) concluded, that iPad use can redefine learning spaces and Contribute to the creation of innovative pedagogies, as teachers RESPOND to the iPads versatility and mobility features. The potential, and limitations, of Digital Technologies to Contribute to students' learning Opportunities Explored have been here, through analysis of the perceptions, stories and actions of teachers, students and parents. Thanks to the iPad and selected applications we can keep the experiment for future use: the form of photos, videos, interactive books.

4.1 Application Magniscope

Due to the intellectual abilities and individual differences of students in special elementary schools, it is possible to include working with the iPad as a "computer aided teaching of science. "into teaching process. In practice, we mean adoption and approach of substances features - solubility, density, surface detail. This allows students to work with the iPad and applications Magniscope. Applications Magniscope - it is an easy used application "magnifying glass for everyone." Holding iPad of about 10 centimetres above the paper. We can see *„small letters printed sentences through the lens of the camera on the iPad.*" (App Store, online, 2016).

1. area of shot subject
2. object detail - microscope function
3. button "Information"

Figure 3. Magniscope applications operating environment.

Students are able to work independently with the iPad and applications Magniscope. They enclose the iPad in front of the object of their interest, they wait for the focus of the object. Once it is focused, they „freeze“ the object by touching the screen. This will keep a preview of the inspected object. Students can independently create screen display by double touching (pressing a Power button and home Button - simultaneously). This created screen is saved to the iPad in the Photos app. Pupils already know where exactly find the resulting images.

4.2 Experiment process

In the first part of the lesson, we talked about living and nonliving nature. I explained the importance of non-living components for living nature. In the next part of the lesson, pupils were given several different subjects and they were supposed to assess them in terms of state - solid, liquid and gas. Together we have gathered the main common characteristics of these three types of state. To be able to see details of surveyed objects, we used the iPad app Magniscope. Pupils were able to see the structure of sugar, salt, a carpet, a stone, a paper tissue, oil in water, ice. At the end of our experiments we demonstrated, that some substances can be found in all three states. The proof was water, which we brought to boil, and we saw it going up in the form of gas, which is steam. We let freeze part of the water in the freezer, so that at the end of the lesson it was in the form of solid - ice. Thanks to the fact that we introduce most of the demonstrative aids continuously to our observations, we were able to keep their attention on the maximum level. Bílek, Tobořiková (2010) states, that the real experiment should not disappear from the school practice, but also, we cannot avoid vicarious observing and working with models. It is necessary to search for an appropriate combination of both approaches applications. For pupils with special educational needs, the experiment is working with Magniscope application and observation of details.

4.3 Findings record

To record the findings of knowledge in a special elementary school, feedback is very important. Based on meta-analysis of series of studies, Hattie and Timperleyová (2007) indicate, that various types of feedback can be variously effective. Primarily, feedback focused on the process fosters deeper understanding. On the contrary, they oppose to feedback, focused on the personality, which has no direct connection with actual pupils' performances. Applications Book Creator can be used in any field, regardless of age, from the age of 4 and up. "Using Book Creator we can create our own learning resources, or work on their own materials with pupils:

- interactive stories,
- digital documents,
- journals,
- poetry books,

- science write-up,
- instructions for use." (Redjumper, online, 2016).

Thanks to the book created with book Creator , the educator gets interactive material to which he can return at any time and can easily update it, edit, share. For the pupil, the feeling of a well done job naturally increases, reinforces key skills for learning, skills for problem solving and social personnel and especially communicative competence. If the student has an interactive book content created by himself, he recalls information more easily. *„All educational content must face the formation and development of key competencies , methods and forms of education and activities taking place at school. By respecting the specific needs of students with moderate intellectual disability, the focus is on key communication skills, social and personal work.* " (RVP ZSS, 2008, p. 13).

5. BENEFITS OF WORKING WITH IPAD

For children lacking motor skills, touch screens are more intuitive devices. **Fine motor skill** - experiment in teaching, using the tablet, has clearly demonstrated a reduction in claims on fine motor skills. Students are unable to work with ordinary keyboard due to these difficulties. Typing on the virtual keyboard of the tablet is very fast interactions: eye - hand. A pupil sees immediately what he writes. For students, who have not embraced writing letters, using common writing instruments -a pencil, a pen, tablets are a new mean of working, which he couldn´t do before. **Working with the media** - pupils work with the tablet, using the camera application. They can create photographs, video recordings together with the teacher. With those they work in Book Creator and create interactive books. That lesson is still "alive". It means that students can always come back to their interactive books in their tablets. They can look at the photos, videos. If the teacher only created a "passive" book that would be printed, photos would reduce the effect of re-call of the phenomenon. **New possibilities** - using ICT, in the form of a tablet, in the classroom, offered a completely new form of work and a completely new tools for working. Working with classic microscope is impossible in elementary school. Working with Magniscope, which simulates a microscope, was very helpful and efficient. Students were given the opportunity to examine the details of substances and objects. **Motivation and imagination** - working with the tablet is still a very strong motivator. Pupils enjoy working with tablets. Tablet can increase their attention at work. Pupils are focused, concentrated, are keen to explore and research. This phenomenon is very valuable. We could see their interest in object details. We can reinforce imagination very effectively, which is characterized by "narrow-mindedness, fragmented and unclear connections, which can be seen in stereotypical and content-poor activities of the play, which persists even in compulsory schooling." (Zezulková, Kaleja, 2013,p. 25).

6. CONCLUSION

Methods of work, forms of education and access to pupils with special educational needs are very specific. Limited to some extent. From both sides - students - intellectual ability and personal oddities, and from the teaching materials - they are very outdated, inadequate. Nevertheless, using innovative features and approaches, usually encountered in elementary schools of an ordinary type, we can try even in special elementary schools to maximize the development of students. When working with an iPad we can use several forms of teaching. Frontally - illustration of Magniscope applications; individually - helping pupils with the creation of the Screen, Screen inserting and the creation of interactive books; We can individualize the teaching process - capable students perform their tasks independently with their own pace. They reach the goal = creating an interactive book.We should not forget one thing. Using mobile touch technologies, which tablets represent, bring new possibilities for pupils. We naturally raise their motivation, enthusiasm, new possibilities of gaining knowledge. Pupils in special elementary schools can work as ordinary pupils. They use the same options, only in a limited extent.

REFERENCES

Act no. 82/2015 Coll., Amending Act no. 561/2004 Coll., On preschool, primary, secondary, higher professional and other education (Education Act), as amended, and certain other acts

Allen M.,L., Hartley C., Cain K. (2016) *iPads and the Use of "Apps" by Children with Autism Spectrum Disorder: Do They Promote Learning?* Front. Psychol. 7: 1305th doi: 10.3389 / fpsyg.2016.01305

App Store. *Magniscope.* [online]. 2016 [cit. 18/12/2016]. Available at www: https://itunes.apple.com/gb/app/magniscope-easy-to-use-magnifying/id577370129?mt=8)

Apple. *iMovie.* [online]. 2016 [cit. 18/12/2016]. Available at www: http://www.apple.com/imovie/)

Bílek M., Tobořiková, P.: *Current challenges for computer-aided school chemistry experiments. In: Chupáč, A., Veřmiřovský, J. (eds.): Current aspects of undergraduate training and postgraduate education of chemistry teachers* - Proceedings of the International Conference Ostrava: University of Ostrava, 2010, pp. 32 - 35.

Concordia university. 6 *Strategies for Teaching Special Education Classes.* [online]. [quote. 25-12 2015]. Available at http://education.cu-portland.edu/blog/special-ed/6-strategies-for-teaching-special-education-classes/

Decree no. 27/2016 Coll., On the education of pupils with special educational needs and gifted pupils [online]. [feeling. 5. 5. 2016]. Available from http://www.nuv.cz/t/nadani/vyhlaska-c-27-2016-sb

Education week: digital directions. *Educators Evaluate Learning Benefits of iPad.* [online]. [quote. 25-12 2015]. Available at http://www.edweek.org/dd/articles/2011/06/15/03mobile.h04.html

Flewitt, R., Kučírková, N., Messer, D. (2014). *Touchingthe virtual, touching thereal: iPads and enabling literacy for students experiencing a disability. Aust. J.Lang.Literacy* 37,107-116.

Gybas V., Kostolányová K. *Mobile touch screen devices as compensation for the teaching materials at a special primary school* in the 12th International conference on mobilelearning 2016. Algarve, Portugal. pp. 157-161, 5 pp.

Hattie, John; Timperley, Helen. *The Power of*Feedback. 2007.

Johnson G.M./ Curtin University (2013): Using Tablet Computers with Elementary School Students with Special Needs: The Practices and Perceptions of Special Education Teachers and Teacher Assistants, [online]. [quote. 2-2 2017]. Available at http://www.cjlt.ca/index.php/cjlt/article/viewFile/767/381

Macdonald, P., Hill B., Brown G. S. Is Apple transforming special education? Assessing the effcacy of the iPad as an assistive technology for students with special education needs. In Special Education perspectives. [online]. [quote. 25-12 2015]. Available at http://aase.edu.au/wordpress/wp-content/uploads/documents/SEP-Contents-Vol-23-No-1.pdf

Malčík M., Mechlová E. *Methodology for the use of measurement systems - general section.* [online]. 2016 [cit. 18/11/2016]. Available from http://prvedyss.zvas.cz/files/MET/metodika-OBECNA.pdf

Müller, O., Valenta M. *Psychopedie.* Theoretical foundations and methodology. Prague: Parta, 2013.

Pipeková, J., Vítková, M. *Therapy in special educational care.* 2nd ed. Brno: Paido, 2001, 165 pp.

Redjumper. *Book Creatorapp.* [online]. 2016 [cit. 18/11/2016]. Available at www: http://bookcreator.com/education/)

RVP ZSS. *Framework educational program for the field of education special elementary school.* 1st edition. Prague: Research Institute of Education, 2008.

Wainwright A. 8 Things to Remember When Preparing for iPads in the Classroom. [online]. [quote. 25-12 2015]. Available at http://www.pearsonfoundation.org/downloads/PF_Tablet_Survey_Summary_2012.pdf , http://www.securedgenetworks.com/blog/8-Things-to-Remember-When-Preparing-for-iPads-in-the-Classroom

Zezulková E., Kaleja M. *The basic resources of education of pupils with special educational needs.* Ostrava. 2013.

Zounek, J. *Computer, Internet and Multimedia in teacher's work.* In Novotný, Petr, Pol, Milan (ed.). Selected Chapters from school education. Brno, 2002. pp. 61-73

MOBILE LEARNING IN THE THEATER ARTS CLASSROOM

Dr. Zihao Li (Michael)
Office 1024, E33, Faculty of Education, University of Macau, Macau

ABSTRACT

Mobile learning (m-learning) challenges the traditional definition of teaching and learning. M-learning concept is gaining popularity because it enables learning across multiple contexts and disciplines by using portable mobile devices. In recent years, it has attracted increasing attention at the tertiary level as some institutions adopt Bring Your Own Devices (BYOD) in classrooms. While m-learning is becoming ubiquitous as educators often hear about it at conferences and encounter it in literature, one might assume that many educators know about and use it in teaching. It is not, especially in theater arts classrooms. In Dance and Drama education, for instance, the use of mobile teaching and learning is extremely limited both in literature and in practice. This study looks at 146 undergraduate students in three General Education (GE) classes (two Drama and one dance) over fourteen weeks at a comprehensive university in Southern China. During lectures, in class and online, smartphones were integrated in learning and they were used in a variety of class related activities including ZOOM, virtual presentations, online polls, and video making to further engage students in deep learning. This study finds that though challenges exist, the fusion of the multichannel teaching approach (m-learning, blended learning, in class/online lectures) has enhanced teaching and learning experiences among theatre arts students.

KEYWORDS

Mobile learning; In-class/online teaching; Dance and Drama; Theater arts education.

1. INTRODUCTION

Mobile learning (m-learning) is a relatively new learning model as it integrates mobile technology to enhance learning experiences (Yuen & Yuen, 2008). In recent years, m-learning has gained sufficient momentum that it is seen in research studies, publications, at conferences, and among educators, particularly those teaching at the tertiary level. M-learning encompasses three characteristics: portability; connectivity; context sensitivity (Cheon et al., 2012). The combination of these m-learning features constructs a unique learning environment (Traxler, 2007, 2008, 2010). Researchers in this study calls this learning environment a "simulated learning space."

1.1 Disadvantages

Despite the abundance of mobile devices, the usage of new technologies in higher education is sporadic, uneven and rigid (Selwyn, 2007). The readiness to incorporate m-learning is discussed (Park, 2011; Wang et al., 2009) and mixed views are shared among educators. Some studies show that many learners are inclined to use their mobile device for music, social media/network, and games instead of for educational purposes (Park, 2011; Wang et al., 2009). WeChat, Twitter, WhatsApp, and other instant messages are exchanged among family and friends members (Pew Research Center, 2015). In education, text messaging is incorporated into classes for content learning (Cifuentes & Lents, 2010), class discussion (Hou & Wu, 2011) and team support (Timmis, 2012). On the flip side, researchers have found that m-learning including text messaging could disrupt regular in-class teaching (Corbeil & Valdes-Corbeil, 2007; Park, 2011; Wang et al., 2009). Their concern was that the focus of the class might be carried away when mobile device activities were implemented. In short, the integration and the promotion of m-learning still faces great challenges due to its unique social, cultural, organizational, socio economic, and psychological factors (Cheon et al., 2012; Corbeil & Valdes-Corbeil, 2007; Traxler, 2007, 2010).

1.2 Advantages

Gikas and Grant (2013) have found that mobile systems could facilitate learning during lectures by posing questions and activating exercises via mobile devices. This approach increases the level of the student's engagement and participation during lectures (Markett et al., 2006), and motivates them to achieve better learning outcomes (Wang et al., 2009). Research also found that instructors preferred to use mobile devices in teaching because they generated instant responses and feedback on teaching methods and gathered insights from students on certain topics or concepts (Wang et al., 2009). However, Arrigo, Kukulska-Hulme, Arnedillo-Sanchez, and Kismihok (2013) suggest that most of the studies on m-learning were centered on the distribution of content instead of on social interaction between tutors, teachers or peers using mobile devices. Educators use learning apps (e.g., Moodle and Blackboard) on mobile devices to post reading materials or assign homework. That is not an effective use of mobile devices in education as Laurillard (2010) states that the application m-learning actually supports learning through instruction, sharing, construction, discussion, and collaboration (Laurillard, 2010).

1.3 M-learning in theatre arts (Dance and Drama)

In Dance and Drama classes, the use of mobile technology in teaching is limited (Robinson, 2016). To many people, dance and drama are linked to popular culture where subjects are shared on smartphones through social media such as Facebook and WeChat. Dance and Drama teaching methods, nonetheless, are still quite traditional and conservative (Calvert et al., 2005). Research on the use of technology, especially about mobile devices in Dance and Drama teaching remain as an uncharted territory for many educators and researchers. On the other hand, technology has been successfully used in various theater performances on stage and at site-specific locations. Some scholars suggest that these embodied arts [Dance and Drama] are less likely to be associated with technology (Calvert et al., 2005). Others argued that for better teaching outcomes and learning engagement, technology integration provides a strengthened approach for teaching Dance and Drama (Doughty et al., 2008). This paper aims to fill the gap by investigating the impact of m-learning on theater arts education.

2. METHODOLOGY

This study used mixed methods, one of which was a nonrandom sampling technique (convenience sampling) to gather data (Creswell, 2012). It also utilized qualitative case studies along with survey distribution, data collection through formal and informal semi-structured interviews, class observations, open polls, social media posts, and course assignments/projects analysis.

The participants in this study were 160 undergraduate students at a large public funded comprehensive university located in Southern China. It also categorized itself as a research-intensive institution. These students were enrolled in "Introduction to Dance Studies" and "Introduction to Drama Studies" which were general education (GE) courses. In other words, they were elective courses that students could take among hundreds of other GE courses ranging from Microbiology to Japanese language. Researchers announced the study at the beginning of the semester and stressed that the participation was entirely voluntary. All students had the same instructor, course content (two Drama classes and one Dance), and teaching schedule (3-hour lecture, once a week for a total of fourteen weeks). Students signed a consent form and were informed that the study would be used for academic purposes including scholar paper publication and conference presentations. They were also told of their rights to withdraw at any time during the study. Among all participants, 146 students from two Drama (n= 105) and one Dance (n=41) successfully completed the study. The rest of the students 16, were not included due to missing responses and absences.

The 10-item survey measured participants' views on the use of mobile devices in teaching with a 5-point Likert scale, ranging from frequently to never or extremely important to not important. Other questions were seeking their perceptions on mobile learning and their familiarity with mobile apps functions. All surveys were conducted as open polls, which were anonymous. All students were given an invitation letter to participate in a semi-structured interview but only the first twenty who handed in the consent form were recruited. All interviews were conducted on the university premises according to students' and the instructor's availability. All interviews were recorded, numbered, transcribed, and color coded.

3. PARTICIPANT PROFILE AND RESULTS

Among 146 students who completed the survey, there were more female students (females n=89) than males students (males n=57) in Dance and Drama classes. Students were from different faculties and majors: 31 per cent came from the Faculty of Social Sciences, which represented the largest student body in the study. There was only one student from the Institute of Chinese Medical Sciences due to its research based nature and most of its students were graduate students. Figure 1 shows students' representation.

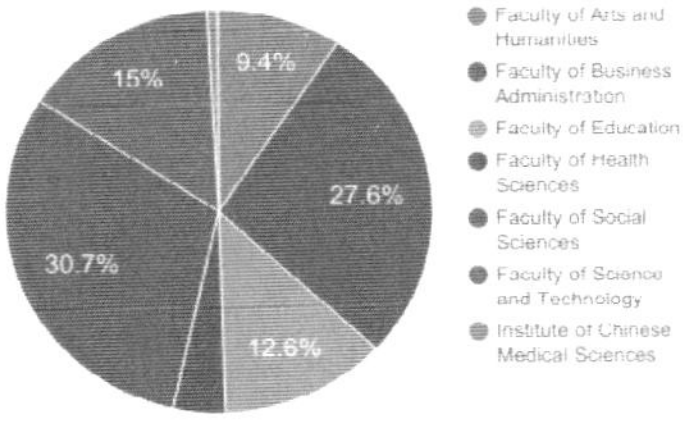

Figure 1. Student body representation.

The majority of GE courses at this university used English as the teaching language. A few GE courses used different languages due to their cultural, language acquisition nature. For instance, Portuguese and Japanese as instructional language for Culture and Language studies. Many students were fluent in three languages: English, Mandarin, and Cantonese. Local students spoke Cantonese as their mother tongue language and they represented 80 per cent of the student population. In these two courses, English was the language for instruction, assignments, and in-class/off-class communications. An online poll (diagnostic test) was conducted in the first class to find out the students' background training in Dance and Drama. The poll was made and conducted on Polleverywhere, an online survey that students could use on their mobile device. With a quick scan on Quick Response (QR) code, they were able to complete the survey in few minutes. The poll showed that a vast majority of students had little or no previous dance/drama training background. In the Dance class, 39 per cent had limited informal dance training in the past. The Poll in Drama classes indicated that 98 per cent of them had never had any theater training background. Researchers observed that every student owned at least one mobile device in these two classes. In fact, many students at this university owned multiple mobile devices and they were comfortable with mobile technology and aware of its capabilities. On average, each student owned between two and four mobile devices on campus (Tan, 2016). These findings matched previous studies (Roschelle & Pea 2002; Campbell, 2006) that young people would embrace mobile technology quickly.

3.1 Mobile learning – Student perspectives

The majority of students rated the use of a mobile device as important and effective in helping them with daily life and school work. Of all participants, close to 90 per cent rated the use of mobile devices in Drama and Dance classes important to extremely important in helping them learn the subject. This finding was in line with a previous study that the integration of technology enhances Dance and Drama teaching (Doughty et al., 2008). The percentage is almost the same when the same question was applied to students' learning in other subjects. Among Dance and Drama students, 21 per cent thought the use of mobile devices important; 42 per cent considered it very important; 33 per cent believed the use of it extremely important. This finding matched Roschelle and Pea's (2002) study, in which they predicted that young people, K-12 classrooms, would embrace portable technologies in the near future to communicate and socialize (Campbell, 2006). When asked what kind of activities students liked the most, text messaging came up to the top of the list. This finding was in line with Pew Research Center's study (2015) on instant messages' popularity. Students also indicated that simultaneous text message/feedback/comment on educational platform (Polleverythere and Qualtrics) were effective tools to help them understand the subject (Cifuentes & Lents, 2010), stimulate in-class discussion (Hou & Wu, 2011) and promote peer collaboration (Timmis, 2012). Figure 2 and 3 show student perceptions on the effectiveness/importance of using mobile devices in learning.

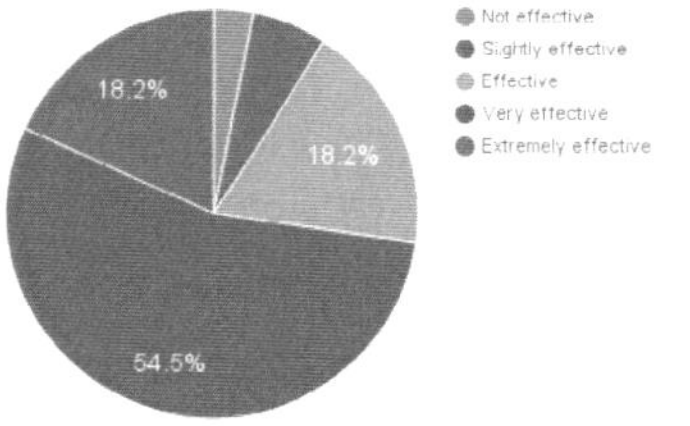

Figure 2. Attitude on the effectiveness of using mobile devices in Dance & Drama classes.

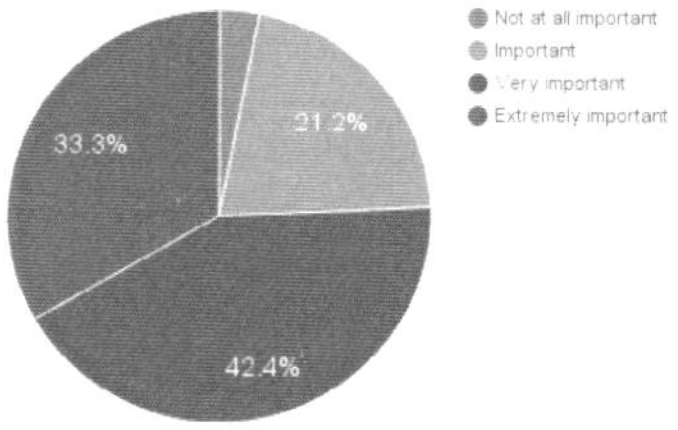

Figure 3. Important of using mobile technology in learning in general.

3.2 Mobile teaching on campus

Status of mobile teaching on campus. The entire campus including all classrooms, hallways, other learning spaces, including the dance studio and drama theater were equipped with free wifi to students and educators. Researchers observed that many students were quite accustomed with their mobile device and apps' functions and capabilities. What made this happen? Where did student learn about it? Were other professors using mobile devices in teaching on campus? Since 146 participants came from different faculties on campus, the question on the status of mobile teaching by other educators was raised. Data showed that only 6 per cent of the teaching staff (junior lectures to full professors) used mobile devices in teaching frequently; 20 per cent used it sometimes; 20 per cent incorporated it every once in a while; the majority, 44 per cent used it rarely during lectures. The study also found that approximately 9 per cent of the educators never used any mobile device in teaching. Some professors even requested students to turn off mobile devices during classes. Interviews with students found that mobile device apps were easy to use and almost all of them did not require special training. Many students admitted that they had already obtained "mobile skills" at the high school level, which was confirmed by Campbell's study on young people's familiarity with mobile device applications (Campbell, 2006). Interview with the instructor revealed difficulties in applying mobile devices in teaching, especially at the beginning stage. That partially explained why so few educators on this campus used mobile devices in teaching. Figure 4 shows mobile teaching among teaching staff on campus.

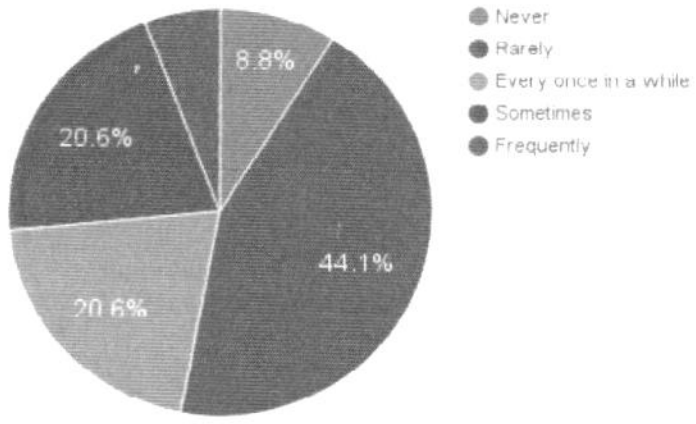

Figure 4. Mobile teaching among other Professors in the same university.

4. CONCLUSION

This study finds that all Dance and Drama students own at least one mobile device and they are familiar with mobile technology. Students can figure out certain apps to help them learn, translate, and complete assignments. On the other hand, students are easily distracted by their mobile devices' stimulating and interactive capabilities that connect them with non-course related activities. In other words, students are easily pulled away from focusing on class content. The study also reveals that few teaching staff utilize m-learning but students view m-learning as effective and important ways in enhancing their learning experience. Students view traditional ways of lecturing, top-down style disengaging and they would like to see more professors use mobile technology in course delivery. Dance and Drama GE students consider the integration of mobile devices during lectures stimulating and beneficial. In Dance and Drama classes, mobile device become a tool by which students and educator communicate within a private educational group, research on different topics, share resources, reflect on issues in/out of the class, and create projects effectively and efficiently. The limitation of the study on the number of students and subjects in fact points to the potential areas of research in this emerging field. While Dance and Drama classes are viewed as least likely to be associated with technology, findings from this study show promising signs that m-learning is effective. Furthermore, if m-learning benefits theater arts education, it can also enhance teaching and learning in other subject areas, locations, and students.

REFERENCES

Arrigo, M., Kukulska-Hulme, A., Arnedillo-Sanchez, I., & Kismihok, G. (2013). Metaanalyses from a collaborative project in mobile lifelong learning. *British Educational Research Journal*, 39, 222-247.

Campbell, S. W. (2006). Perceptions of Mobile Phones in College Classrooms. *Communication Education,* 55, 280–94.

Cheon, J., Lee, S., Crooks, S. M., & Song, J. (2012). An investigation of mobile learning readiness in higher education based on the theory of planned behavior. *Computers & Education*, *59*(3), 1054-1064.

Cifuentes, O., & Lents, N. (2010). Increasing student-teacher interactions at an urban commuter campus through instant messaging and online office hours. *Electronic Journal of Science Education*, 14(1), 1–13.

Corbeil, J. R., & Valdes-Corbeil, M. E. (2007). Are you ready for mobile learning? *Educause Quarterly*, 30(2), 51–58.

Creswell, J. W. (2012). *Educational research: Planning, conducting, and evaluating quantitative and qualitative research* (4th ed.). Upper Saddle River, NJ: Pearson Education.

Doughty, S., Francksen, K., Huxley, M., and Leach, M. (2008). Technological enhancements in the teaching and learning of reflective and creative practice in dance. *Research in Dance Education*, 9(2), 129-146.

Grant, M., & Gikas, J. (2011, November). *Strategies for mobile teaching and learning.* In Paper presented at the annual convention of the association for educational communications and technology, Jacksonville, FL.

Hou, H., & Wu, S. (2011). Analyzing the social knowledge construction behavioral patterns of an online synchronous collaborative discussion instructional activity using an instant messaging tool: A case study. *Computers & Education*, 57(2), 1459–1468.

Laurillard, D. (2010). *Effective use of technology in teaching and learning in HE*. In P. Peterson, E. Baker, & B. McGaw (Eds.), International encyclopedia of education (3rd ed.) Vol. 4, 419–426.

Markett, C., Sanchez, I. A., Weber, S., and Tangney, B. (2006). Using short message service to encourage interactivity in the classroom. *Computers & Education*, 46, 280-293.

Park, Y. (2011). A pedagogical framework for mobile learning: categorizing educational applications of mobile technologies into four types. *International Review of Research in Open and Distance Learning*. 12(2), 78–102.

Peters, K. (2007). m-learning: positioning educators for a mobile, connected future. *International Review of Research in Open and Distance Learning*, 8(2), 1–17.

Pew Research Center (2015). *U.S. smartphone use in 2015.* http://www.pewinternet.org/2015/04/01/us-smartphone-use-in-2015/ [Accessed 28.02 2017].

Roschelle, J., & Pea, R. (2002). A walk on the WILD side: How wireless handhelds may change computer-supported collaborative learning. *International Journal of Cognition and Technology*, 1 (1), 145-168.

Selwyn, N. (2007). The use of computer technology in university teaching and learning: a critical perspective. *Journal of Computer Assisted Learning*, 23, 83-94.

Timmis, S. (2012). Constant companions: Instant messaging conversations as sustainable supportive study structures amongst undergraduate peers. *Computers & Education*, 59(1), 3–18.

Traxler, J. (2007). Current state of mobile learning. *International Review of Research in Open and Distance Learning*, 8(2), 9–24.

Traxler, J. (2008). Learning in a mobile age. *International Journal of Mobile and Blended Learning*, 1(1), 1–12.

Traxler, J. (2010). Sustaining mobile learning and its institutions. *International Journal of Mobile and Blended Learning*, 2(4), 58–65.

Wang, M., Shen, R., Novak, D., & Pan, X. (2009). The impact of mobile learning on students' learning behaviours and performance: report from a large blended classroom. *British Journal of Educational Technology*, 40, 673-695.

Yuen, S. C., & Yuen, P. K. (2008). *Mobile learning*. In L. A. Tomei (Ed.), Encyclopedia of information technology curriculum integration. Hershey, PA: Idea Group.

NOMOPHOBIA: IS SMARTPHONE ADDICTION A GENUINE RISK FOR MOBILE LEARNING?

Neil Davie and Tobias Hilber
South Westphalia University of Applied Sciences
Lindenstrasse 53, 59872 Meschede, Germany

ABSTRACT

Repeated surveys have shown that all students at our university have smartphones and use them regularly both at home and in the university. Excessive regular use of anything, including digital devices, can lead to addiction which has promoted researchers to classify and label smartphone addiction as "nomophobia". Using a self-assessment survey developed at Iowa State University this papers evaluates whether nomophobia is a problem at the institution and to what extent. A non-representative sample of 104 students showed that a small minority (<3%) could be classified as having severe nomophobia and almost 40% as moderately nomophobic. The remaining students were classed as mildly nomophobic with absolutely zero students being categorized as not nomophobic. This creates a potential risk for any teacher-led activities, such as mobile learning, which encourage further use of mobile devices. It is therefore recommended that this situation be monitored and that the issue of nomophobia be included in future programs teaching digital literacy. Further research using qualitative methods is recommended to gain more accurate data and a deeper insight into how students are using their smartphones and how aware they are of the dangers of nomophobia.

KEYWORDS

Nomophobia, smartphone, addiction, mlearning.

1. INTRODUCTION

New technologies have brought new forms of addiction with them. Traditional addictions to alcohol, drugs or gambling have now been joined by addictions to videogames, the internet and even mobile phones. Mobile phone addiction, commonly termed nomophobia, is one of the newest forms of digital addiction and as such has been less researched than other forms, such internet addiction, for example. However, researchers in South Korea (Kim, 2013; Kwon et al., 2013) have found that levels of smartphone addiction are even higher than internet addiction. One of the causes posited for this was the convenience of mobile devices. One of the same factors which makes mobile learning so interesting and useful may therefore also be leading to a dangerous addiction. As an institution which has actively encouraged students to make use of mobile devices it would therefore seem prudent to investigate this topic before further expanding the use of mobile learning.

2. NOMOPHOBIA & LEARNING

Kim's study in South Korea found that smartphone addiction has genuine consequences which affected student success (Kim, 2013). Sufferers were unable to do school work, found that interpersonal relationships suffered and felt anxiety and loneliness without their smartphones. In research on undergraduate students in the US Emanuel found that one-fifth of respondents were classed as totally dependent on their smartphones and about one-half were overly dependent (Emanuel et al., 2015). Their literature review also concluded that college age students are the group most likely to be nomophobic. Evidence from a study in Saudi Arabia supports this view and the negative consequences of smartphone addiction (Alosaimi et al., 2016). This study of university students found that they suffered from a lack of sleep and a loss of energy, had a more unhealthy lifestyle and that 25% of the participants attributed smartphone use to a drop in academic performance. Hawi & Samaha (2016) also found a correlation between excessive smartphone use and GPA test results. This was seen to be partly due to the students´ tendency to multitask with their smartphones, even when doing coursework, rather than just concentrating on one thing at a time. Alijoma et al. (2016) found that Bachelor degree students have the highest degree of addiction. Significant differences were also found on the health dimension in favour of participants with lower monthly income (Alijoma et al., 2016). Al-Barashdi et al. (2014) found that some studies of their literature review have shown significant gender differences in smartphone addiction and other studies have shown no gender differences. Some studies have examined the relationship between addiction and the course of studies (Al-Barashdi et al., 2014). The study by Haug et al. (2015) provides the first insights into smartphone addiction and predictors of smartphone addiction among young people from a European country (Switzerland).

3. RESEARCH METHODOLOGY

To assess the amount of nomophobia at the South Westphalia University of Applied Sciences a convenience sample of 104 undergraduate students of business and engineering programs completed an online survey based on research at Iowa State University (Yildirim & Correia, 2015). After answering initial demographic questions on age, gender, degree program and smartphone ownership students were asked if they had already used a smartphone for learning purposes and if they had their phone with them in class. Students then responded to the 20 questions from the Iowa study on a scale of 1 (strongly disagree) to 7 (strongly agree). The survey questions were translated into German to ease understanding. In Yildirim & Correia's assessment of nomophobia, participants receive between 1 and 7 points per answer giving a minimum total of 20 points and a maximum of 140 points. Four possible degrees of nomophobia are identified: 20 points and under – not nomophobic, 21 – 60 points – mild nomophobia, 61 – 100 points moderate nomophobia, 101 – 120 points – severe nomophobia.

3.1 Findings

The majority of the participants were in the age range 20 to 25 years – the age group which previous studies have identified as most at risk from nomophobia (Emanuel, 2015).

Table 1. Participant age.

	<20	20 - 25	26 – 30	> 30	Total
Female	3	38	9	1	51
Male	3	34	11	5	53
	6	72	20	6	104

All of the students who participated confirmed that they owned a smartphone. The questions regarding the use of mobile phones in class revealed how ubiquitous these devices have become. 99% of the students surveyed stated that they regularly had their smartphones with them and switched on during class. Although 86% had their phone switched to silent mode, the remaining 12% had their phones on as normal with the ringer activated. Incoming calls or messages could therefore create a disturbance and disrupt class. The students were also asked how often they used their phones for private (non-class related activities) during a lesson. Only 3% answered never, 59% sometimes and 36% often. 95% did however state that they had already also used their smartphones for learning purposes – either inside or outside of class.

The demographic and general questions were followed by the 20 questions from the ISU study.

Table 2. Results of nomophobia self-test (Part 1).

Somewhat/Mostly/Completely disagree	Neither agree nor disagree	Somewhat/Mostly/Completely agree
I would feel uncomfortable without constant access to information through my smartphone.		
42	20	42
I would be annoyed if I could not look information up on my smartphone when I wanted to do so.		
23	12	69
Being unable to get the news (e.g., happenings, weather, etc.) on my smartphone would make me nervous.		
66	17	21
I would be annoyed if I could not use my smartphone and/or its capabilities when I wanted to do so.		
30	19	55
Running out of battery in my smartphone would scare me.		
64	15	25
If I were to run out of credits or hit my monthly data limit, I would panic.		
89	9	6
If I did not have a data signal or could not connect to Wi-Fi, then I would constantly check to see if I had a signal or could find a Wi-Fi network.		
66	14	24
If I could not use my smartphone, I would be afraid of getting stranded somewhere.		
88	7	9
If I could not check my smartphone for a while, I would feel a desire to check it.		
51	16	37

Table 3. Results of nomophobia self-test (Part 2).

If I did not have my smartphone with me ...		
Somewhat/Mostly/Completely disagree	**Neither agree nor disagree**	**Somewhat/Mostly/Completely agree**
I would feel anxious because I could not instantly communicate with my family and/or friends.		
64	17	23
I would be worried because my family and/or friends could not reach me.		
48	20	36
I would feel nervous because I would not be able to receive text messages and calls.		
69	13	22
I would be anxious because I could not keep in touch with my family and/or friends.		
59	21	24
I would be nervous because I could not know if someone had tried to get a hold of me.		
60	22	22
I would feel anxious because my constant connection to my family and friends would be broken.		
71	14	19
I would be nervous because I would be disconnected from my online identity.		
100	0	4
I would be uncomfortable because I could not stay up-to-date with social media and online networks.		
99	3	2
I would feel awkward because I could not check my notifications for updates from my connections and online networks.		
98	4	2
I would feel anxious because I could not check my email messages.		
80	7	17
I would feel weird because I would not know what to do.		
89	7	8

Firstly the students were asked whether they would feel uncomfortable without permanent access to information on their smartphone. 40% of the respondents agreed or strongly agreed with this statement however an equal amount disagreed or strongly disagreed. The results were however clearer when asked whether they would be annoyed if they could not access information on their phone when they wanted to do so. 65% agreed or strongly agreed with this statement and only 22% disagreed or strongly disagreed. 53% of the participants agreed or strongly agreed that they would be annoyed if they could not use their smartphone or its capabilities when they wanted to do so. Only 29% disagreed or strongly disagreed with this statement.

Issues of personal connectivity have been highlighted as important in other studies. However, when asked if they would feel nervous if they didn't know if someone had tried to contact them, 57% of students disagreed or strongly disagreed.

Based on the total survey results nomophobia is a serious problem for only a small group of students (less than 3%). However, almost 40% of the respondents were in the category "Moderate nomophobia". This is therefore the group that perhaps requires most caution when encouraging students to use their mobile devices for learning purposes. The results also show that male students were more likely to be nomophobic than female students, given the size of the survey group this is however not statistically significant.

Table 4. Total results of nomophobia self-test.

	Not nomophobic	Mild nomophobia	Moderate nomophobia	Severe nomophobia	Total
Female	0	31	19	1	51
Male	0	29	22	2	53
	0	60	41	3	104

4. CONCLUSION

The nomophobia test was conducted as a self-analysis by only a small part of the student body (approximately 10% of the full-time undergraduate population). Whether the students answered honestly is therefore questionable as is how representative the participants were of the group as a whole. The project does however raise student and staff awareness of the risk of smartphone addiction and gives pause for thought when implementing mobile learning initiatives. The results suggest that creating new or expanding existing programs to raise student digital literacy, especially in relation to addiction, would be a wise step for any institution promoting mobile learning.

A further qualitative study is recommended to explore what extent students are using their mobile devices and what percentage of this time is actually used in relation to learning. Also further qualitative methods are recommended to provide better understanding of smartphone addiction and its impact on the academic achievement of the students. Also more studies are needed to find out if nomophobia can be linked to family relations or gender differences.

ACKNOWLEDGEMENT

Our gratitude to the students who voluntarily took part in the nomophobia survey. We hope the results may make them think about how attached they are to their devices and whether they are using them in the most productive way.

REFERENCES

Journal

Al-Barashdi, H. S. et al., 2014. Smartphone Addiction among University Undergraduates: A Literature Review. *Journal of Scientific Research & Reports*, Vol. 4, No. 3, pp. 210-225.

Aljomaa, S. S. et al., 2016. Smartphone addiction among university students in the light of some variables. *Computers in Human Behavior*, Vol. 61, pp. 155–164.

Alosaimi, F. D. et al., 2016. Smartphone addiction among university students in Riyadh, Saudi Arabia. *Saudi Med J.*, Vol. 37, No. 6, pp. 675-683.

Emanuel, R. et al., 2015. The truth about smartphone addiction. *College Student Journal*, Vol. 49, No. 2, pp. 291-299.

Gökçearslan, S. et al., 2016. Modelling smartphone addiction: The role of smartphone usage, self-regulation, general self-efficacy and cyberloafing in university students. *Computers in Human Behavior*, Vol. 63, pp. 639–649.

Haug, S. et al., 2015. Smartphone use and smartphone addiction among young people in Switzerland. *Journal of Behavioral Addictions*, Vol. 4, No. 4, pp. 299-307.

Hawi, N. S. & Samaha, M.., 2016. To excel or not to excel: Strong evidence on the adverse effect of smartphone addiction on academic performance. *Computers & Education*, Vol. 98, pp. 81-89.

Kim, H., 2013. Exercise rehabilitation for smartphone addiction. *Journal of Exercise Rehabilitation*, Vol. 9, No. 6, pp. 500-505.

Kwon, M. et al., 2013. The Smartphone Addiction Scale: Development and Validation of a Short Version for Adolescents. *PLoS ONE*, Vol. 8, No. 12, e83558.

Liu, C. H. et al., 2016. Smartphone gaming and frequent use pattern associated with smartphone addiction. *Medicine (Baltimore)*. Vol. 95, No. 28, e4068.

Roberts, J. A. et al., 2014. The invisible addiction: Cell-phone activities and addiction among male and female college students. *Journal of Behavioral Addictions*, Vol. 3, No. 4, pp. 254-265.

Samaha, M. & Hawi, N. S., 2015. Relationships among smartphone addiction, stress, academic performance, and satisfaction with life. *Computers in Human Behavior*, Vol. 57, pp. 321–325.

Yildirim, C. and Correia, A-P. 2015. Exploring the dimensions of nomophobia: Development and validation of a self-reported questionnaire. *Computers in Human Behavior*, volume 49, August 2015, pp 130-137.

Webpage

Gregoire, C. 2015. *This Scientific Test Will Tell You How Addicted You Are To Your Smartphone.* The Huffington Post, Available at http://www.huffingtonpost.com/2015/05/18/nomophobia-smartphone-sep_n_7266468.html [Accessed 11/12/2016]

ANALYSIS OF MEANS FOR BUILDING CONTEXT-AWARE RECOMMENDATION SYSTEM FOR MOBILE LEARNING

Larysa Shcherbachenko[1,2] and Samuel Nowakowski[1]
[1]*Université de Lorraine, LORIA, UMR 7503, Vandoeuvre-lès-Nancy, F-54506, France*
[2]*Faculty of Applied Mathematics, National Technical University of Ukraine "Igor Sikorsky Kyiv Polytechnic Institute" Peremohy Ave, 37, Kiev, 03056, Ukraine*

ABSTRACT

One of the rapidly developing tools for online learning is learning through a mobile environment. Therefore, developing and improving mobile learning environments is an active topic now. One of the ways to adapt the learning environment to the user's needs is to use his context. Context of the user consists of the current context in online learning environment and physical context. This paper concentrates on the physical context and ways to improve the user's experience in a learning environment. For this an ontology-based system is presented, and Learning Context ontology is extended for User Context ontology. Also, a use-case is provided to show situations which will be covered by such an approach.

KEYWORDS

Context, Context-Awareness, Adaptive Learning, Learner-Centered, Mobile Learning.

1. INTRODUCTION

In recent years, we have witnessed a rising interest in and acceptance of Vygotsky's social development theory (Wertsch & Sohmer, 1995), connectivism (Siemens, 2005) and other modern pedagogical theories, which argue for learners' active involvement in the learning process and construction of knowledge through social interactions.

Success in online teaching and learning can largely depend on the available means or tools students have to be connected to pedagogical resources. These, in turn, rely on the information related to the learners' current context in online learning environments as well as in social networks and instant messaging systems, and furthermore on physical context such as locations, current activity, or place. Such information reveals how present the student is and what could be an appropriate resource to recommend to him to reinforce his learning strategy. If employed in an appropriate way, this information could greatly increase the learning efficiency.

One of the main development of the online presence approach concerns mobile learning environments. Indeed, mobile learning environments have to take into account many parameters of the learners' context including location, current state of mind, activity and the user's environment. Furthermore, mobile learning environments, because of the worldwide deployment of smartphones, are one of the most active developing fields now: for example, e-learning applications make up 10% of all mobile applications (Focus RH, 2017). Thus, designing an app which is able to recommend an appropriate pedagogical resource according to the physical context of the learner is an important challenge. Learners are connected through their mobile phones, and this mobile phone is like a "part of them". So, for efficient user-application interaction the mobile phone should provide an automatic adaptation of its content and system behavior to learner state and needs.

2. RELATED WORK

Context-aware applications have been the subject of debates among researchers in different domains (Armstrong et al., 2000). Based on the requirements and characteristics of each of these domains, the term "context" has been interpreted in different ways (Bazire & Brézillon, 2005), and different approaches have been applied to capture the contextual information. One of these domains is Ubiquitous Learning environment. This approach contains two underlying contexts, namely the learning context and the mobile context.

2.1 Definition of context

We follow the definition of context provided by (Anind, 2001): "context is any information that can be used to characterize the situation of an entity. An entity can be a person, place, or object that is considered relevant to the interaction between a user and an application, including the user and applications themselves".

In our project, context dimensions are time, user's physical activity (walking, biking, running etc.), user's location and calendar information. The User Context ontology is based on these context dimensions. Learning situation is presented as a set of parameters: 1) learning activity; 2) learning content; 3) learner –whether the user involved in learning process; 4) context of the learner.

2.2 Formal description of domain

For providing common underlying language of the items in domain, ontology approach is chosen.

There are several metadata standards for description of learning objects. The Dublin Core metadata initiative (dublincore, 2017) contains base description of learning resources, but it does not contain attributes describing the pedagogical perspective of a document. Also, there is IEEE LOM (Learning Object Metadata) that was developed under (imsglobal, 2006). IEEE LOM has technical standards, recommended practices, and guidelines. Technical standards allow taking into account more details about learning objects. So, in this work IEEE LOM is used.

According to the best practices of reusing domain ontologies, most of used ontologies are inherited. Therefore, consequent ontologies will be used for describing learning systems. LOM-FR (LOM-FR, 2017) that is a IEEE LOM extension for France. Learning Context Ontology (IntelLEO D3.2, 2010) describes learning situations: learner activity and the result of it, the time when the activity takes place, online environment where it takes place etc. The User Model ontology (IntelLEO D3.2, 2010) provides a formal representation of a learner: his profile information, short / long term goals, and preferences. The Competences ontology (IntelLEO D3.2, 2010) provides information about the level of skills that the subject has. The subject can be represented as a user or a LOM object. The User Context ontology represents the context of a learner based on concepts such as Time, Place, Calendar, PhysicalActivity (Madkour et al., 2013). (Torniai et al., 2008) provides information about equipment (smartphone). The activities ontology (IntelLEO D3.2, 2010) allows modeling the learner's activities as reading, quizzing, etc. The Annotations ontology (IntelLEO D3.2, 2010) allows modeling user's ratings of materials for keeping it as user's history.

3. DESCRIPTION OF THE SYSTEM ARCHITECTURE

In spite of the fact that the provided architecture of recommendation system takes into account the user's long-term goal, it makes recommendation relevant to current user's state and doesn't provide a plan for future learning. The first time the user opens the system, it creates a model for him based on his profile information. Further usage of the system makes the user's model more accurate. User's context can be subject to change his model even during the offline time. To take into account these changes, user's calendar will be used.

Considering the user as a person that supports life-learning approach. In this case, she has some learning strategy. Therefore, the following user's characteristics can be specified. First, the user has an e-learning resource system that specifies material that the user learns on his own or in school or university (e.g. a university system that provides structured learning content divided in lessons). Second, the user makes planning in his calendar and connects the calendar events to learning materials in the e-learning resource system if it is possible. If it is not, the user comments the events by adding keywords or topics relevant for the event. Also, in the end the user makes notes whether the event was accomplished or not.

3.1 Description of the learning environment

Actions, performed by the system when the user opens the application, are provided below.

First, it gathers information about the user's context: his local time; where he is (location); his activity; makes rough estimate of the number of people around him (many people, few people, nobody); checks if headphones are plugged in or not and if the user is particularly close to a specific location.

Second, it checks the user's calendar: processing all events which have happened since the last session. Processing events means enriching the user model with the skills that user has obtained or honed while offline. If the learning event is specified in the calendar and there is some learning material attached, the system should analyze the LOM description of this learning object and add it to the model of user. It impacts the upcoming user events and extracts user current needs and predicts the time that the user could spend in the system.

Then, the system makes recommendation in the following way: it determines and ranges domains, topics, or keywords that will be interesting based on base information like user's profile, user's history, long-term goals and the gathered information etc. Then, it estimates the level of expertise of the user in these areas. It will be useful if the user forgets some material and wants to review it. Also, it is easier to learn new material by making association rules with the one that is already learned or being learned; after that, it makes recommendation of some learning material as presented in Figure 2.

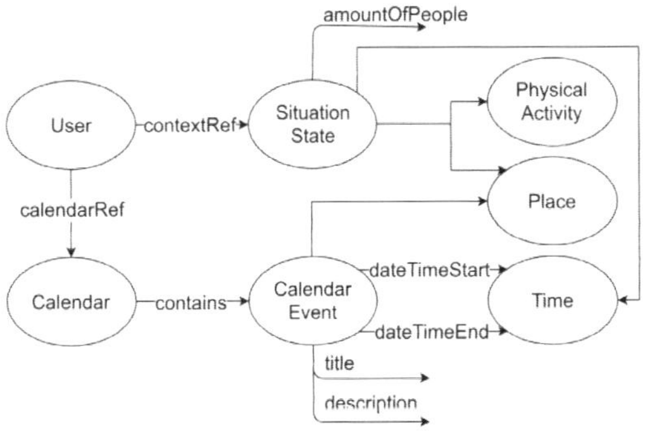

Figure 1. User context ontology.

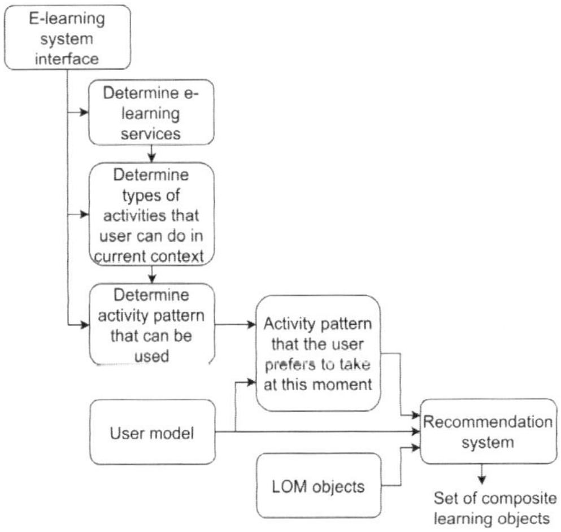

Figure 2. Structure of the proposed recommendation system.

3.2 Design of the recommendation system

The recommendation system uses mix content-based and context-based techniques. The user context defines the type of activity that the user can do and the LOM objects that are appropriate to him in this current situation. Firstly, the system checks available e-learning services (for example, spell checker, quizzes engine, text / audio / video viewer, etc.). Then, it determines the types of activities and activity patterns that are suitable to the user based on the available e-learning services and the user's context. The type of activity is a composition of learning resource type (evaluation, questionnaire, guide, etc.) and the LOM format.

Determine learning pattern as a way of learning data representation. Examples of learning patterns are different types of quizzes (yes-, no- questions, one choice or multiple choice tests, etc.), video, audio, text material with or without quizzes build in the lesson or at its end, etc. Composite learning object can be built as a combination of atomic learning objects. This allows learning object to be a combination of a learning pattern and learning data. Figure 2 shows the structure of our recommendation system.

3.3 Use Case

Consider the following use case of our system. The user is a student. He uses a calendar for planning his time. In the calendar, the events are labeled with such information as full description, the topics, and the location. Now, the user is going by tram to his classes. Usually he has a few different lessons a day, so, he has a large variety of things to review: prepare to his classes and for the upcoming events or explore the domains within the scope of his interest. To cope with this amount of learning materials, the user uses the provided system. This system does not make the choice for him, but it provides him with recommendations on what to study in the current period of time, taking into account his plans for the day and the available amount of time that he could spend in the system. After system approves with user amount of time that he plans to study it provides him with learning material.

4. CONCLUSION

In this work we design the architecture of a context-aware e-learning system to enrich user's model with his context that accurate recommendations. To demonstrate the designed system we suggest a use case. Our next step will be to implement the system's prototype and to evaluate its effectiveness in real environment. One of the directions for future work is to connect calendar events with learning objects provided an external e-learning resource system and then take them into account when measuring the user's growing competence outside of provided system.

REFERENCES

Anind, D., 2001. Understanding and Using Context. *Personal and Ubiquitous Computing*, 5, pp.4-7.

Armstrong, S., Morse, D.R. & Dey, A.K., 2000. CHI EA '00 CHI '00 Extended Abstracts on Human Factors in Computing Systems. In *The what, who, where, when, why and how of context-awareness*., 2000.

Bazire, M. & Brézillon, P., 2005. Modeling and Using Context. CONTEXT 2005. Lecture Notes in Computer Science. In *Understanding Context Before Using It*. Berlin, Heidelberg, 2005. Springer.

Bazire, M. & Brézillon, P., 2005. Understanding Context Before Using It. In *Modeling and Using Context*. pp.29 – 40.

dublincore, 2017. *Dublin Core Metadata Initiative*. [Online] Available at: http://dublincore.org/ [Accessed January 2017].

Focus RH, 2017. *Les Apps, nouvelle révolution du e-learning ?* [Online] Available at: http://www.affen.fr/affencafe/formation/les-apps-nouvelle-revolution-du-e-learning/ [Accessed 31 January 2017].

imsglobal, 2006. *IMS Meta-data Best Practice Guide for IEEE 1484.12.1-2002 Standard for Learning Object Metadata*. [Online] Available at: http://www.imsglobal.org/metadata/mdv1p3/imsmd [Accessed January 2017].

IntelLEO D3.2, 2010. *IntelLEO - Intelligent Learning Extended Organisation, Deliverable D3.2 IntelLEO Implementation Framework*. [Online] (First Version, FP7 Project no. FP7-ICT-231590.) Available at: http://intelleo.eu/uploads/tx_abdownloads/files/D3.2_ver09_100.pdf.

LOM-FR, 2017. *LOM-FR*. [Online] Available at: http://www.lom-fr.fr/ [Accessed January 2017].

Madkour, M., Driss, E.G. & Maach, A., 2013. Context-Aware Service Adaptation: An Approach Based on Fuzzy Sets and Service Composition. *Journal of Information Science and Engineering*, (29), pp.1-16.

Siemens, G., 2005. *Connectivism: Learning as Network-Creation*. [Online] Available at: http://www.elearnspace.org/Articles/networks.htm [Accessed 17 February 2017].

Torniai, C. et al., 2008. m-LOCO: An ontology-based framework for context-aware mobile learning.

Wertsch, J. & Sohmer, R., 1995. Vygotsky on Learning and Development. *Human Development*, 38, pp.332–337.

RUNJUMPCODE: AN EDUCATIONAL GAME FOR EDUCATING PROGRAMMING

Matthew Hinds, Nilufar Baghaei, Pedrito Ragon, Jonathon Lambert, Tharindu Rajakaruna, Travers Houghton and Simon Dacey
Unitec Institute of Technology, Private Bag 92025, Victoria Street West, Auckland 1142, New Zealand

ABSTRACT

Programming promotes critical thinking, problem solving and analytic skills through creating solutions that can solve everyday problems. However, learning programming can be a daunting experience for a lot of students. *RunJumpCode* is an educational 2D platformer video game, designed and developed in Unity, to teach players the fundamental concepts of C# programming. The game enhances the player's programming knowledge by providing a fun range of challenges and puzzles to solve. We promoted the interaction of programming through a 'Code Box', allowing players to enter lines of predefined code that modifies in-game objects. This tool is essential in completing the challenges and puzzles we designed. To allow alterations of its properties, we made further manipulation of each object possible, which would give the player creative freedom to complete each level. Quizzes and journals were utilized to assess and collate their learnt material for future reference. In addition, we created a mobile application to track each player's statistics throughout the game and compare their progress with other users. A full evaluation study has been planned, the goal of which is to examine the effect of using the system on students' learning.

KEYWORDS

Game design, education, programming.

1. INTRODUCTION

Programming promotes critical thinking, problem solving and analytic skills through creating solutions that can solve everyday problems. Technology in the 21st century has evolved in many ways, helping us to be connected. Through each of these innovations comes a need to develop and design new solutions. Getting into programming can be a daunting experience and has shown to be too overly complex, frustrating and unenjoyable for many novice students (Lahtinen, Ala-Mutka, and Jarvinen, 2005; Milne and Rowe, 2002).

Current easy to access resources consist of articles and written tutorials. There has also been attempts in improving teaching through classes, video and auditorial – being able to learn through a fun interaction can be a more enjoyable and knowledge retention experience. Video games are not a new concept and while they are popular and generally created for entertainment purposes, they can be adapted and used for engaging users with educational materials.

Determining the age group in designing educational programming video games comes from identifying the curriculum of which is planned to be taught. The more complex the content, the higher the recommended age bracket is. However, current video games that teach programming generally cater towards the ages 16 and below. This can be attributed to the fact that more complex and involved topics require a dedicated classroom teaching environment that offers live guidance through a teacher. Current educational video games, e.g. Code Spell (https://codespells.org/), Kodu (www.kodugamelab.com/) and Scratch (https://scratch.mit.edu/) typically teach the basic fundamentals and later on expand each topic resulting in a progressively increasing learning curve of content difficulty, which in turn can reduce the overall retention of players and learning speed.

While progressing the content naturally increases its difficulty, it is important to present the new material in a way that is easily accessible and personalise it towards the knowledge of the player. In this project, we slowed down the progression of new information and packaged it together with new gameplay mechanics so that players learn through naturally completing each level. In addition, after every three levels we included a quiz that recaps the previous levels' content. By doing so, players are reminded to pay more attention throughout each level so they can successfully pass the quiz and proceed to the next level.

Video games first emerged since the successful proof of concept by Physicist William Higinbotham in October 1958 using circuitry revolving around the use of resistors, relays, capacitors and transistors ("The First Video Game of William Higinbotham," n.d.). Since then during the next decade, video games have seen a radical change as general computing became more developed and commercially viable.

With the release of the first video game console, the Magnavox Odyssey the video game industry saw its first leap towards public interest and the industry began its capitalization of the at home entertainment system (Schilling, 2003; Williams, n.d.). Popularity with video games made its first big break with the release of the Atari 2600 in 1977 (Bellemare, Veness, and Bowling, 2012) and the Nintendo 64 in 1996 (Schilling, 2003); since then video games have caught the attention of millions of children and families which has strengthen its status as a must have electronic of the modern household.

Video game interaction revolves around user input on a touchscreen, gamepad or keyboard and mouse to control and perform the appropriated directed action desired on screen. These repetitious actions are fundamental in playing and through studies have shown to help improve motor functionality and hand eye coordination. The video game experience in particular allows gamers to develop perceptual and cognitive skills in many aspects that exceeds those of their non-gamer counterparts (Green and Bavelier, 2004).

The educational games genre has yet to see their popularity boom, as most players tend to use video games as a form of entertainment rather than education. However, in more recent times the use of video games to develop educational tools has expanded due to the rise of affordable and accessible technology, especially in smart tablet devices. It allows them to be an effective classroom tool to help students learn and reinforce a variety of skills and knowledge (P. Rossing, Miller, Cecil, and Stamper, 2012).

Rewards should be given out to players for completing specific tasks that range from easy to hard. The drive to seek out higher rewards come from video games tendency to promote competitiveness amongst players and their peers. Such behavior can be exploited to promote higher engagement and retention rates as players are more likely to work to completing more difficult tasks if they are tempted with a greater reward for completion. Such rewards are built around how the game is developed, but should be meaningful so that they do not feel worthless. For example, giving new unlocks for levels, badges, medals, titles or character customization options are suitable rewards and can garnish players' attention.

An educational game designer should first thoroughly understand the contents and methodologies of its subject. Without a strong and accurate background, it would be difficult to have confidence in the teaching material and curriculum. One can then decide on the best way to represent that content in a meaningful way. Each dimensional environment (2D or 3D) has its own strengths and weaknesses, one being more immersive through freedom of a three-dimensional world, but heavier on hardware taxing reducing the potential adoption of low end system players. While the other is less engaging through a lack of connection that is brought in from a two-dimensional world, it also allows a wider adoption due to less hardware constraints.

Following a teaching structure that is similar to a classroom curriculum will help build a path of content that is easy to grasp in the beginning and later becoming more difficult. Progressively expanding the content allows players to start off with the basics and slowly move up to more in-depth and complex concepts, giving them a natural curve of increasing knowledge.

2. RUNJUMPCODE GAME DESIGN

RunJumpCode is a 2D platform with basic left, right jumps & gravity idea. It was adopted from Super Mario Bros. (Pedersen, Togelius, and Yannakakis, n.d.) due to its high success rate (Ryan, 2011, Baghaei 2016), simplicity and level of entertainment. User have to learn theory, solve problems and apply learned knowledge in order to progress through the game.

Once launched, the player is taken to the main menu where items are clear and easy to understand. The idea behind the simplicity is so that the players on a broad age group will be able to figure out the workings of the GUI with minimal effort. And since this is the user's first point of contact with game and as a first impression, it was imperative for the design to be cluster free and easily understandable.

RunJumpCode was developed with a diverse age group in mind, mainly senior high school students and/or undergraduate tertiary students. The first step is to login which is done either with a new account or an existing account. Once logged in, the player will be taken to the level selection window where the completed levels and the next level are highlighted. Once clicked on a highlighted it will show the level name, description and the difficulty to give the user an idea as to what they are about to do and learn in order to complete the level. Once the user selects a level and click play, the level will be initiated. The first thing the user sees on the level is the level information screen. Key information shown here is the programming tutorial section, which highlights what is taught and the exclusions section, which highlights the restrictions applied to the level. This helps the users to familiarize themselves with the level so they know what to expect for the coming session.

The game character moves by detecting arrow key presses. The user has to navigate the game space to reach the endpoint by clearing obstacles along the way. Each obstacle poses a learning curve to the user. This is an approach to promote logical thinking. Logical thinking is by far the most important aspect of software engineering and this is where some people struggle. With our application, the users are actively encouraged to come up with solutions to each problem. To make things more interesting, each level also comes with a set of restrictions just like lifelike scenarios where not all the options are available. On each level these restrictions are different, to ensure the user cannot interact with a problem same way if it occurs multiple times, thus forcing them to think differently.

Obstacles also require object manipulation, meaning the user may have to spawn, scale, enable & disable objects to progress. This approach was encouraged by need to teach syntax. As an example to spawn a box a player has to enter *"player.spawnItem(Box);"*. If the user makes an error a syntax error will be shown with the cause, helping the user to understand how important it is to follow syntax in coding.

Apart from that, the user also has a theory section as well, giving the user key theory knowledge required to progress with the game such as explaining what Integers are in Level 1. This is further elaborated with examples which in our past experience helped with memorizing theory. Before the user can complete any level, there is a minimum number of coins to be collected, which is another measure taken to make sure the player gets a minimum level of knowledge before progressing forward.

The game starts at a very simple level, which is made even easier with hints and lots of mouse clicks and less coding. As the game progresses, it involves more and more coding and less GUI operations. This is also a systematic approach since people who are not very technical, seem to need more help till they get more familiar with the concept of coding. Although hints are available, it is not free to use them. The user loses some marks for using hints. This helps to discourage the player from using them and guides them more towards thinking and independent learning. Both of which are again quite important for software developers.

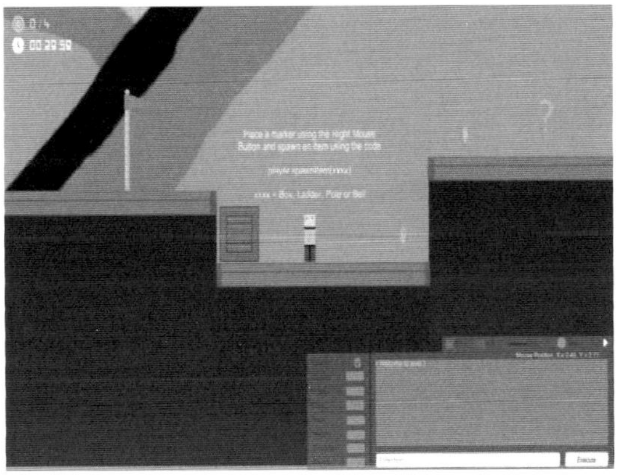

Figure 1. *RunJumpCode* Level 1.

In level 1 (shown in Figure 1) the obstacles are very simple to overcome. All the player needs to do is to place a box, jump on it and continue on. As the player progresses, the obstacles get progressively trickier. In figure 2 one box is not allowed so the user has to summon a ladder. Merely summoning one ladder is not enough as the player also has to scale the ladder. This makes the user interact more with the game on a creative level. With development tools such as Unity[1] and Unreal Engine[2] being available for free, 3D development has become slightly easier. Having said that, budget plays a role on how a game is being developed. 2D game development cost less as teams can be smaller in size and development is less complex. Math and art are more complicated in 3D. As for gameplay, 2D game has simpler physics mechanics and basic intuitive controls. Players would be able to identify interactive objects in the environment easily. Interactive tutorials and Code Box also work well on 2D because of the said simpler layout and should cater well to users of all ages compared to 3D. 2D development requires low system requirements thus the game can be played on a very low end system without sacrificing the gameplay. Another issue with 3D development is having to use more memory and resources thus producing inconsistent framerate could greatly impact player's experience on a slow machine.

Building a good programming foundation is one of the goal of this game. It aims to enhance player's knowledge by solving a wide range of challenges and puzzles as they go through each stage. The primary focus was the introduction of programming in a way that is mentally stimulating while being engaging and fun. This would provide the user an engaging experience and help increase knowledge of programming fundamentals.

3. TARGET AUDIENCE

The game is designed to cater for teenagers and young adults. It is easy to understand and would be attractive to Senior High School students and young professionals. It can feed their interest with both gaming and programming. Those who are new to gaming should find an easy take on into the game. *RunJumpCode* is also challenging enough for regular game players and we believe parents might be interested in trying it out too.

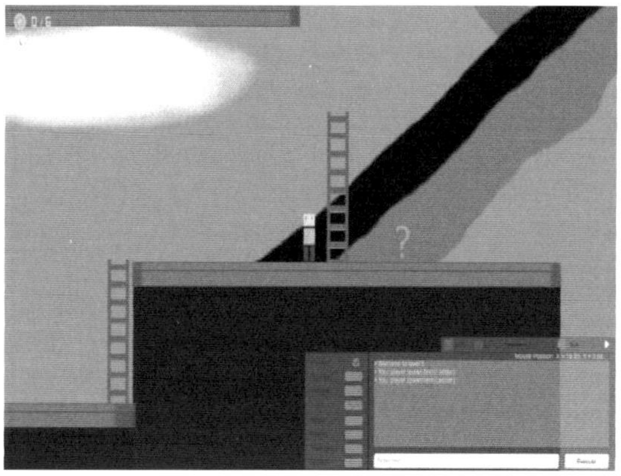

Figure 2. RunJumpCode Level 3.

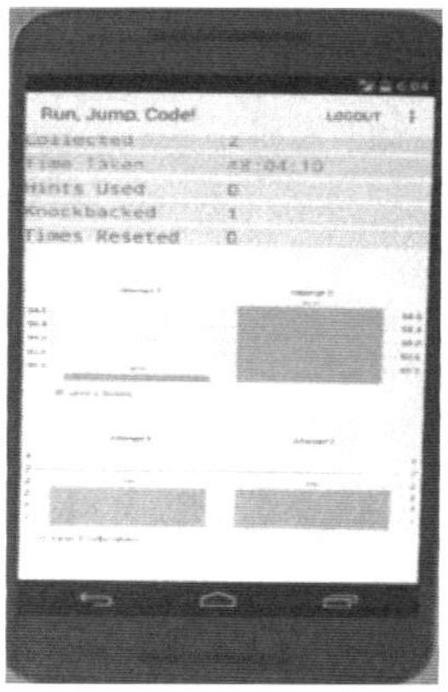

Figure 3. Mobile App collecting myRunJumpCode statistics

The elements of this game are tailored carefully, with the aim of eliminating the possibility of the user getting deterred, confused, or bored easily. As the game progresses, it challenges players more based on an increasing learning curriculum. Each stage is focused on teaching one programming skill. The more stages the player goes through, the more skills they learn and utilize to progress. This way, anticipation is being fed to avoid boredom among players but at the same time keeping the process simple enough to cater for teenagers and young adults who have basic computer knowledge. The game provides a Code Box in which the user learn how to write a code. By using the code the player writes in the box, they are able to manipulate the object in the game. The number of stages reached should equate to the user's interaction with the computer and his acquired programming skills.

---

[1]https://unity3d.com/

[2]https://www.unrealengine.com/

Finally, Figure 3 shows the player's interaction data collected by the mobile application we have implemented. Users, researchers and/or parents can view the statistics for each level (picked from a drop down menu), e.g. total scores, time taken to complete the level, number of hints received, number of times reseted etc. We will be analysing this data for the upcoming study to see how engaged players are with the game in addition to assessing the improvement in their programming knowledge.

4. CONCLUSIONS & FUTURE DIRECTIONS

We presented *RunJumpCode*, an educational game to teach the fundamental concepts of programming. We used C# for this project, as we have two C# programming courses in our undergraduate curriculum. The game enhances the player's programming knowledge by providing a fun range of challenges and puzzles to solve. We promoted the interaction of programming through a 'Code Box', allowing players to enter lines of predefined code that modifies in-game objects. This tool is essential in completing the challenges and puzzles we designed. To allow alterations of its properties, we made further manipulation of each object possible, which would give the player creative freedom to complete each level. Quizzes and journals were utilized to assess and collate their learnt material for future reference. In addition, we created a mobile application to track each player's statistics throughout the game and compare their progress with other users.

Going forward, we plan to conduct an evalution study with 20-30 undergraduate tertiary students to measure the effectives of *RunJumpCode* in teaching C#. We will have a control group who will complete a pre-test, do an introductory C# course followed by a post-test. We will also have an experimental goup of students who take the same course, sit the same pre-test and will be given the game to play in their free time. They will complete the post-test at the end of the course. We will be measuring the learning outcome, engagement with game and enjoyment via pre-test, post-test and subjective questionnnaire as well as analysing the data logged during the players' interaction with the game features. We hypothesise that those students who play the game enjoy their experience and enhace their programming knowledge significantly more than their control group. We believe our research paves the way for the systematic design and development of full-fledged eductional games dedicated to teaching fundamental conceptos of programming.

REFERENCES

Baghaei, N., Nandigam, D., Casey, J., Direito, A., & Maddison, R. (2016). *Diabetic Mario: Designing and Evaluating Mobile Games for Diabetes Education*. Games for Health Journal: Research, Dev, and Clinical Applications (Vol. 5(4)), pp.270-278.

Bellemare, M.G., Veness, J. and Bowling, M. (2012) *Investigating Contingency Awareness Using Atari 2600 Games*. University of Alberta, Edmonton, Canada, 1-2.

Green, C.S. and Bavelier, D. (2004) *The Cognitive Neuroscience of Video Games*. Messaris & Humphreys, 5-7.

Lahtinen, E., Ala-Mutka, K. and Jarvinen, J.M. (2005). *A Study of the Difficulties of Novice Programmers*. Tampere University of Technology Institute of Software Systems. 15-17.

Milne, I. and Rowe, G. (2002) *Difficulties in Learning and Teaching Programming—Views of Students and Tutors*. Kluwer Academic Publishers, 59-62.

Pedersen, C., Togelius, J. and Yannakakis, G.N. *Modeling Player Experience in Super Mario Bros*. IT University of Copenhagen (n.d.), 1-4.

Rossing, J.P., Miller, W.M., Cecil, A.K. and Stamper, S.E. (2012). *iLearning: The future of higher education? Student perceptions on learning with mobile tablets*. Journal of the Scholarship of Teaching and Learning, 12(2), 13-16.

Ryan, J. (2011) *Super Mario: How Nintendo Conquered America*. Penguin, 155-162. Schilling, M. (2003) *Technological Leapfrogging: Lessons from the U.S. Video Game Console Industry*. California management review, 7-10.

Williams, D. A *Brief Social History of Game Play*. Univeristy of Illinois at Urbana-Chappaign (N.D), pp. 3-5. Wall-Montgomery, M. (2015) *Facebook launches TechPrep: 'By 2020 there will be 1M programming jobs left unfulfilled'*. Retrieved from http://venturebeat.com/2015/10/20/facebook-launches-techprep-by-2020-there-will-be-1m-programming-jobs-left-unfulfilled/

READINESS FOR MOBILE LEARNING: MULTIDISCIPLINARY CASES FROM YAROSLAVL STATE UNIVERSITY

Vladimir Khryashchev, Natalia Kasatkina and Dmitry Sokolenko
P.G. Demidov Yaroslavl State University
Sovetskaya 14/2, Yaroslavl, Russia

ABSTRACT

The survey data suggest a high technical and sufficient psychological readiness of Yaroslavl State University students to use mobile devices in learning. The results of the research prove that students have an above the average level of interest and motivation in learning with the help of mobile devices. Nevertheless, it is obvious that there is a need for popularizing mobile learning among students through organization of explanatory talks and encouragement on the part of the teaching staff. Two multidisciplinary cases with using modern IT-technologies in university educational process are presented.

KEYWORDS

Mobile application, multidisciplinary cases, blended learning, cross-platform development.

1. INTRODUCTION

The organization of mobile learning in a classical university is a very complicated process requiring serious planning and coordinated actions of the educational establishment administration and teaching staff. The educational process organizers face the following challenges while implementing mobile technologies (Golizyuna, 2011):

– choosing the mobile technology's role and place in learning. Mobile devices can be used in different ways in educational process: both in the classroom and outside it, as an obligatory element of a course or as an additional one.

– assessing students' readiness for mobile learning. It is advisable to assess the level of students' technical facilities and competence as well as their psychological readiness before implementing mobile technologies in the educational process. It is reasonable to make a survey (questionnaire), the results of which will help make a deliberate decision about the necessity of using mobile devices in teaching and learning.

– choosing the strategy for providing students with portable devices:

1) BYOD (bring your own device) strategy – each student uses their own portable device This strategy answers the purpose of mobile learning – to gain knowledge at any time and place – most of all. It is useful when students are technically well-equipped, thus avoiding considerable material costs.

2) providing the group with the devices belonging to the educational establishment – the supporters of this strategy mention such advantages as unified technical features of all the devices, the possibility to control learning activity and other such things that are impossible to do when students use their own devices.

The research concerning the level of Russian students' mobile devices facilities, which is a key factor in implementing BYOD strategy, shows that 100% of students have mobile phones and use them every day, while about 90% have smartphones with the Internet access and application installation facilities (Eremin, 2014; Son, 2013; Titova, 2013). Thus, the data, collected by different researchers, corroborate the students' mobile competence. Nevertheless, I.S. Son has pointed out that both students and teachers are ill-informed about the effective use of mobile devices in educational process (Son, 2013). Students in U.V. Eremin and E.F. Krylova's study expressed the same opinion: 75% of students voice fears that they might not be able to cope with such activities without the teacher's advice and supervision because they "don't know where to start" (Eremin, 2014). These findings demonstrate the importance of the organizational factor in mobile learning as well as the necessity to give proper attention to the mobile learning organization issues in higher educational establishments.

Apart from the importance of having a mobile device with a necessary set of functions, it is essential for students to be psychologically ready to make their learning efficient. Psychological readiness for any activity indicates a psychological state when a person mobilizes resources to carry out some specific short-term or long-term activities or tasks (Titova, 2013).

Nevertheless, mobile learning, as any other type of learning, is based on the students-and-teacher interaction, taking place both in virtual setting and physical environment. Only one in six studies analyzed the problem of teachers' readiness for mobile learning. The survey (questionnaire) made by I.S. Son showed that only 15 out of 38 teachers approved of using mobile technologies in English language learning, while some teachers demonstrated skepticism and even disapproval of such learning (Son, 2013) .

Besides analyzing students' technical and psychological readiness it is important to find out the advantages and disadvantages of using mobile technologies in learning activities. In the study devoted to students' foreign languages mobile learning, U.V. Eremin and E.F. Krylova pointed out the following positive features: a smartphone is always close at hand; one can get information at any place and time; one can devote time spent in public transport, queues and traffic jams to learning a foreign language; there is access to video and audio content in a foreign language (Eremin, 2014). Accumulator discharge and instability of the Internet access were mentioned among mobile technologies shortcomings (Titova, 2014). Such a project, devoted to foreign languages learning, was implemented in Yaroslavl State University (YSU) (Laure, 2016).

2. ANALYSIS OF MOBILE TECHNOLOGIES APPLICATION IN YSU

Below we analyze the results of the students' survey at YSU revealing their readiness for using mobile technologies in learning.

2.1 Student Initial Testing

The students' survey (questionnaire) at Yaroslavl State University was based on a scheme of assessing students' readiness for mobile learning, which is described in different literary works. The first- and second-year students of the Law Faculty, the Faculty of Philology and Communication and the Faculty of Information and Computer Science took part in this survey. There were 121 respondents. According to the questionnaire data, all students have at least one type of portable device; 94,2% have smartphones, 26,5% - mobile phones, 43,8% - tablets, 30,6% - netbooks. In accordance with the presented data we can state that almost all participants are fully equipped with portable technical devices.

The next step after assessing the level of students' technical facilities is analyzing their skills to use different technical devices' functions, work with applications and employ mobile devices while learning. All these skills form the concept "competence in using mobile devices" or "mobile competence". Students were asked to estimate the frequency with which they use different functions and applications in learning. The results of the survey are presented in Figure 1.

The results of the survey show that students almost fully exploit the potential of their portable devices both in everyday life and in learning. While learning, students use Internet access, search engines, e-reference books/ e-dictionaries and applications for reading e-books. The frequency with which students use specific functions and applications corroborates their mobile competence.

The results of the research prove that students have an above the average level of interest and motivation in learning with the help of mobile devices. Nevertheless, it is obvious that there is a need for popularizing mobile learning among students through organization of explanatory talks and encouragement on the part of the teaching staff.

The survey also showed that about 17% of students have mobile learning experience. In general, portable devices were employed while preparing for the Unified State Examinations in Russia, learning foreign languages and other school subjects. The students' responses about such experiences are mostly positive, but many students mention inconveniences in using mobile devices in learning concerning the screen size, low quality of the teaching material and its design and the lack of timely consultations on the topic under study.

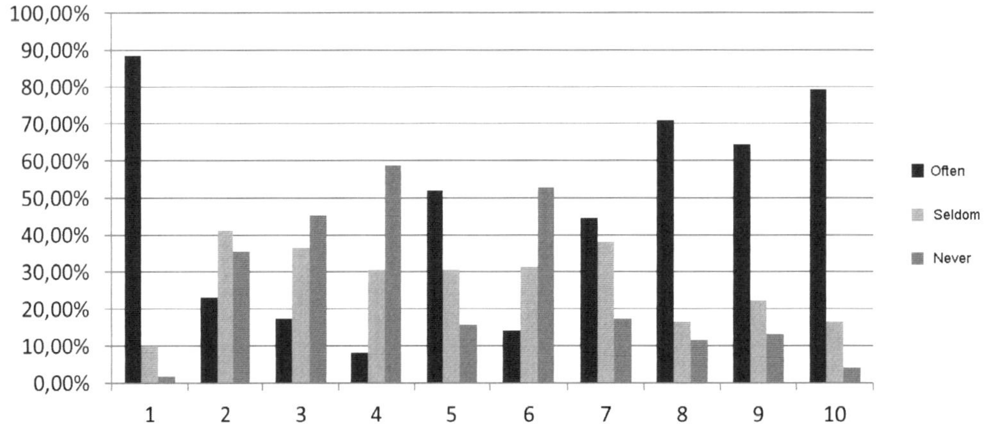

Explanation: 1 – Internet access; 2 – watching video files; 3 – listening to audio files; 4 – SMS/MMS messengers; 5 – applications for social networks (VK, Facebook, etc.); 6 – messenger-applications (WhatsApp, Viber, Telegram, etc.); 7 – e-mail; 8 – e-reference books/ e-dictionaries; 9 – applications for reading e-books; 10 – search engines (Google, Yandex).

Figure 1. The frequency of using different applications on portable devices in educational process.

Let's look at two pilot projects for employing mobile technologies in the current educational process at YSU.

2.2 City Guide Application

The purpose of this multidisciplinary project is the development of the "City Guide" application, including a set of excursions around Yaroslavl for a specific user. The teachers and students of the Faculty of Information and Computer Science, the History Faculty, the Faculty of Philology and Communication took part in this process. The main stages of the project designing presented in the 'Project Activity' section for each group of students are shown in Table 1.

While developing the project, the client's role was played both by the teachers and students. It was an iterative application development: after critical analysis, the developers had to make a lot of improvement to the seemingly finished program with consideration for the defects detected during the previous cycle.

During the work on the project, the following training targets and learning tasks were achieved:

– reconstructing the specialist's future activities context: the students of the Faculty of Information and Computer Science went through the full mobile application development cycle, the students of the History Faculty planned a real excursion, the students of the Faculty of Philology and Communication translated the presented material.

– reconstructing the future professional activity sociocultural context: the students worked in a real professional team adopting particular roles, interacting with each other.

– learning the specific features of other students' future professions and professional activities.

– developing personal qualities and professional skills while developing a high-technology product.

– working on a real, topical present-day problem: unlike classical laboratory and practical work where the test subject is mostly trivial and outdated and the task is artificially created, the students worked with real material in natural working conditions fulfilling an actual task to develop a product which is in a high demand on the market.

The result of the project is a completely developed application, City Guide, which can be useful both for the citizens of Yaroslavl and its guests.

Table 1. The main stages of the project designing for different groups of students.

	The students of the Faculty of Information and Computer Science	The students of the History Faculty	The students of the Faculty of Philology and Communication
Needs assessment	Assessing social and educational significance of the product under development.		
	Examining the existing products in application stores for portable devices.	Accumulating information about the existing excursion routes, discovering 'blank spaces' on the tourist map of the city.	Gathering information about the tourist services market, including the necessity of creating a bilingual version of the application.
Planning	Joint analysis of the data, accumulated during the first stage. Evaluating resources and costs necessary for the application development. Initial schematic introduction of the application structure and interface that ensures the tasks understanding by each group of students.		
	Modelling of application domain, choosing the platform, defining objectives, developing software architecture.	Collecting material for the excursion.	Collecting material for the excursion.
Implementation	Joint selection of the specific logical implementation model, subsequent assessment of the work coordination of the implemented components set		
	Developing an application with a definite set of functions and a user-friendly interface, inputting the content, created by humanitarian students for the application	Developing several excursions, gathering visual and audio content for each part of the excursion.	Translating the texts of the excursions, created by history students into English. Recording audio files in English.
Critical analysis	Assessing final application functionality and functioning correctness, evaluating learning significance of the work performed		
	Elimination of defects, code optimization.	"Full-scale testing" of the application on relatives and acquaintances; completeness analysis of the submitted information.	"Full-scale testing" of the application on students with a good level of English; assessing the quality of the translation and pronunciation on the record.

2.3 Study24Seven Application

This project is aimed at developing and testing the system of a blended educational project for pursuing a Masters in technical and computer sciences (Horn, 2014). The humanitarian course "The history and methodology of science" for YSU postgraduate students, specializing in "Information and communication technologies and communication systems", was chosen as a pilot project (Kovarik, 2011).

The choice of the pilot project is based on the following factors:

– students with the technical specialization have an extremely low level of humanitarian knowledge the existing methods of giving lectures and presentations don't work properly);

– a very low percentage of technical students go to the library;

– such students demonstrate low activity during the term;

– there is an immense body of high-quality materials on the history of science (e.g. films by Leonid Parfenov "Zworykin-Muromets", films about Nicola Tesla, video materials devoted to the invention of radio, the Silicon Valley and other innovation clusters), which are publicly available.

To work out the cloud system of blended learning, it was decided to choose the cross-platform mobile and web-development (Corral, 2012; Xanthopoulos, 2013). The most popular today are the mobile iOS and Android platforms. The advantage of this product is that one can use this app on several initially incompatible platforms using one code. This minimizes the product costs as it is enough to have only one software developer create the mobile application suitable for all platforms. The shortcomings of the product are the limited apps characteristics in comparison with native apps. The second drawback, the general design of the interface, is, to some extent, an advantage as well. No matter which platform is used it will have the same interface and screen logic. The complete application is compiled in the form of installation packages for every mobile operating system. The developers created a system with 4 quick login options: via e-mail, facebook, vk and twitter.

3. CONCLUSION

The survey data suggest a high technical and sufficient psychological readiness of Demidov Yaroslavl State University students to use mobile devices in learning. The City Guide project creates the interaction of students of humanitarian and technical specialties: having the experience of collaboration with colleagues with a different mentality is useful for both the students of humanities (it increases their competence in the field of ICT), and for technical students (it raises their level of culture, language knowledge, etc.).

The developed mobile application Study24Seven is cross-platform and is suitable for modern versions of the iOS and Android operating systems. This result is achieved both through the application architecture and the use of PhoneGap/iOnic technology. The development of appropriate methods of the blended learning system will increase the efficiency of teaching the Humanities to students of technical specialties.

ACKNOWLEDGEMENT

This work was supported by Vladimir Potanin Foundation (http://www.fondpotanin.ru).

REFERENCES

Corral, L. et al, 2012. Potential advantages and disadvantages of multiplatform development frameworks – a vision on mobile environments. Procedia Computer Science, vol. 10, pp. 1202–1207.

Eremin, Yu. and Kryulova E., 2014. The use of mobile technology in the students tasks in a foreign language study. In Izvestia: Herzen University Journal of Humanities & Science. No. 167, pp. 158-166.

Golizyuna, I. and Polovnikova N., 2011. Mobile Education as a new Education Technologies. In Education technology and Society, No. 1, pp.205-211.

Horn, M. et al., 2014. Blended: Using Disruptive Innovation to Improve Schools. Jossey-Bass, Wiley.

Kovarik, B., 2011. Revolutions in Communication: Media History from Gutenberg to the Digital Age. Bloomsbury Academic.

Laure, D. et al, 2016. Cross-platform Development for Sailfish OS and Android: Architectural Patterns and "Dictionary Trainer" Application Case Study. Proceedings of 19th Conference of Open Innovations Association (FRUCT). Jyvaskyla, Finland, pp. 145-150.

Son, I., 2013. Mobile Education for foreign language study. Proceedings of International Conference "Education in modern world: theory and practice. Sankt-Peterburg, Russia, pp. 164-167.

Titova, S. and Avramenko A., 2013. The evolution of learning tools in teaching foreign languages: from the personal computer to smartphones. In Vestnik of Moscow State University (Linguistics and Intercultural Communication Series), No. 1, pp. 4-12.

Xanthopoulos, S. and Xinogalos, S., 2013. A comparative analysis of crossplatform development approaches for mobile applications. Proceedings of the 6th Balkan Conference in Informatics. Thessaloniki, Greece, pp. 213–220.

THE M-LEARNING EXPERIENCE OF LANGUAGE LEARNERS IN INFORMAL SETTINGS

Emine Şendurur[1], Esra Efendioğlu[2], Neslihan Yondemir Çalışkan[1], Nomin Boldbaatar[1], Emine Kandin[2] and Sevinç Namazli[1]
[1]*Ondokuz Mayis University, Turkey*
[2]*Turkish Ministry of National Education, Turkey*

ABSTRACT

This study is designed to understand the informal language learners' experiences of m-learning applications. The aim is two-folded: (i) to extract the reasons why m-learning applications are preferred and (ii) to explore the user experience of Duolingo m-learning application. We interviewed 18 voluntary Duolingo users. The findings suggest that mobile language learning applications are perceived as complementary tools. They believe that it is impossible to learn a complete language only through the use of these apps. They find them convenient, because they spend tiny periods of their leisure such as coffee breaks at work on these applications. Duolingo is one of the most downloaded apps in the market. The participants like the method the app follows. Step-by-step flow, gamification, immediate feedback, high usability, and effortless use of the app can be considered as the good parts of user experience. Notifications could turn into a burden for some users. For advanced level users, the level of challenges is quite low. However, the flexible features and being almost completely free can contribute to the user experience in a positive manner.

KEYWORDS

UX; m-learning; language learning app; gamification.

1. INTRODUCTION

Throughout the history of instructional media, the integration of technology into education generally did not go beyond formal learning scenarios. The expectations were quite high, but the outcomes were not very different from those of the traditional educational settings consisting of blackboards and textbooks. The advancements of computer technologies offering high interactivity, the accessibility of personal computers, the introduction of graphical user interfaces, the development of Internet, prevalence of wireless technologies, and growing acceptance of mobile devices, especially the smartphones with advanced features made a difference in everyday life. Today, we frequently use online banking, store and share digital documents via clouds, exchange any information, and even learn online. Unlike its antecedents, mobile devices have the advantage of "anytime, anywhere, and anyone" flexibility, which enhances the opportunity for mobile-learning (m-learning).

In its early history, m-learning was directly associated with the mobile devices. Early definitions included device names such as handhelds (Traxler, 2005) or approached more general concepts such as mobile devices/environment (Polsami, 2003; Trifonova, 2003). It is obvious that m-learning is viewed beyond traditional learning, but there is no unique universal definition. As Peters (2007) stated the definition of m-learning is heading towards flexible learning owing to rapid developments. Recently, communication among users within mobile environment (Sharples et al., 2010) and sociocultural potential of those (Kearney et al, 2012) are the focus of these definitions. Despite the variety of definitions, it is seen that people use mobile devices to learn something as well as to communicate, and furthermore it may be bringing about new forms of learning (Khaddage et al., 2016).

The literature of m-learning grows day by day, but there are certain fields of study benefiting the mobility features. Mobile language learning is one of those fields. Some researchers try to contribute the theoretical issues (Stockwell & Hubbard, 2013), whereas some of them design and develop their own m-learning applications (Wu, 2015). One of the recent studies, Liu, Hwang, Kuo, and Li (2014) developed an innovative language learning material with smartphone and QR code integration. In this way, people were learning fitness related words as they engage in reading the materials in a fitness center. Another example is the use of handhelds to improve listening and vocabulary skills in language learning. In their study, Hsu et al. (2013) provided students with different caption options as they watch videos. Although students' vocabulary learning results were different across groups, no differences were observed in terms of listening skills. In its early history, the integration of mobile devices was challenging considering limited screen size, virtual keyboard usage, and power capacity or even audiovisual quality, which is crucial for language learning (Chinnery, 2006). Today, people are getting used to be proficient in mobile device usage and multimedia quality is quite high. That can be the reason why Mobile Applications for Language Learning (MALL) are popular recently with the increased positive effects on learning (Flores, 2015; Ketyi, 2016). The success of these apps can be sometimes attributed to gamification features, the inclusion of game-like elements in a design, which is not game-like at all (Deterding et al., 2011). Thereby, the motivation is preserved at a high level.

In application stores of different platforms, the number of MALL is considerably high as well as the number of downloads. Not all of them provide m-learning experience; some of them just serve as a translator or a dictionary. However, such popular applications as Duolingo offer users simple m-learning experiences with gamification (Flores, 2015), and thus have millions of downloads. There are many others in the market. For example, Busu, Babbel, and Italki have millions of users or Mondly has 100,000 users. They are generally free of charge but offer in-app purchases.

In this study, we are going to explore the m-learning experiences of Duolingo users. It is a very popular application having 50 million users and has versions in different languages. There are studies including many MALL, but this study is designed to have insights of user experiences in a specific MALL. The following research questions will be utilized: (RQ-1) Why do the participants prefer m-learning applications?; (RQ-2) What are the user experiences of Duolingo m-learning application?

2. METHOD

In this study, we designed a single-case study (Yin, 2009). The unit of analysis consists of Duolingo users. We deliberately choose a group of adult language learners having m-learning experience on Duolingo mobile application. 18 users accepted our invitation for the interview. They use at least one language learning application in addition to other apps. The mostly studied language is English (N=13), then German (N=4), Spanish (N=3), and finally Italian (N=1). Their occupations of participants were: student (N=4), teacher (N=4), engineer (N=2), accountant (N=2), civil servant (N=2), ship-broker (N=2), interpreter (N=1), and graphic designer (N=1). We collected data through semi-structured individual interviews lasting about 10-15 minutes. The questions were shaped to have insight of users' experiences with Duolingo. The questions were categorized into three: (i) demographics, (ii) usage patterns of m-learning app, (iii) perceived advantages and problems of Duolingo app. We recorded transcribed, and then coded the interviews. The content analysis was performed in the light of research questions with the help of literature. The themes and categories were discussed among researchers, thus received its final form. We both used direct quotations of users and frequencies.

3. FINDINGS

The collected data were analyzed and the themes and categories were extracted. In this section, the findings will be summarized in line with the research questions. Table 1 summarizes the sample coding.

Table 1. Coding Scheme.

Reasons for MALL (RQ1)	UX
Perceptions	**Positive**
Complete tool	*Effectiveness*
Not enough to learn a language	Ad-free
Complementary tool	Step-by-step (smoothness)
Repetition	*Efficiency*
Practice (Vocabulary; Grammar)	Free
Life-long Learning	Rich examples (vocabulary; grammar; pronunciation)
Self-improvement	
Career	Feedback (immediate; summary of performance)
Convenience	
Flexible	Flexible (Shortcuts; customization)
Time (shorter periods)	*Satisfaction*
Location	Design (simple/friendly; high-quality visuals)
Home (before bed; while watching TV; at dinner)	
	Gamification (entertaining; Interesting; helpful
Commute (avoiding boredom)	
Work (Coffee/lunch breaks)	notifications)
	Negative
	Restrictions
	Technical (Internet connection; headphones; screen size; battery; system bugs)
	Affective (Timeless notifications; decreasing levels)

3.1 Why M-learning Apps?

The participants reported frequent use of mobile language learning apps. In addition to Duolingo, the popular m-learning apps were identified as follows: Busuu, Memrise, Mondle, HelloTalk, Toeic Game, English Central and others. They all have and use dictionary apps frequently.

In order to understand the reasons why users download and use m-learning apps, we asked a few questions. First of all, all participants (N=18) stated that using such applications is not enough on its own to completely learn a foreign language. According to them, those can serve as complementary tools (N=10) for the purposes of repetition (N=15), vocabulary learning (N=9), and basic grammar practice (N=6). The participants all have life-long learning purposes, and therefore self-improvement (N=8) is crucial for them. They believe that learning a language can create new opportunities for them in terms of their career (N=10).

In its basic definitions, m-learning includes such terms as anytime and anywhere. The analyzed interview data indicate similar structure. In other words, one of the main reasons why m-learning language apps are preferred is becase they are convenient to use. Some of the participants (N=4) do not have time for a formal language education, but using such apps is possible since they do not demand long attention periods (N=2). The analysis showed that the participants use m-learning apps everyday (N=16) as long as they have free time (N=16). Unlike traditional PC-based ones, m-learning apps enhance the context. The participants emphasized how convenient the m-learning apps due to the usage anywhere (N=16). They use them at home (N=7) before going to bed (N=6). Instead of reading a book, they practice with apps. They also use them while watching TV (N=3) and having dinner (N=4). The majority of the participants (N=11) use the apps during morning/evening commutes in order to avoid boredom. For the same reason, they also complete a few levels during their coffee/meal breaks at work (N=4).

3.2 User Experience (UX) of Duolingo Users

Duolingo offers wide range of exercises in a gamification manner, which seems to be attracting many users. In this study, except for 2 participants, all of them reflected positive feelings about the app. Moreover, they expressed their satisfaction through their many statements. For example, they admitted that they learn something but in an entertaining (N=12) and interesting (N=2) way. Being free of charge (N=8) and having no embedded advertisements (N=3) are the positive sides of the app, according to users.

The method of Duolingo consists of many features that users appreciate. The participants enjoy the step-by-step flow of the app (N=10). Each step comprises of small pieces of information. The overall aim of this app is to enable learners moving forward in a smooth way with repetitions, which attracts the participants' attention (N=15). In addition to vocabulary (N=9) and basic grammar (N=6) practices, the app offers a rich pronunciation (N=11) practice, which was perceived as a valuable feature by users. One of the most powerful features of the app is immediate feedback and performance summary (N=13), especially during the pronunciation exercises. Earning points as you gain skills enriches the flow of app (N=4), so that some of the participants defined Duolingo as a game (N=7).

In terms of design features, participants agreed that the interface is simple and usable (N=12). According to them, the quality of visuals are high (N=8). One of the important points in user experience is the flexibility of the system. The participants remarked the value of available shortcuts and customizations (N=4). For example, slowing down the pronunciation, skipping the exercises requiring the use of microphone, and moving to the next level with a simple test rather than completing the whole lesson were all mentioned shortcuts in this study.

Like many other apps, Duolingo sends notifications when the user skips the daily practice. Although the aim is to motivate people to spend time for a little practice, this may not always serve this purpose. For example, 2 participants reflected that they had to delete the app due to timeless reminders. Because, according to them, notifications made them feel guilty. They could not manage to use the app due to lack of time. On the other hand, 11 participants were affected in a positive way. The notifications served as either the regulators of their performance (N=11) or motivators to start studying (N=4). Some of the participants had neutral attitude (N=3) because they already can regulate their own study habits.

The general user experience of Duolingo seems quite positive, but there are some problems that users face in real settings. The app requires Internet connection (N=4), which is a restriction according to some users. Moreover, for listening and pronunciation exercises one needs headphones within crowded places, and therefore it limits the usage (N=2). Small screen sizes (N=2) and high demand of battery (N=1) are the other bad experiences reported by our participants. The software is not without bugs, therefore the users sometimes experience and have to leave the system especially during the recording of pronunciation exercises (N=3).

The comments of participants revealed the affective dimension of the experience. Its gamification approach seems to appeal the target audience (N=3), but sometimes can be time consuming (N=3). Some of the participants found the reward/punishment discouraging (N=7).

4. CONCLUSION

The body of m-learning literature is growing rapidly in the last decade. In this case study, we focused on user experiences of Duolingo, the mobile language learning application having 50 million users. We interviewed with 18 voluntary Duolingo users. First, we tried to understand the reasons why they prefer m-learning applications and then explored the user experiences of Duolingo. The findings suggest that our participants find m-learning apps convenient, which is included in the definitions of m-learning in the literature (Kearney et al, 2012). They do not have time to participate in a formal leaning environment. Instead, they find using such apps more convenient because they already have those bits of time that are useless otherwise. However, they are all aware that one cannot learn a language via m-learning apps without previous experience. They should be integrated into formal classes to practice (Chen, 2013).

In user experience, effective and efficient use of the app is very important in addition to the satisfaction. If people perceive the ease of use then the frequency and the probability of the good experience may occur (Hsia, 2016). The majority of the participants were very positive about the interface and the overall experience. Duolingo supports multiple types of practices ranging from vocabulary to pronunciation. Such a rich environment can increase the flow of the usage. Gikas and Grant (2013) suggest that the quick access, situated learning, and various learning options are the advantageous parts of m-learning. Practicing vocabulary, grammar, speaking, and listening with repetition were seen crucial according to the participants. Duolingo offers an extensive series of practice, which may appeal the users, so that they continue to use it. Such apps can be used not only informally out of the school, but also during the formal learning period to support the user (Steel & Levy, 2013). Although the aim of the notifications is to encourage users to log in the system, for some participants those notifications were the main reason why they leave the system eventually. At this point, the designers should carefully analyze the needs of the stakeholders (Stockwell & Hubbard, 2013). Recently, adaptive learning environments are on the spot. For such popular m-learning apps, adaptive features should be embedded in the future.

REFERENCES

Chen, X.-B., 2013. Tablets for Informal Language Learning: students Usage and Attitudes. *Language Learning & Technology,* Vol. 17, No. 1, pp.20-36.

Chinnery, G.M., 2006. Going to the MALL: Mobile Assisted Language Learning (Emerging Technology). *Language Learning & Technology,* Vol. 10, No. 1, pp. 9-16.

Deterding, S. et al, 2011. Using Game Design Elements in Non-gaming Contexts, *CHI 2011.*

Flores, J.F.F., 2015. Using Gamification to Enhance Second Language Learning. *Digital Education Review,* Vol. 27, pp. 32-54.

Gikas, J. & Grant, M.M., 2013. Mobile Computing Devices in Higher Education: Student Perspectives on Learning with Cellphones, Smartphones, and Social Media. *The Internet and Higher Education,* Vol. 19, pp. 18-26.

Hsia, J.-W., 2016. The Effects of Locus of Control on University Students'Mobile Learning Adoption. *Journal of Computing in Higher Education,* Vol. 28, No. 1, pp. 1-17.

Hsu, C.K. et al, 2013. Effects of Video Caption Modes on English Listening Comprehension and Vocabulary Acquisition Using Handheld Devices. *Educational Technology &Society,* Vol. 16, No. 1, pp. 403-414.

Ketyi, A., 2016. From Mobile Language Learning to Gamification: an Overlook of Research Results with Business Management Students over a Five-Year Period. *Porta Linguarum,* pp. 45-60.

Kearney, M. et al, 2012. Viewing Mobile Learning From a Pedagogical Perspective. *Research in Learning Technology,* Vol. 20, pp. 14406.

Khaddage, F. et al, 2016. Advancing Mobile Learning in Formal and Informal Settings via Mobile Application Technology: Where to From Here, and How? *Educational Technology & Society,* Vol. 19, No. 13, pp. 16-26.

Liu, G.Z. et al, 2014. Designing Dynamic English: A Creative Reading System in a Context-Aware Fitness Center Using a Smart Phone and QR-Codes. *Digital Creativity,* Vol. 25, No. 2, pp. 169-186.

Peters, K., 2007. M-learning: Positioning Educators for a Mobile, Connected Future. *The International Review of Research in Open & Distributed Learning,* Vol. 8, No. 2, pp. 1-17.

Sharples, M. et al, 2010. A Theory of Learning for the Mobile Age Learning through Conversation and Exploration Across Contexts.

Steel, C.H. & Levy, M., 2013. Language Students and Their Technologies: Charting the Evolution 2006-2011. *ReCALL,* Vol. 25, No. 3, pp. 306-320.

Stockwell, G. & Hubbard, P., 2013. Some Emerging Principles for Mobile-Assisted Language Learning. Monterey, CA: *The International Research Foundation for English Language Education.* Retrieved from http://www.tirfonline.org/wp-content/uploads/2013/11/TIRF_MALL_Papers_StockwellHubbard.pdf

Traxler, J., 2005. Defining Mobile Learning. *Proceedings IADIS International Conference Mobile Learning.* Malta, pp. 261-266.

Wu, Q., 2015. Designing a Smartphone Application to Teach English (L2) Vocabulary. *Computers & Education,* Vol. 85, pp. 170-179.

Yin, R.K., 2009. *Case Study Research: Design and Methods.* Sage, California, USA.

Reflection Papers

NEW MODEL OF MOBILE LEARNING FOR THE HIGH SCHOOL STUDENTS PREPARING FOR THE UNIFIED STATE EXAM

Airat Khasianov and Irina Shakhova
Higher School of Information Technology and Information Systems, Kazan Federal University
Kremlyovskaya St., Kazan, Russia

ABSTRACT

In this paper we study a new model of mobile learning for the Unified State Exam (*USE*) preparation in Russian Federation. USE - is the test school graduates need to pass in order to obtain Russian matura. In recent years the efforts teachers put for preparation of their students to the *USE* diminish how well the subject is actually mastered by the students. The problem lays in the key performance indicators the teachers must reach. The *KPI* is not unified across the country, but often it includes, in one or another form, the *USE* score the students get.
The main proposition of this research is to use gamification in order to transfer the *USE* preparation out of the classroom activities. The most natural platform for this gamification is the ecosystem of the smartphones and social media available to the students. We build the *USE* preparation didactical model that addresses the challenges the teachers currently have. Then we discuss the architecture and the implementation for the whole solution.

KEYWORDS

Mobile learning, education, software engineering, education technology, pedagogy, unified state exam.

1. INTRODUCTION

We have been studying gamification for different settings (Khasianov et al., 2016, Suleymanov et al., 2016). Now we shall consider the unified state exam (*USE*) school graduates have to pass in order to apply for the tertiary education institutions. Often the teacher has the bonus reduced if the students perform below certain threshold in the *USE*. Thus the teacher is not motivated to invest time in teaching really complex topics, neither the teacher is motivated to pursue the deep understanding of the subject. The students in turn only get to master very basic competences just enough to perform above the threshold. This sort of the extra work does not improve the understanding of the subject by the students.

There are two challenges: a) remove the unnecessary workload from the teachers without compromising performance of their students according to *USE*, b) increase the students' involvement, and let the teachers spend their time to actually teach the subject.

We propose to a) remove the *USE* activities from the classroom; b) involve the students in the self-sustained process of the subject mastery, while thoroughly learning the subject; c) measure what *USE* score the students get.

Our proposal is to shift the most routine tasks from the classroom to the mobile application. Then we "gamify" process of solving the typical tasks one by one. We make the students get involved in the competition. We also motivate the students to help each other in learning how to solve the typical cases their classmates don't understand. We already have started the experiment in one of the schools, we have collected the teachers feedback, and implemented their user stories in the application the children will get on their smartphones. During the next two years we shall be collecting the data on the general mastery of the subjects involved, and the *USE* performance of the participants of the experiment. All the activity is done extracurricularly, the teacher's participation is limited to the roles shown below in the model description. The children use the smartphone application to solve problems, search for tutors and tutees and improve their scores.

2. DESCRIPTION OF THE MODEL

The project called *Gamified preparation for the Unified State Exam (GUSE)* can shortly be described with the use-case diagram. We follow here the *three agent systems* design pattern described earlier in Suleymanov et al., 2011 and Khasianov et al., 2017. According to the *three agent* approach the digital education environment is build around the three agents: the *teacher*, the *student*, and the *system itself as an actor*. In this case the student can take one of the two roles, or even both at the same time for different topics: the *tutee* and the *tutor*.

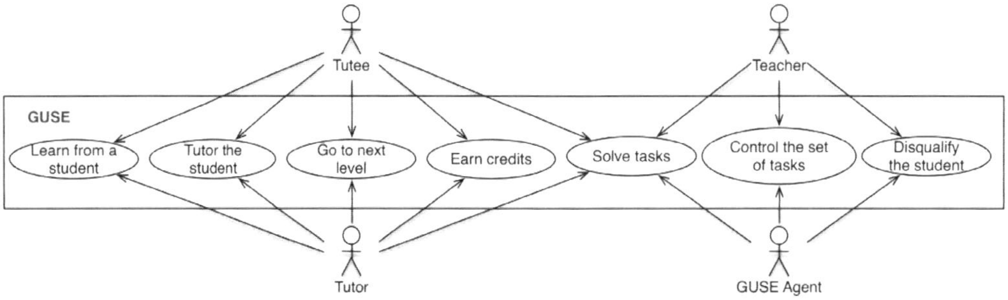

Figure 1. Use case diagram for the GUSE.

The *teacher* and the *intelligent agent* can both *control the set of tasks* the system takes form the open sets of the assignments. Both of the two actors may also *disqualify* a students for certain inappropriate use of the system. The student can either *tutor* another student, or *learn* from a *tutor* student. According to the performance and the achievements the student in either role (*tutor* or *tutee*) can earn credits, and even can be *promoted to the next level*. The *level* is the rough representation of how far the student will get in the actual *USE* exam according to the currently demonstrated performance. Some tasks the student solves as a *tutee* may need a human peer review, therefore the *teacher* is still involved in the activity. But the total amount of workload of the teacher is dramatically reduced when using the system, since major part of the work related to assigning unique test sets and control of the students feedback is done without the teacher's intervention.

For some cases a *tutor* student can also be involved in the solutions evaluation. Thus we extend the range of possible solutions the students get introduced to. We thus also further reduce the teacher's workload. The tutoring also speeds up the student's transition from the unconscious incompetence to the conscious incompetence, and then further through the conscious competence to the unconscious competence (Sprague and Stuart, 2000). The feedback is crucial for the knowledge acquisition (see e.g. Butler and Winnie, 1995), and both the submissions feedback and the tutee-tutor interaction gives the student the right kind of feedback for the *self-regulated learning* setting we create. The general principles of cognitive tutors design are well presented as early as in Anderson et.al., 1995. For the rather simple *GUSE Agent* we follow the same guidelines.

This model is an instance of the blended learning approach (see Bonk et.al., 2006). The teacher can't be excluded from the system. We don't want the learning degrade down to the automated *USE* training. Our main objective is to let the teacher do the job, while the routine tasks of *USE* preparation are taken care off.

The process of tutoring and learning, where the *tutor* and the *tutee* are involved, happens outside the application. Preferably, in a face-to-face manner. The application only registers the shear fact of the relation and the topics being tutored. The application also lets the students evaluate each party, and then tracks the performance gains of the *tutees,* within the topics worked through with the *tutor,* in order to increase the credits of the *tutor* student.

We should be careful with the motivation (see Atkinson, 1964). Our goal is to reinforce the students' motivation of mastering the subject and performing their best at the *USE.* But we should not replace that motivation with the *game*. In order to create the right *motivation* we a) let the student expect better performance at the *USE* after doing what the model suggests; b) show that the higher *USE* score opens better future tertiary education opportunities - that assigns value to mastering the subject.

The model creates the setting where the students not only have a lot of practice, but also assign clear goals to their practice. Thus we expect the goal-provided students to perform measurably better than average as a result of their goal-directed practice (Rothkopf and Billington, 1979).

The *Levels* communicate the students relevant information on how close they have come to reach their *goals*. This information is timely provided when the students still can correct their learning strategies. Moreover, there are motivated *tutors* that would seek for the *tutees,* in order to increase their own credits and understanding. The *tutor-tutee* relationship also gives the students feedback on the concrete reasons the students underperform in certain tasks, unveil the blind spots and particular flows in the *tutors'* understanding of the material. That in turn improves learning (Cardelle and Corno, 1981).

The application limits how much practice the student can take in a day. Thus we let the students have time to develop knowledge (Carey, 2014).

The gamification made right also creates productive and positive climate around the *USE* preparation. Provides the students with the feel of control, and makes the whole (normally stressful) preparation for one of the most important exam in their lives a bit fun. We know that the climate the students live in, while learning, has tremendous effects on what and how well they learn (Astin, 1993).

3. GAME MECHANICS

According to Salen and Zimmerman, 2003, game has three important aspects: *rules*, *play* and *culture*. All of the objects in the game should be in the system of well-defined relationships that create clear rules. The players choose strategies to reach their goals within the rules of the game. Social and cultural context of the real life apparently affects the players' behavior in the game. Thus, any game has three aspects: *cognitive, emotional and social* (Lee & Hammer, 2011). Each of these aspects is reflected by the corresponding game mechanics.

The *cognitive* component of the game supports experimentation and discovery. Understandable and achievable *goals* and *challenges* that gradually increase their difficulty according to the skills development of the players are also essential to keep the students in the proximal development zone (Vygotsky, 2005). It is also important for the *goals* to be desired by the students (Atkinson, 1964), while leaving the freedom of how the goals are actually achieved. In our case, the *goal* would be passing the USE with the highest possible score, and the *challenges* are the tasks to solve in order to achieve the desired score (Khasianov et al., 2016).

The next aspect is the *emotional*. The *USE* preparation takes time, and the absence of the continuous feedback may diminish the students' motivation. It is crucial for the student to receive the continuous feedback. We implement this through the progress indicators, that show the players how close they have come to their goals, and correct their strategies if needed. The progress indicators are presented in terms of *points, levels* and *badges*. *Points* are the progress units the student receives when completing a tasks. The total number of *points* creates an individual *score* of the student that can be used to show his/her rating. *Levels* represent the difficulty levels that correspond to the parts of the *USE*. *Badges* are awards that can be received by the student doing certain activities. A *goal achievement* is awarded with a *badge*, in addition, the *badges* can be obtained by performing certain *challenges* or combinations of certain actions in the mobile application. In order to create positive emotional climate, and avoid the stress accumulation. It is very important to let the students do mistakes.

The *social component* allows players to try new social roles, and establish communications in the game environment. In the *GUSE* context a player who has achieved certain rating level can become a *tutor* and help other players to reach their *goals*. It allows to strengthen the positions of the students (as a *tutor* and a *tutee*) in the social environment. One more way to organize effective communication and involvement is a *competition* which provides another opportunity to get the proper feedback about the exam preparation progress.

4. CONCLUSION

We propose a model that puts the right weight for the course mastery and the test preparation activities during the graduation year at the high school. We start the experiment with the high school students in order to prove our approach right or wrong, although we put thorough theoretical basis under our development. There are several aspects of the model that can be listed shortly: a) the teacher is relieved from the routine activity; b) the students get timely informative feedback in terms of approaching their goal and in terms of what is wrong with their mastery of the subject in particular; c) the systems provides a lot of practice, but the problem sets and the time limits a set individually with accordance to the student's workload, performance, and the assignments other students get; e) the model works only as a part of *blended learning* paradigm; f) the model encourages social interactions and creates positive climate giving the goal, the value, the feel of control and introduces a bit of a fun game with friendly competition in the initially very stressful situation - we take the attention away from the actual moment of the *USE* that is glooming over the cohort in the nearest future; g) the model supports inherent motivation, and this is important; h) the general architecture is built around *three-agent* concept for educational digital tools, where the system can take actions, depending on the individual and social dynamic of the learners.

There certainly will be further research of the subject, as well as the analysis of the experimental data.

REFERENCES

Anderson, J.R. et al., 1995. Cognitive tutors: Lessons learned. *Journal of the Learning Sciences,* 4(2), pp. 167-207.

Astin, A.W., 1993. *What matters in college? Four critical years revisited.* Jossey-Bass, San Francisco, CA.

Atkinson, J., 1964. *An introduction to motivation.* Van Nostrand, Princeton, NJ.

Bonk, C.J. et al., 2006. *The Handbook of Blended Learning: Global Perspectives, Local Designs.* Pfeiffer Publishing, San Francisco, CA.

Butler D. and Winne P., 1995. Feedback and Self-Regulated Learning: A Theoretical Synthesis. *Review of Educational Research,* Vol. 65, No. 3, pp. 245-281.

Cardelle, M. and Corno, L., 1981. Effects on second language learning of variations in written feedback on homework assignments. *TESOL Quarterly,* 15(3), pp. 251-261.

Carey, B., 2014. *How we learn: The surprising truth about when where and how it happens.* Rabdom House, NY.

Khasianov, A. et al., 2016. Gamification in higher education: Kazan Federal University primer. *Proceedings of the 12th International Scientific Conference eLearning and Software for Education.* Bucharest, pp. 519-522.

Khasianov, A. et al., 2017. Three agent platform approach for digital education environment. *Proceedings of the 11th annual International Technology, Education and Development Conference (to appear).*

Lee, J. J. and Hammer, J., 2011. Gamification in Education: What, How, Why Bother? *Academic Exchange Quarterly,* 15(2), pp. 146-150.

Rothkopf, E.Z. and Billington, M.J., 1979. Goal-guided learning from text: Inferring a descriptive processing model from inspection times and eye movements. *Journal of Educational Psychology,* 71, pp. 310-327.

Salen, K. and Zimmerman, E., 2003. *Rules of play: Game design fundamentals.* MIT Press, Cambridge, MA.

Sprague, J. and Stuart, D., 2000. *The speakers' handbook.* Harcourt College Publishers, Fort Worth, TX.

Suleymanov, D., 2011. Methodology and principles of the intelligent agent design for the textual dialogue systems. *Proceedings of System analysis and semiotic modelling*, pp.31-37.

Suleymanov, D. et al, 2016. *Education looking to the future. Socio-cognitive study of youth media and computer technology education.* The Academy of Sciences of Republic of Tatarstan Press, Kazan, Russia.

Vygotsky, L.S., 2005. Psikhologiya razvitiya cheloveka. Moscow: Eksmo (in Russian).

RE-MENT - REVERSE MENTORING AS A WAY TO DECONSTRUCT GENDER RELATED STEREOTYPES IN ICT

Kathrin Permoser
University College of Teacher Education in Lower Austria,
Mühlgasse 67, A-2500 Baden, Austria

ABSTRACT

In applying a reverse mentoring approach, the project *re-ment* aims at raising the interest of female students for Information and Communication Technology (ICT) professions and at contributing to the deconstruction of gender stereotypes in this field. This approach offers a completely new and innovative perspective in the field of gender equality and advancement of girls in technology. This innovative mobile learning approach is applied in *re-ment* as the mentors and the mentees communicate via a social network. The project implements reverse-mentoring programs in four partner schools in Austria, the main result being a comprehensive course for teacher education.

KEYWORDS

Innovative mobile learning approaches, e-mentoring.

1. INTRODUCTION

Re-ment is a research project that develops and implements a reverse-mentoring approach in four upper secondary schools in Austria. The aim of this project is to raise girls' interest in ICT (Information Communication Technologies) and sciences professions and to demonstrate gender specific segregation as well as to deconstruct gender related stereotypes. One major element of *re-ment* is the e-mentoring approach as the mentoring process itself will be online via a social network. Combining reverse mentoring and e-mentoring is identified as an innovative mobile learning approach.

2. REVERSE MENOTRING IN ICT

Reverse-mentoring opens new perspectives and equal opportunities for girls in the ICT branch. *Re-ment* focuses on the girls' competences and not their deficits. Especially regarding ICT competences, young people have higher competences than older people as published by the PIAAC (Program for the International Assessment of Adult Competences) study in 2013. According to Bozeman and Feeney, mentoring takes place between a mentor, who is "a person who is perceived to have greater relevant knowledge, wisdom or experience" and a mentee, "a person who is perceived to have less" (Bozeman and Feeney, 2007, p. 731). In *re-ment*, female students, aged between 16 and 17, who have higher competences in ICT will be mentors and teachers or parents will be mentees. Consequently, girls' ICT competences will be raised on an individual level as well as gender related stereotypes will be deconstructed. It is well known that reverse mentoring mainly implements ICT questions or issues as the younger people are the digital natives and support older people with latest developments in ICT and, therefore, both – mentors and mentees – will benefit and it is an innovative way to encourage learning (Prensky, 2001).

Reverse-mentoring turns the traditional mentoring concept upside down. It is an internationally well developed and often used method. According to Hsueh-Hua-Chuang and Ann Thomson there are two well spread projects in the USA that make use of the reverse-mentoring concept and focus on ICT competences of pupils and students (Hsueh-Hua Chuang and Ann Thompson, 2005, cited by Peterson, 2012). In these two projects, pupils and students act as a kind of help desk regarding ICT questions to support school management staff or teachers. These two projects are called Mouse (Making Opportunities for upgrading Schools and Education) and GenYES. Mouse's mission is "to empower students to create with technology to solve real problems and make meaningful change in our world." One central focus of Mouse is on "creating more diversity in STEM (Science, Technology, Engineering and Mathematics) [...]" (https://mouse.org/). GenYes aims at "closing the digital divide and empowers students to become leaders in their schools by using technology to solve crucial problems in education, while also becoming interested in STEM careers" (http://genyes.org). The benefit that is outlined by Peterson is that teachers and management staff profit from the ICT support and pupils and students profit from the preceding trainings that they received by professional mentors (Peterson, 2012). Consequently, reverse mentoring implements a high potential for innovative improvements in educational settings, especially in ICT. For the purposes of the research project *re-ment*, reverse-mentoring is defined as

> *"Reverse-mentoring is a specific form of mentoring and refers to a reciprocal and timely stable developmental partnership between one or more less experienced mentor/s providing specific expertise and one or more experienced mentee/s who want/s to gain this knowledge. The partnership is characterized by reciprocity and mutual respect and it aims at both, the development of the mentors and the mentees. In applying a networked perspective, it may take advantage of digital technology."*

One key element of this innovative mobile learning approach in *re-ment* is the online mentoring process that is often referred to as e-mentoring. A definition of e-mentoring that is offered by Stöger states that e-mentoring is "a special form of mentoring where communication takes place online, at least partly" (Stöger, 2009, p. 229). This online mentoring process faces new challenges and opportunities for mentees and mentors regarding their ICT competences as outlined by Williams, Sunderman and Kim (2012) and consequently trainings have to be offered in the course of this project. For the purposes of the research project *re-ment*, a social network is used to facilitate communication between mentors and mentees. The social network that is used is called *yammer* which is primarily used by enterprises to connect employees across the company. *Re-ment* makes use of *yammer* that mentors and mentees are able to connect and collaborate online as well as to provide a secure online platform (www.yammer.com).

Using the social platform *yammer* for the online mentoring process is beneficial for mentors and mentees. Giddens and Phillips outline the positive experiences using the Web 2.0 for their reverse-mentoring concept in a company that can be identified in an educational environment as well:

> *"Reverse mentoring is an innovative way to encourage learning and facilitate cross-generational relationships."*

„The most positive outcome for us was, that web 2.0 was a catalyst for the strengthening of our professional relationship, underpinned by deeper levels of honesty, trust and respect for each other." (Giddens and Phillips, 2009, p. 9)

Therefore, using *yammer* as the online platform in *re-ment* will help mentors and mentees in the mentoring process as the relation between the girls and teachers or parents will be supported and intensified. According to Bargh & McKenna online relationships conducted through e-mentoring programs can be similar to those developed in person in terms of their breadth, depth and quality (Bargh and McKenna, 2004, cited by Shpigelman, 2014). Shpigelman concludes that there is a considerable potential of e-mentoring for personal growth and empowerment of children as well as adolescents (Shpigelman, 2014). Consequently, mentors and mentees in *re-ment* will experience the online reverse mentoring process positively.

3. CONCLUSION

In conclusion it can be stated that this innovative mobile learning approach that combines a reverse mentoring concept and an online social platform to facilitate the mentoring process will be an innovative setting for both, mentors and mentees. In *re-ment* girls who are the mentors support their parents or teachers who are their mentees regarding ICT questions or issues and, therefore, both will benefit as it is an innovative way to encourage learning. Finally, the project itself and the results will be published and the findings of the accompanying quantitative and qualitative evaluation will be the basis for the development of teacher trainings and teaching material. The course will consist of a face-to face seminar that will also be offered online, and a module for the new upper secondary school in Austria will be designed.

ACKNOWLEDGEMENT

The prototype implementation is funded by the Austrian Ministry of Traffic, Innovation and Technology within the 4th Call Talente/FemTech: “re-ment” (www.rement.at) is currently in progress.

REFERENCES

Arnold, P. et al, 2013. *Handbuch E-Learning: Lernen und Lehren mit digitalen Medien.* W. Bertelsmann Verlag GmbH & Co. KG, Bielefeld.

Beddoes-Jones, F. and Miller, J., 2006. “Virtual” mentoring: can the principle of cognitive pairing increase its effectiveness? *International Journal of Evidence Based Coaching and Mentoring,* Vol. 4, No. 2, pp. 4–60.

Bellinger, A., 2009. E-Mentoring im Kontext von E-Beratung. Der Einsatz neuer Medien zur Förderung von Frauen in akademischen Karrieren am Beispiel des Projekts E-Mentoring. In Stöger, Heidrun, Ziegler, Albert, & D. Schimke (Eds.), *Mentoring: Theoretische Hintergründe, empirische Befunde und praktische Anwendungen,* pp. 269–283. Papst Science Publishers, Lengerich.

Bozeman, B. and Feeney, M. K., 2007. Toward a Useful Theory of Mentoring: A Conceptual Analysis and Critique. *Administration and Society,* Vol. 39, No. 6, pp. 719–739. retrieved from http://aas.sagepub.com/content/39/6/719.full.pdf+html

Bozionelos, N., 2004. Mentoring provided: Relation to mentor’s career success, personality, and mentoring received. *Journal of Vocational Behavior*, Vol. 64, No. 6, pp. 24-46.

Brondyk, S. and Searby, L., 2013. Best practices in mentoring: complexities and possibilities. *International Journal of Mentoring and Coaching in Education*, Vol. 2, No. 3, pp. 189–203.

Buahene, A. K. and Kovary, G., 2009. Reversing roles: Why Gen Ys can make great mentors. Canadian HR Reporter. *The National Journal of Human Resource Management,* Retrieved from www.hrreporter.com

Butler, A. J. et al, 2013. Technology´s role in fostering transformational educator mentoring. *International Journal of Mentoring and Coaching in Education,* Vol. 2, No 3, pp. 233–248.

Chaudhuri, S. and Gosh, R., 2012. Reverse Mentoring: A Social Exchange Tool for Keeping the Boomers Engaged and Millennials Committed. *Human Resource Development Review,* pp 55–76.

Chuang, H.-H. and Thompson, A., 2005. Students Teaching Teachers. *Educational Leadership*, Vol. 63, No. 4, pp 70–71.

Cotunga, N. and Vickery, E. C., 1998. Reverse-mentoring: A twist to teaching technology. *Journal of the American Dietetic Association,* Vol. 98, No. 10, pp. 1166–1168.

Crawford, K. et al, 2013. Change, challenge and choice: being a student mentor. *International Journal of Mentoring and Coaching in Education,* Vol. 2, No. 2, pp. 137–148.

DeAngelis, K. L., 2013. *Reverse Mentoring at the Hartford: Cross generational transfer of knowledge about social media.* Sloan Center on Aging and Work, Boston College. retrieved from http://www.bc.edu/content/dam/files/research_sites/agingandwork/pdf/publications/ha rtford.pdf

Fransson, G. and MacMahan, S. K., 2013. Exploring research on mentoring in education. *International Journal of Mentoring and Coaching in Education,* Vol. 2, No. 3, pp. 218–232.

Gibson, L. and Sodeman, W., 2014. Millennials and Technology: Addressing the Communication Gap in Education and Practice. *Organization Development Journal*, pp. 64–75.

Giddens, D. and Phillips, R., 2009. *Reverse Mentoring: Finding a new way of working while discovering Web 2.0* (ALIA National Library and Information Technicians Conference). Adelaide Convention Centre, Adelaide, SA, Australia.

Larson, L., 2009. A Descriptive Study of Mentoring and Technology Integration among Teacher Education Faculty. *International Journal of Evidence Based Coaching and Mentoring,* Vol. 7, No. 1, pp. 119–135.

Peterson, M. J., 2012. *Switching roles: an investigation into the use of reverse-mentoring by students to encourage teachers' uptake of ICT in their pedagogical approach.* Curtin University, School of Education.

Prensky, M., 2001. *Digital Natives, Digital Immigrants,* Vol. 9, No. 5, pp. 1-6, Horiz. MCB Univ. Press.

Shpigelman, C., 2014. Electronic mentoring and media. In Dubois and Karcher (Eds.), *Handbook of Youth Mentoring, 2nd edition,* pp. 259-272, SAGE Publications, United States.

Stöger, H., 2009. E-Mentoring: eine spezielle Form des Mentorings. In Stöger, Heidrun, Ziegler, Albert, & D. Schimke (Eds.), *Mentoring: Theoretische Hintergründe, empirische Befunde und praktische Anwendungen,* pp. 227–243, Papst Science Publishers, Lengerich.

Williams, S. and Kim, J., 2011. E-mentoring in Online Course Projects: Description of an E-Mentoring Scheme. *International Journal of Evidence Based Coaching and Mentoring,* Vol. 9, No. 2, pp. 80–95.

Williams, S. et al, 2012. E-mentoring in an Online Course: Benefits and Challenges to E-mentors. *International Journal of Evidence Based Coaching and Mentoring*, Vol. 10, No. 1, pp. 109–123.

Zauchner-Studnicka, S., 2013a. Genderforschung. Ihr Blick auf das Lernen und Lehren mit neuen Technologien. In M. Ebner and S. Schön (Eds.), L3T *Lehrbuch für Lernen und Lehren mit neuen Technologien.* Retrieved from http://l3t.eu/homepage/das-buch/ebook- 2013/kapitel/o/id/122/name/genderforschung

ACADEMIC SUCCESS FOUNDATION: ENHANCING ACADEMIC INTEGRITY THROUGH MOBILE LEARNING

Alice Schmidt Hanbidge[1], Amanda Mackenzie[2], Nicole Sanderson[1], Kyle Scholz[2] and Tony Tin[1]
[1]*Renison University College*
[2]*University of Waterloo*
Waterloo, Ontario, Canada

ABSTRACT

How do we close the gap between the lack of academic experience incoming students have - with the expectation that students know the rules of writing and taking exams? Academic integrity (AI) is essential in post-secondary academia yet insufficient time is allocated to teaching and practicing its concepts. Talks at orientation, lectures in the first class, and notations in the course syllabus have been used to assist students with the academic transition to university, but have been less effective at increasing the student's level of academic integrity (Bertram Gallant, 2011; Josephson Institute of Ethics (see www.josephsoninstitute.org/reportcard). One solution is to provide students with information about institutional academic expectations in advance of the first day of classes yet, a number of barriers exist, including limitations in the learning management systems (LMS) and firewalls blocking access to external content.

Developing a mobile AI learning application would circumvent the LMS and firewall issues and enable information to be made available prior to students' arrival, thereby acculturating them to university values and academic integrity rules to help support student success well before classes begin.

KEYWORDS

Academic integrity, mobile learning, academic misconduct.

1. INTRODUCTION

Globally, college and universities often struggle to identify the best pedagogical approach to engaging students with academic integrity content. Academic Integrity (AI) "refers to a set of conventions that scholars follow in their work, and which generates credibility, trust, and respect within the academic community" (http://www.yorku.ca/spark/academic_integrity/index.html). When students cheat on exams or purchase completed assignments online, academic integrity is lost and academic institutions lose their validity and credibility. Unless the importance of honesty, originality and learning is internalized, students could receive a degree without the requisite skills. Hence, it is imperative that students understand academic rules and demonstrate them in their scholarship. Most universities rely on instructors to cover this foundational information in class; however, consistency and quality in its delivery varies widely. Moreover, many post-secondary institutions post their AI resources and policies deep within institutional websites. As a result, this information is often not visible nor does the static nature of the content readily engage students.

As the needs and interests of student's change, so must pedagogy. Hence, to better reach and resonate with students, we propose to develop an interactive mobile AI application. Specifically, to educate students about the values of honesty, trust, respect, responsibility, fairness and courage, which form the basis of academic integrity (http://www.academicintegrity.org/icai/resources-2.php).

Compounding this is a lack of institutional resources dedicated to raising awareness of academic integrity (Bertram Gallant, 2011), as well as the dearth of research on AI in higher education. Limited pre-existing research indicates the need for more support to encourage academic integrity. Several customized strategies employed at various institutions are not standardized nor applicable to other schools. This proposal seeks to develop an engaging instructional mobile application available across post-secondary institutions.

2. LITERATURE REVIEW

2.1 Academic Integrity

The International Center for Academic Integrity (ICAI) defines academic integrity as "a commitment, even in the face of adversity, to six fundamental values: honesty, trust, fairness, respect, responsibility, and courage" (Fundamental Values Project, 2014, p. 16). Over the last 20 years, institutional approaches to AI have shifted from being punitive or rules-focused to being educative and values-based (Bertram Gallant, 2011). A punitive approach emphasizes strict consequences as a behavioural deterrent (e.g. suspension from school), whereas, educational approaches support students to learn why they should follow the rules (e.g. workshops and training). Bertram Gallant (2011) emphasizes that "schools should aim to infuse the value of integrity into structures, processes and cultures of the organization" (p. 13). Therefore, to embrace the tenets of AI, students need to have scholarship and integrity role-modeled by educators and nurtured in classes for written assignments, quizzes/tests and exams within an educational institution (Glendinning, 2014).

Traditionally, scholarly rules to maintain AI are passed to students directly from their instructors, yet practices vary among instructors, resulting in inconsistencies in both the AI content shared and the depth of such discussions. Studying faculty attitudes on students' AI at 17 Canadian universities, MacLeod (2014) concluded that "[every university] mentions the importance of academic integrity and affirms that they expect students to act ethically… regrettably, there are often no follow-up provisions for actually teaching students to do so" (p. 11). With this in mind, we advocate that students receive this foundational knowledge in a consistent manner.

Boehm, Justice and Weeks (2009) identify numerous AI best practices. Surveys of three US higher educational institutions indicated that instructors identified that training for instructors, adhering to classroom management strategies to reduce the chance of cheating, and providing clear examples of what academic integrity constitutes as most beneficial in supporting AI initiatives. However, these are mostly instructor-led initiatives; the student is considered a passive recipient of knowledge. To inspire active learning, the ultimate goal of educating students, Pfeiffer and Goodstein (1983) support ensuring that students recognize the importance of fundamental AI values and their application to their personal lives and careers.

East (2016) suggests that AI modules should be engaging to students; use more images than text to convey meaning; incorporate games to immerse students into the content and to provide immediate and memorable feedback; and provide opportunities for students to practice and apply these concepts. Mobile learning is one approach to empower students to better learn and understand the values of academic integrity, but there is currently only one other mobile application that offers similar content (uomfair.info), and this information is not contextualized to the Canadian higher education landscape.

2.2 Mobile Learning

Mobile learning (m-learning) entails using mobile devices to deliver learning materials with integrated strategies to allow access to knowledge from anywhere at any time (Ally, 2004). M-learning or "education on the go," through devices such as phones and tablets, expands the boundaries of anytime, anywhere learning (Wu et al., 2012). As this is an emerging field, its full educational potential is untapped and best-practice guidelines for m-learning are still unknown and require formulation (Schmidt Hanbidge, Sanderson & Tin, 2015).

McGraw-Hill Education's (Aug 2016) report, *The Impact of Technology on College Student Study Habits*, surveyed 2,657 US higher education students and found that two-thirds (61%) of college students reported using their smartphones to study. Although mobile learning applications exist that were developed for monetization purposes through advertising revenue, and largely succeeded by gamifying the experience (see Duolingo or Khan Academy), few institutions explicitly support the use of mobile learning to address specific learning outcomes (Herrington & Herrington, 2007). The *New Media Consortium's Horizon Report* (Johnson et al., 2016) suggests that mobile learning has great potential to address many of the emerging trends in higher education, such as a growing focus on measuring learning and blended/hybrid learning environments. Mobile initiatives have the potential to transform learning in Canada by bridging the digital divide through augmented learning.

3. PROJECT CONTRIBUTIONS

Given that communication technology is rapidly changing information delivery and processing, the means by which AI content is delivered needs to keep pace with the best and most innovative ways to educate students. By providing visually stimulating and interactive content, as well as incorporating gamification elements to stimulate and motivate learners, we aim to appeal to students' desires to engage with content, while making this information readily available without being confined to a classroom site or a LMS. East (2016) insists, "all students take time and practice to become versed in academic codes and to understand academic culture" (p. 485), and this project solution will provide students this opportunity.

With the financial and administrative support from our university, developing the mobile *Foundations for Academic Success (FAS)* m-learning tool will allow us to make information available to students at their convenience, thereby acculturating them to the values held by the university before classes begin. Currently, our university has a mandatory tutorial for all incoming graduate students however, but technical restrictions make this material inaccessible until the first day of class. In addition, this platform does not easily track completion, making monitoring and following-up an arduous process. The proposed FAS tool not only will track module completion, but also has capacity to recognize effort and completion by issuing badges and certificates of completion. Once completed, the mobile application will be freely accessible for adoption to interested institutions to help alleviate common AI instructional challenges. Additional research from a user perspective is needed to discover the best strategies for maximizing m-learning (Schmidt Hanbidge, Sanderson & Tin, 2015). As advocates of mobile learning, we intend to enhance learning experiences rather than replace instructor and student interactions. Our dedication to helping learners better understand AI using mobile technology provides a unique opportunity to shape the project research framework.

4. PROPOSED METHODOLOGY

The FAS project meets objectives to develop strategies for enhancing student AI knowledge with innovative mobile technology to connect learners with timely, relevant multimedia content through six interactive modules. Our research study entails a mixed-method (quantitative and qualitative) non-experimental approach, including both pre- and post- tests, student questionnaires and tool testing. All data will be tracked using learning analytics to aid in iterative design of the mobile application. The mobile application will use ProProfs (http://www.proprofs.com/quiz-school/), a web–based service that allows educators to create and deliver online modules and assessments. Students achieving a passing grade in the modules earn an e-certificate, demonstrating AI competency. FAS tool testing will occur at multiple points to ensure quality and to enhance tool reliability. Contributing research activities (Table 1) include test groups to pilot the FAS tool. Following development of the modules, Focus Group A will review the content of lessons and quizzes. Test Group B will test the prototype model. Next, modules will be translated into Chinese and Test Group C will pilot test the tool. A final round of FAS tool testing (Test Group D) addresses all technical system challenges. A comparison student group (Control Group E) provides a benchmark against results with those who completed the AI modules.

Table 1. Research activities.

	Research Activities						
Testing Groups	Discussion Group	Pre-Test	AI Lessons	AI Quizzes	Final Quiz	Post Test	Questionnaire
Focus Group A: Review Lesson Content (N = 50)	X	O	X	X	X	O	O
Test Group B: Students Pilot Prototype (N = 150)	O	X	X	X	X	X	X
Test Group C: Chinese Translation (N = 100)	O	X	X	X	X	X	X
Test Group D: Final Trial (N = 150)	O	X	X	X	X	X	X
Control Group E: No Tool, only Pre-Post Test(N = 50)	O	X	O	X	X	X	X

All six AI modules will be comprised of the following instructional sequences:

- Definition of values and examples that demonstrate value interconnections (i.e. scenarios)
- Scenarios depicting diverse student life (i.e. cultural differences, peer pressure, time constraints)

• Multimodal tasks such as drag and drop, ordering of responses, videos and games
• Quizzes on all modules (i.e. true/false, multiple choice, fill in the blanks)
• Final test on all content testing integration of knowledge (i.e. badges and e-certificate)

First to fifth year undergraduate students will be recruited to participate in the study. Participants will use their personal smartphones, mobile devices or computers to access the modules.

5. CONCLUSION

Due to current LMS limitations, AI modules are not available in online formats before students arrive on campus. Through the design and testing of our proposed FAS tool, we aim to contribute to the scholarly discourse on m-learning and AI in higher education, while adding our own Canadian context. By offering open access resources to facilitate anytime, anywhere learning, higher education institutions benefit.

We envision multiple benefits to students and university instructors, including having a clear understanding of key aspects and values of AI, and, understanding of academic integrity transferred into their course work, fieldwork and ultimately, their workplace. AI resources will be accessible to all course instructors thus reducing the responsibility on instructors to develop and deliver AI information.

Demonstrated benefits for the learning community will be measured with pre-post outcome tests (and compared with control group test results) while experiences of mobile technology users will be investigated. It is here that we position our solution, envisioning a mobile learning experience that embraces the affordances offered by m-learning, while ensuring that the academic integrity platform solution we design enables successful implementation and dissemination of the FAS initiative to meet the emergent trends in higher education.

REFERENCES

Accessibility for Ontarians with Disabilities Act (AODA). (2005). Integrated accessibility standards regulation (IASR). Retrieved Oct 20, 2016, from https://accessontario.com/aoda/

Ally, M. (2004). Designing effective learning objects for distance education. In R. McGreal (Ed.), *Online education using learning objects* (pp. 87-97). London: Routledge Falmer.

Bertram Gallant, T. (2011). Building a culture of academic integrity: Based on the Magna online seminar, "Helping students learn from ethical failures" [White Paper]. Magna Publications, WI.

Boehm, P. J., Justice, M., & Weeks, S. (2009). Promoting academic integrity in higher education. *The Community College Enterprise,* 15(1), 45-61.

East, J. (2016). Educational responses to academic integrity. In Tracey Bretag's (Ed.) *Handbook of academic integrity,* (pp. 481-496). Springer, Singapore.

Fundamental Values Project. (2014). *International Centre for Academic Integrity.* Retrieved from http://www.academicintegrity.org/icai/resources-2.php

Glendinning, I. (2014). Responses to student plagiarism in higher education across Europe. *International Journal for Educational Integrity*, 10(1), 4-20.

Herrington, A. & Herrington, J. (2007 November). Authentic mobile learning in higher education. Paper presented at the *AARE International Educational Research Conference*, Fremantle, Western Australia.

Johnson, L., Adams Becker, S., Cummins, M., Estrada, V., Freeman, A., & Hall, C. (2016). *NMC Horizon Report: Higher Education Edition.* [Report]. Austin, Texas: The New Media Consortium. Retrieved from http://cdn.nmc.org/media/2016-nmc-horizon-report-he-EN.pdf

MacLeod, P.D. (2014). An exploration of faculty attitudes toward student dishonesty in selected Canadian universities. (Unpublished doctoral dissertation). University of Calgary, Alberta.

Schmidt Hanbidge, A., Sanderson, N., & Tin T. (2015). Using mobile technology to enhance undergraduate student information literacy skills: A Canadian case study. *IAFOR Journal of Education, Technology and Education Special Edition*, 3(2), 108 -118.

SPARK, (Student Paper and Academic Research Kit), York University. [Website]. What is Academic Integrity? Retrieved from http://www.yorku.ca/spark/academic_integrity/index.html

Wu, W. H., Wu., C. J., Chen, C. Y., Kao, H. Y., Lin, C. H., & Huang, S. H. (2012). Review of trends from mobile learning studies: A meta-analysis. *Computers and Education*, 59(2), 817-827.

USING TABLET AND ITUNESU AS INDIVIDUALIZED INSTRUCTION TOOLS

Libor Klubal, Katerina Kostolanyova and Vojtěch Gybas
University of Ostrava, Pedagogical Faculty
Frani Sramka 3, Ostrava, Czech Republic

ABSTRACT

The paper is aimed at the possibilities of the implementation of individualized instruction in a regular classroom using a tablet and the iTunesU tool. It compares the course of collective frontal instruction and individualized instruction. The results show that the tools make instruction more effective and help increase the students' motivation. The described method of individualization can be easily implemented in a regular class.

KEYWORDS

Tablet, individualized teaching, iTunesU.

1. INTRODUCTION

In the Czech education system, collective frontal instruction with the dominant position of the teacher is used extensively. According to annual reports of the Czech School Inspectorate, the above form of instruction is used mainly in upper primary schools and high schools. However, this form of instruction does not allow for the development of every student's individual skills as the majority of the students remain passive.

Individualized instruction is one of the forms of instruction which is aimed at the development of a child's creative abilities while respecting their needs (Průcha, Walterová, Mareš, 2003). The paper describes the practical realization of a class in which the iTunesU e-learning tool and the tablet are used in order to achieve an individualized approach in a regular class with a full classroom.

The Pedagogical dictionary defines individualization of instruction as "a way of differentiation of instruction where heterogeneous classrooms remain a basic social unit, and differentiation takes place at the inner, content and methodical levels, respecting the students' individual needs" (Průcha, Walterová, Mareš, 2003). Abroad, individualization is perceived in a similar manner. For instance, a study on the need for change in Norwegian schools states that "the individual instruction methods are an appropriate tool to push through changes in the yet uninvolved Norwegian schools" (Carlgren et al., 2006). Moreover, the study also stresses the need to set one's own pace of learning, which it refers to as "self-regulated work". In a regular class is customization of time one of the basic elements of individualization.

The aim of this paper is to compare two types of lessons and to compare the differences in the levels of knowledge acquired through the individualized approach in an experimental group and through the classic frontal approach in a control group, respectively.

2. IMPLEMENTATION OF TWO TYPES OF LEARNING

2.1 Realization of Class in Experimental Group

The described class was 45 minutes long and was attended by 27 12-13-year-old students. All of the students were from the same classroom (first grade of grammar school). The aim of the class was practicing simple equations.

Using the iTunesU tool, a course was created to be used in the class where each student was working with an iPad in the shared device mode. At the beginning of the class, the students were told how to operate the device. Afterward, they worked at their own pace. From then on, the teacher provided individual help to those students who needed it.

The first activity was practicing equations using the Algebra Touch application, in which the student is solving equations with the use of interactive tools – moving terms, distribution of terms, cancelling out terms. Working with the application, the students had to solve 10 equations, writing down only the problem and the solution.

The second activity was a written exercise when a problem in PDF form was inserted into the iTunesU tool. In this case, the students had to not only solve the problem alone, but also had to write the entire solution (including the proof) down in their notebooks. As a result, the tablet was only used to display the common assignment.

The final activity involved Orbit Integers, a game application which is used to practice integer calculations. The application is based on the maximum of 4 students competing against one another in solving problems involving addition and subtraction of integers. The quickness and correctness of the calculation influences the speed of a car on the racetrack. Using internet connection, the application can put as many as four students on one racetrack. The students were divided into the competing groups on the basis of the previous results. This activity develops general math skills of students that are necessary and solving equations.

2.2 Description of Course of Class in Experimental Group and Indentified Observations

The course of the class was monitored by the teacher and a researcher. While the teacher was doing their usual work, the researcher was only there to monitor the students' and teacher's activities and did not become involved in them.

At the beginning of the class, the teacher handed the students tablets, through which they then logged into the iTunesU course using the QR code they saw on the projection screen. The teacher explained to the students what the class would look like, how to work with iTunesU and defined the rules for writing in the notebook. This part took 4 minutes. In two cases, the teacher had to help the students to reload the QR code in order to log into the course.

The students began to solve the 10 equations using the Algebra Touch application. The teacher had reminded the students that they need to write down the problem and the solution in their notebook and then monitored their problem-solving process. The teacher had to help five students with the application as they did not understand the problem-solving process. The remaining students did not find it problematic. However, it was evident that in some case the students helped each other with the application. The activity of the students made transition to the second part of the class easy to monitor. The student that had finished solving the problems in the Algebra Touch application started to write down in the notebook, i.e. stopped using the tablet. It also signalled to the teacher that they could start to evaluate the Part 1 tasks. Moreover, the teacher knew which students had difficulty solving the task and therefore could help them. The transition from Task 1 to Task 2 took 13 to 22 minutes from the beginning of the class.

The second part of the class was regular. The students were writing solutions in their notebooks while teacher was helping them, highlighting errors, telling them to do a proof, etc. Two students realized that they could enter the task into the Algebra Touch application and verify the result. The remaining students then followed their example. As each student used the application different number of times to verify their results, the exact number of students who did so could not be determined. However, it was less than 10 students.

With 26 minutes having elapsed from the class, first students proceeded to the third part of the class. The teacher supervised the division of students into groups. The entire process was natural based on the order in which the students finished the second part of the class. As a result, students with similar mathematical skills were placed in the same group. As the students had already been familiar with the game, they did not need any help. With 35 minutes having elapsed from the class, as many as 19 students were competing. At that time, the teacher checked up on the remaining eight students, helped them finish the current task and allowed them to proceed to the final activity. 6 of those 8 students had 1-2 problems left to solve to complete the entire set, while the other two 3-4. With 39 minutes having elapsed, all of the students were playing the mathematical game.

With two minutes remaining, the teacher ended the game, repeated the basic rules of solving simple equations and demonstrated them on examples in the Algebra Touch application.

2.3 Realization of Class in Control Group

The control group consisted of 26 students who attended a parallel classroom in a grammar school. Again, the students were 12 to 13 years old. The class was based on the regular frontal scheme. The teacher had prepared a set of equations. To maximize similar content, the equations were generated using the Algebra Touch application. The teacher showed the entire set to the students using a projector. Following the instructions, the students started to solve the equations, writing solutions in their notebooks, highlighting the result and the proof. The teacher helped the students individually. After the students had finished the above task, they were handed a task similar to that of the experimental group. At the end of the class, the students were handed tablets on which they played the Orbit Integers game.

2.4 Description of Course of Class in Control Group and Indentified Observations

The course of the class was monitored by the teacher and a researcher. While the teacher was doing their usual work, the researcher was only there to monitor the students' and teacher's activities and did not become involved in them.

At the beginning of the class, the teacher told the students the objective of the class – to practice solving simple linear equations. The first part of the class started 3 minutes later with the teacher showing the 10 equations using a projector and giving the students instructions. The students solved the individual problems on the blackboard while discussing it with the teacher. Therefore, the teacher paid attention only to the student at the blackboard. Half of the students solved the problems by themselves and then compared their result with the result on the blackboard. Only few of the students paid attention to the teacher. This activity ended 29 minutes into the class.

In the second part of the class, the students solved the tasks on the worksheet the teacher had handed to them. The teacher helped the students individually. The first students finished the tasks 42 minutes into the class. As there were only 3 minutes left, the teacher decided not to proceed to the following activity.

With 43 minutes having elapsed from the class, the teacher learned (by asking the students) that 6 students solved all of the problems, 8 students had 1-2 problems left to solve, 10 students had 3-4 problems left and 2 students had more than 5 problems left to solve. To conclude the class, the teacher repeated the basic rules of solving simple equations using the Algebra Touch application.

3. DISCUSSING RESULTS

The class in which tablets and the iTunesU were used showed optimal distribution of activities, therefore making better use of time which resulted in the students solving more problems. Moreover, the students could practice their skills by playing a game, which the other students could not due to time constraints. Both the researcher and the teacher agreed that the students in the experimental group were more motivated than those in the control group. But this is only a subjective opinion of a teacher and researcher.

Table 1. Comparing the number of solved problems in groups.

Number of solved problems	**Experimental Group**		**Control Group**	
	Number	Share of total	Number	Share of total
11	19	70.37 %	6	23.08 %
9–10	6	22.22 %	8	30.77 %
7–8	2	7.41 %	10	38.46 %
Less than 7	0	0 %	2	7.69 %

4. CONCLUSION

The implementation of individualized instruction in a regular classroom with a great number of students is usually difficult. The iTunesU tool makes it possible to replace the dominant position of the teacher with the students working individually. The mobile touch device not only guides the student through the curriculum, but is also used for special activities. Another advantage of the described solution is natural division of students into groups based on their skills. Such division is necessary, especially during competition.

The content of the described class is not much different from the content of the regular frontal class. However, due to the implementation of the elements of individualized instruction, more students are involved in the class. The experiment also showed that the teacher still plays an important role – they had to instruct the students on how to work with the application, help the students solve some of the problems and modify the problem in order to make it easier for the weaker students.

REFERENCES

Carlgren, I., Klette, K., Mýrdal, S., Schnack, K. & Simola, H. 2006, "Changes in Nordic teaching practices: From individualised teaching to the teaching of individuals", Scandinavian Journal of Educational Research, vol. 50, no. 3, pp. 301-326.

Moura, A. 2015, "iPad program in K-12 education: Pilot year" in Handbook of Mobile Teaching and Learning, pp. 601-616.

Outhwaite, L.A., Gulliford, A. & Pitchford, N.J. 2017, "Closing the gap: Efficacy of a tablet intervention to support the development of early mathematical skills in UK primary school children", Computers and Education, vol. 108, pp. 43-58.

Park, Y. 2011, "A pedagogical framework for mobile learning: Categorizing educational applications of mobile technologies into four types", International Review of Research in Open and Distance Learning, vol. 12, no. 2, pp. 78-102.

Průcha, J., Walterová, E., Mareš, J.. *Pedagogický slovník*. 7., aktualiz. a rozš. vyd. Praha: Portál, 2013. ISBN 978-80-262-0403-9.

DUOLIBRAS - AN APP USED FOR TEACHING-LEARNING OF LIBRAS

Erick Nilson Sodré Filho, Lucas Gomes dos Santos, Aristóteles Esteves Marçal da Silva, Nidyana Rodrigues Miranda de Oliveira e Oliveira, Pedro Kislansky and Marisete da Silva Andrade
Faculdade Dom Pedro II, Rua Miguel Calmon,S/N, Praça da Inglaterra. Comércio. Salvador, Bahia, Brazil

ABSTRACT

This paper describes an application for learning Libras (Brazilian Sign Language). The application was developed as an initiative of a group of students and teachers in order to promote innovative ideas. The product is for people that are not hearing impaired as an important linguistic tool for social inclusion. We developed the application on android platform because of its popularity. As this is an work is in progress, we didn't do formal tests yet. However, preliminary tests reveal optimistic results and good acceptance.

KEYWORDS

Libras, mobile learning, android, and hearing impaired.

1. INTRODUCTION

The Brazilian Sign Language, also known as ***Libras***, is an important linguistic tool for social inclusion of the hearing impaired into the society. Beyond that, the knowledge of the social, historical, structural and legal aspects of this tool are crucial for improving better society awareness. Concerning the Libras legal aspects, the actual legislation is the federal law 10.436/2002 establishing *Libras* as an official language.

Boninho explains that after the implementation of the federal law, teaching *Libras* became mandatory in all Brazilian schools. She adds a short explanation how the sign language works through combination of hand movements and reference points.

Brito et al. show that Libras was created, specially, for non- hearing impaired people and it is an important tool for communication between them and the hearing impaired population. He also alleges that most students have difficulties for learning Libras, reinforcing the need for applications that can improve the learning of Libras.

This paper describes an ongoing project of an information systems undergraduate course. The faculty is part of the Unidom group and is located in Salvador-Bahia Brazil. The discipline aims to enable students how to build mobile applications and develop innovative ideas.

This work (DuoLibras project) was inspired by the difficulties experienced by Libras students and the need for a project for the above discipline. The application was developed for android platform. The environment is game-like and enables the user to test his expertise on Libras. The application focuses on simplicity and on a learning modality called m-learning. Because it is an ongoing project, it has been tested only inside a classroom with the students of the discipline. The class response was very promisingly and generated the desire for continuing the project as a final graduation work.

Besides this introduction, this paper has other four sections. Section 2 discusses the aspects related to m-learning. Section 3 presents some related works. Section 4 shows the application. Section 5 presents the conclusion of this work and directions for further research.

2. M-LEARNING

M-learning or Mobile Learning is a learning modality that opens new opportunities for the future. It uses mobile application for leaning purposes allowing people to have access to high level education in places where schools and teachers can't be found and education is still considered a privilege of some individual (Heflin et al. 2017; Li 2017).

The Mobile Learning concept has been promoting the researchers' interest all over the world, specially because its organization capacity, its ability for arising a sense of responsibility and for aiding and encouraging new learning-teaching practices (M. Glasemann, Anne Marie Kanstrup 2010). Furthermore, Mobile Learning is suitable for educational processes which have high levels of interactivity, content integration and the easiness of been able to teach-learn anywhere (Ched et al. 2002).

Therefore, technology as general and m-learning specifically represent much more than mastering a language. It is also an instrument used for improving life and learning conditions. Furthermore, the technology and its different variations aim to facilitate the daily life of people. The continuous growth in mobile technology usage has initiated new ways of socio-cultural interaction by narrowing social barriers. The amount of mobile technologies Falibras is a software that enable the user to speak into it so the system translates it for gesture signs and their good acceptance by the students are offering new pedagogical perspectives (Moura 2010).

3. RELATED WORKS

This section presents some works related to mobile learning and sign language.

Falibras is a software that enable the user to speak into it so the system translates it for gesture signs. This interaction allows people that can hear communicate with people that are hearing impaired (Brito et al. 2012). The Falibras messenger uses the Falibras software in order to create a translator from written Portuguese to Libras. It adapts an instant messaging communicator which is integrated to a social network called Telegram. The software enables people to communicate through an adapted interface (Brito et al. 2015).

The Hand Talk application is a translator from written Portuguese to Libras. It is available for both Android and IOS platform. The company responsible for the application received an international award as the world's best social application. The program simulates a character called Hugo which brings an animated and friendly interface for the user (Anon 2017a).

The eSIGN Avatar goes to the next level. Using 3D animation, the system input is a natural language which the system splits it into tokens, hence translates each word which the 3D Avatar animates with sign gestures. The signs are represented by VGuido animation technology

The papers abovementioned describe their efforts for trying to create discrete ways for communication between people who hear and people that do not. The DuoLibras is a project that aims at teaching sign language to people that are not hearing impaired. The idea is to promote people inclusion into the world of hearing impaired.

4. DUOLIBRAS

DuoLibras is simulation software for Brazilian sign language. It was developed for Android platform with native resources. The software tries to create an easy-learning environment where the user can answer to questions based on pre-defined categories, the time is measured and the software records the result and the time spent.

Figure 1 shows the start screen. Here, the participant has to input his name and choose the category he want to play. If he wants to play with substantives, pronouns or verbs.

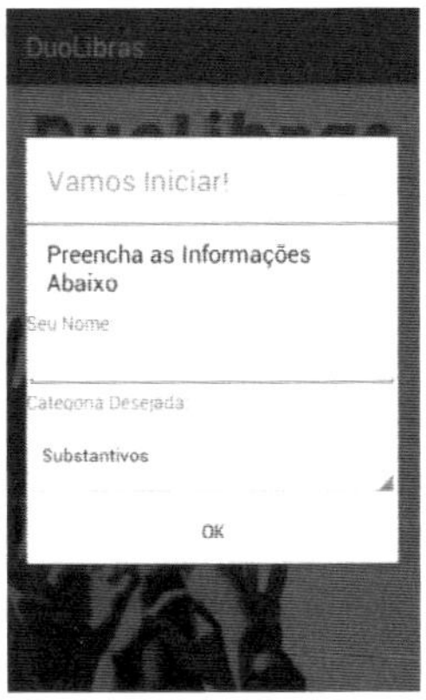

Figure 1. Start screen.

Figure 2 shows the main screen and the history screen. The first has the application's menu. Through it the user can start the simulation, see the simulations' history, know more about the application and finally to exit from the program. The second shows the simulations' history with basic information, such as the participant's name, the number of hits and mistakes, time spent, the date and time and the category chosen by the participant.

Figure 2. The main and simulations' history screen of DuoLibras.

After starting the application and filling basic information, the application shows questions and answers related to the category chosen by the user. The questions are formatted as text and the answers are images that represent sign language (Figure 3). The figure above also shows the result screen. This screen has similar information to the simulations' history screen. The only difference is the percentage of correct answers.

While the player answers the question the application controls the time and the amount of hits and mistakes made by him. After he ended the game the application shows the result with all the information already mentioned before. The categories and images were chosen according to program content described at the teaching plan of the Libras discipline of the Dom Pedro II College.

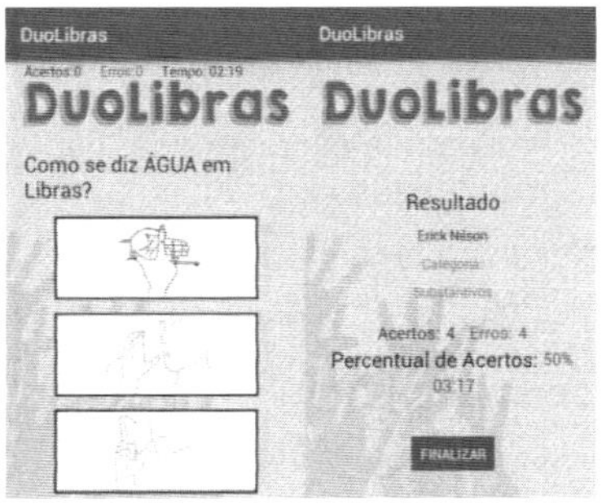

Figure 3. The question-answer and result screen of DuoLibras.

5. PRELIMINARY TESTS

It is an applied research since it aims to work with knowledge from a practical perspective. It is based on the experiences of the interactive processes of teaching-learning and the richness in the sharing of knowledge.

No formal tests were made so far; however, we did an informal test. We asked ten students to use the application for fifteen minutes after a brief explanation about the software. The preliminary results were optimistic. All students liked the simplicity of the application and said that it was very easy to use and understand. Eight said that will continue to use it.

6. CONCLUSION AND FUTURE WORK

There is no doubt that this is a vital research area nowadays. The end of the social barriers between people with disabilities and those who do not have it is imperative. The DuoLibras is an initiative made by students who desire for social changing. It is also a work in progress and already inspired other students to continue the project.

The project is promising and some guidelines were set for future work. The next steps should be to align the Libras discipline with the software content, so it can be helpful during the classes and engage more people with hearing disability to help the project with their unique perspective. Moreover, a better set of tests should be done, especially usability and unity tests.

As said before, this paper represents a work in progress, albeit the preliminary results are positive, still we have much work to do. The students engagement with projects that have social components should be encourage. This contributes for improving the student interest and shows him, in practice, the information technology's potential for changing social reality. The impact on students is surprisingly good and strengths the ties among students, teachers, community and school or college.

ACKNOWLEDGEMENT

We wish to thank the Dom Pedro II College for the technological support and all teachers and people who believed in this work.

REFERENCES

Anon, 2017a. Hand Talk. Available at: http://www.handtalk.me [Accessed January 10, 2017]

Anon, 2002. LEI Nº 10.436, DE 24 DE ABRIL DE 2002. *Presidência da República Casa Civil Subchefia para Assuntos Jurídicos*. Available at: http://www.planalto.gov.br/ccivil_03/leis/2002/L10436.htm [Accessed February 5, 2017].

Anon, 2017b. UNIDOM. Available at: http://unidom.com.br/salvador/ [Accessed February 10, 2017].

Anon, 2017c. Virtual Guido on the Internet. Available at: http://www.sign-lang.uni-hamburg.de/esign/annualreport2003/vguido_internet.html [Accessed February 1, 2017].

Bonino, R., 2007. Os sotaques dos sinais. *Revista Língua Portuguesa*, pp.28–33.

Brito, P. et al., 2012. FALIBRAS: Uma Ferramenta Flexível para Promover Acessibilidade de Pessoas Surdas. *Nuevas Ideas en Informatica Educativa*, (December), pp.87–96.

Brito, P.H. et al., 2015. Tradutor Português-Libras Adaptado a um Comunicador de Mensagens Instantâneas. *Nuevas Ideas en Informática Educativa TISE*, pp.371–378.

Ched, Y. et al., 2002. A Mobile Scaffolding-Aid-Based Bird-Watching Learning System. *IEEE International Workshop on Wireless and Mobile Technologies in Education*, pp.15–22.

Heflin, H., Shewmaker, J. & Nguyen, J., 2017. Impact of mobile technology on student attitudes, engagement, and learning. *Computers & Education*, 107, pp.91–99. Available at: http://www.sciencedirect.com.ezproxy1.library.usyd.edu.au/science/article/pii/S0360131517300064.

Li, X., 2017. Students' acceptance of mobile learning: An empirical study based on blackboard mobile learn. *International Journal of Interdisciplinary Telecommunications and Networking*, 9(1), pp.52–69.

M. Glasemann, Anne Marie Kanstrup, T.R., 2010. Design and Exploration of a Mobile Game Scenario in a Diabetic Youth Camp. In *IADIS International Conference Mobile Learning*. Porto.

Moura, A.M.C., 2010. *Apropriação do telemóvel como ferramenta de mediação em mobile learning: estudos de caso em contexto educativo*. Universidade do Minho. Available at: http://repositorium.sdum.uminho.pt/handle/1822/13183.

EDUCATORS ADOPTING M-LEARNING: IS IT SUSTAINABLE IN HIGHER EDUCATION?

Nicole Sanderson and Alice Schmidt Hanbidge
Renison University College / University of Waterloo
Waterloo, Ontario, Canada

ABSTRACT

Effectively integrating m-learning into higher education necessitates consideration for both student and educator adoption factors. Data collected from 309 Canadian university participants in a Mobile Information Literacy (MIL) research study identified specific student m-learning adoption factors and substantiated those in the literature (Navarro et al., 2016; Wang et al., 2009). Recent m-learning studies (Abu-Al-Aisb, & Love, 2013; Ally & Blásque, 2014) indicated that institutional and educator support is needed to support student m-learning adoption. Our research findings supported this and inspired the researchers to establish a new study to investigate educator attitudes toward integrating m-learning in their teaching and to understand how institutions can support such individuals. Study results intend to support educators focused on pedagogical transformation, to successfully integrate sustainable m-learning in their physical and virtual classrooms.

KEYWORDS

Pedagogy, mobile learning, educator role, institution support, adoption, sustainability.

1. INTRODUCTION

Research literature examining m-learning in post-secondary education predicts it will play an important role in the future of student learning and suggests that "education on the go", utilizing mobile devices such as mobile phones and tablets, expands the boundaries of anytime, anywhere learning (Saunders, 2012; Wu et al., 2012). M-learning, defined as the use of mobile devices to deliver electronic learning materials with built in learning strategies has been introduced and incorporated into the pedagogical repertoire of many educators globally from a variety of academic disciplines (Cheon, 2012; Keengwe, 2014; Schmidt Hanbidge et.al, 2015). A rich body of literature has emerged that utilizes various adoption models of technology to examine and identify students' adoption factors of m-learning (Koole, 2009; Navarro et al., 2016). A study conducted by Schmidt Hanbidge et al. (under review) tested an Information Literacy course (http://bit.ly/milmodules) with Canadian university students that substantiate the student adoption factors outlined in the literature. Key student adoption factors included personal innovativeness of students, ICT literacy, self-management of learning, previous computer experience, ICT anxiety, and confirmation and satisfaction.

Based on recent literature focused on student adoption factors and integration of m-learning into higher education (Cheon, 2013; Keengwe, 2014; Navarro, 2016) and findings from our Mobile Information Literacy (MIL) research study, is a call to examine the role that educators play in m-learning adoption. This call motivated the authors of this paper to appraise the current literature focusing on the role of educators in m-learning adoption and reflect upon the following questions:

- How are educators currently implementing m-learning into higher education?
- What are the challenges of m-learning implementation for university educators?
- What pedagogical and technical institutional supports are available for educators implementing m-learning?
- What is the sustainability of m-learning in higher education?

A notable lack of research focuses on pedagogical transformation and sustainable integration of m-learning into formal education contexts supporting educators and researchers collaborative efforts. Our study will examine how educators implement m-learning into their courses, identify the challenges they face while doing so, highlight the pedagogical and technical supports available to them, identify additional supports needed and reflect upon the sustainability of such m-learning experiences in a Canadian university. Our research will contribute to this gap in the literature and will indicate new directions for developing and enhancing sustainable mobile technology efforts in higher education.

2. HOW CAN M-LEARNING BE INTEGRATED INTO HIGHER EDUCATION?

Al-Emran et al. (2016) assert that Arab Gulf countries take on leadership roles in m-learning research in higher education and surveyed attitudes of fifty-four educators from five Arab Gulf universities towards m-learning in higher education to determine their intentions of using m-learning in educational contexts. Findings indicate that most educators had positive attitudes towards m-learning notwithstanding differences in age, gender, academic rank, academic experience and smartphone ownership. Conclusions suggest that m-learning can be adopted by a variety of educators in higher education. These findings are reassuring for those individuals advocating for the inclusion of m-learning in Canadian higher education, as they suggest the possibility of a positive adoption of this pedagogical approach to teaching and learning.

Lindsay (2016) examined the integration of m-learning by New Zealand educators and contends it is important for educators to consider how they incorporate m-learning into their pedagogy to ensure that m-learning teaching is student-centred, authentic, higher order, and collaborative. Lindsay outlined five characteristics of design approach to m-learning: *associative* (tool substitution to augment existing activities), *individual constructive*, *collaborative* (e.g. augmented reality/game-based learning), *situative* (authentic activities in "real" settings), and *informal* (outside formal education). She contends the pedagogical approaches predominately used by educators were substitutions and augmentations, meaning utilizing technology as a direct tool substitution rather than a transformative approach to teaching and learning. We believe it is important to understand how educators in university institutions incorporate m-learning into their teaching, what design approaches, and what institutional supports are most successful in higher education.

2.1 Challenges of m-learning implementation in higher education

"Ease of use" of mobile devices based on the size of screens and limited information displayed were identified as posing technological challenges for m-learning (Schmidt Hanbidge et. al, 2015). A review of 168 journal articles published between 2006-2014 examined mobile usability showed that only about fifty percent of the m-learning applications performed usability tests (Navarro et al., 2016). These authors recommend that implementation of a pedagogical usability evaluation framework for m-learning. Other studies identified the importance of student adoption of m-learning (Navarro et al., 2016; Wang et al., 2009) while Roblyer et al. (2010) report on differences between students and educators use of technology.

Shadle et al. (2013) from BOISE University identify the importance of "Centers for Teaching & Learning" in bringing together interdisciplinary faculty groups to discuss their experiences with m-learning and their roles in encouraging educators to conduct action research of their teaching. They stressed the importance of providing the required hardware and software needed to access affordable data plans and WIFI. They also stress the importance of weeklong m-learning institutes and mobile days for providing technological support for both students and instructors. Schmidt Hanbidge et al. (2015) and Shadle (2013) illustrate the benefits of librarians and post-secondary educators working together to establish student digital literacy fluency.

While extensive m-learning research has been completed, there has been limited research about educators and m-learning in higher education settings. Institutional support needs to include m-learning in their academic center programs (Teo, 2009). Research conducted on teacher knowledge about using technology as a tool for learning has not yet been adequately explored (Tai & Ting, 2011). We will explore methods to scale up information literacy innovations with educator buy-in to sustain m-learning. We suggest that the role of educators and their openness to explore technology may determine factors about the sustainability of mobile learning in higher education. Huang et al. (2002) contend that the successful integration of technology-facilitated learning depended on teacher attitudes and acceptance.

Our university, located in southern Ontario, Canada has over 3,000 full time faculty and sessional educators and over 35,000 students in various disciplines, heavily focused on mathematics, engineering, health-related fields and arts and humanities. Within our institution, there are supports available to educators, through the *Centre for Teaching with Excellence*, to enhance teaching practices with the learning management system (LMS) and in traditional classroom spaces. However, there is a notable gap in technical and instructional support for teaching with mobile technology that this study aims to address.

2.2 Information literacy integration

In higher education, an apparent gap exists between the information literacy skills that educators expect students to have and those that students actually possess. We advocate that students learn and enhance these skills early in university through an information literacy micro course we developed (http://bit.ly/milmodules) to access m-learning technology. Informally, students accessed information literacy lessons at their leisure and learning was reinforced through practice quizzes. Helping student learners improve their information skills using mobile device was a key outcome of this research study along with developing meaningful and significant contributions to the emerging knowledge in the field of m-learning.

Over the past two years, over 300 students participated in a mobile information literacy course. In the mixed methods (quantitative and qualitative) project, participants completed thirteen online information literacy lessons and quizzes, pre- and post-tests and a questionnaire. Preliminary results indicate that 72% of students maintained or increased their information literacy skills.

Our study confirmed when access to necessary tools is provided, students will use m-learning. Educational institutions should be aware of the student user implications and the consideration of the role of faculty members in such initiatives. As our study focused on student introduction to mobile learning for the specific purpose of developing information literacy knowledge and skills, our data positions us to identify trends in higher education that necessitate further exploration. Understanding student m-learning adoption preferences (Schmidt Hanbidge et al., In Press) helped to frame the next stage of the project. Effective use of technology in the curriculum requires integration of learner characteristics, use of the technology to deliver a sound experience, sound pedagogical curriculum content, and educator and institutional support that integrate these aspects.

Educators play an important role in integrating technology into the learning environment. From our MIL study, it became clear that most educators did not have the experience or the comfort level to independently integrate mobile learning into teaching. We need better understanding about relevant factors that affect their adoption practices in their classrooms. Educators expressed interest in learning, but were not sure of the next steps to take to adopt m-learning. Institutional m-learning technical support and professional development for faculty members is necessary (Gülbahar et al., 2013; Schaffhauser, 2016). Although our university is innovative in many ways, the researchers believe that important institutional support for educators to adopt m-learning may be lacking.

2.3 Next stage: Educator m-learning project methodology

Our study will explore educator adoption of mobile technology into higher education with a focus on educator perceptions about their classroom experiences. This study will incorporate a mixed method approach, collecting both quantitative and qualitative information. A three-phase research design will be implemented.

Phase 1: An in-depth literature review will be conducted to locate and examine resources that currently exist to enhance teaching with mobile technology on campus or virtual spaces.

Phase 2: Educators across our university will be surveyed to determine whether they feel prepared to utilize m-learning in their on campus and virtual classrooms. Semi-structured individual interviews will be conducted to provide input on developing resources to encourage educator adoption, to provide support and tools (both technical and training) to aid in enhancing integration of mobile learning. All educators at the university will be invited to complete online questionnaires that include demographics data and attitudes about integrating m-learning into student learning experiences with mobile devices. Additionally, semi-structured interviews with 10 educators that participated in the original MIL study will determine whether they plan to continue using the information literacy lessons and content in their individual courses. Interviews with faculty from the Center for Teaching Excellence will add further institutional information. All interviews will be recorded, transcribed and analyzed for key themes and trends.

Phase 3: Data analysis identifying themes and trends will occur; subsequently project findings and recommendations will be disseminated.

Based on our earlier project, we intend to explore how to scale up and sustain our information literacy mobile innovation. The research study will consider how this Canadian university and its educators might adopt and sustain this learning innovation.

3. CONCLUSION

Contextual research must be conducted to explore whether Canadian educator experiences differ significantly from their global peers in sharing positive attitudes towards m-learning. Building on our previous research, our new study purports to focus on the pedagogical transformation and sustainable integration of m-learning into higher education contexts with an aim to support educators and researchers collaborative efforts. We will explore how to 'scale up' and sustain our information literacy mobile innovation.

REFERENCES

Abu-Al-Aisb, A., & Love, S., 2013. Factors Influencing Students' Acceptance in M-Learning: An Investigation in Higher Education. *The International Review of Research in Open and Distance Education*, Vol. 14, No. 5, pp. 82-107.

Al-Emran, M., Elsherif, H.M., & Shaalam. K. , 2016. Investigating Attitudes towards the use of Mobile Learning in Higher Education. *Computers in Human Behavior*, Vol. 56, pp. 93-102.

Ally, M. & Prieto-Blázquez, J., 2014. What is the Future of Mobile Learning in Education? [Special Section]. *Revista de Universidad y Socierdad del Conocimiento*. Vol.11, No. 1, pp. 142-155.

Cheon, J., et al., 2012. An Investigation of Mobile Learning Readiness in Higher Education Based on the Theory of Planned Behaviour. *Computers & Education*, Vol. 59, pp. 1054-1064.

Huang, H.M., 2002. Towards Constructivism for Adult Learners in Online Learning Environments. *British Journal of Educational Technology*, Vol. 33, No. 1, pp. 27-37.

Keengwe, J., & Bhargava, M., 2014. Mobile Learning and Integration of Mobile Technologies in Education. *Education and Information Technologies,* Vol. 19, pp. 737-746.

Koole. M.L. (2009). A Model for Framing Mobile Learning. In: M. Ally, ed., *Empowering Learners and Educators with Mobile Learning.* Athabasca, AB: Athabasca University Press, pp. 25-47.

Lindsay, L., 2016. Transformation of Teacher Practice using Mobile Technology with One-to-One Classes: M-Learning Pedagogical Approaches. *British Journal of Educational Technology,* Vol. 47, No. 5, pp. 883-892.

Navarro, C.X., et al., 2016. Framework to Evaluate M-Learning Systems: A Technological and Pedagogical Approach. *IEEE Revista Iberoamericana de Tecnologias del Aprendizaje,* Vol. 11, No.1, pp. 33-40.

Saunders, L., 2012. Faculty Perspectives on Information Literacy as a Student Learning Outcome. *The Journal of Academic Librarianship,* Vol. 38, No. 4, pp. 226–236.

Schmidt Hanbidge, A., Sanderson, N., & Tin, T. 2015. Using Mobile Technology to Enhance Undergraduate Student Digital InformationLiteracy Skills: A Canadian Case Study. *IAFOR Journal of Education*, Vol. 3, No. 2, pp. 108-121. http://iafor.org/archives/journals/education/iafor-education-journal-special-edition-2015.pdf

Schmidt Hanbidge, A., Sanderson, N., & Tin, T., In press. Student Learner Characteristics and Adoption of M-Learning: Are We Effectively Supporting Students? In: M. Ally, ed., *The International Handbook of Mobile and Ubiquitous Learning.*

Shadle, S., et al., 2013. *Leading a Multiple Project Mobile Learning Initiative.* Louisville, CO: EDUCAUSE Centre for Applied Research. Retrieved from http://www.educause.edu/ecar.

Schaffhauser, D., 2016. *Report: Evidence of Tech Use forLlearning in Classrooms Scanty. AdvancedED,* Tempe, AZ.

Tai, Y., & Ting, Y.L., 2011. Adoption of Mobile Technology for Language Learning: Teacher Attitudes and Challenges. *The JALT CALL Journal,* Vol. 7, No. 1, pp. 3-18.

Teo, T., 2009. Modelling Technology Acceptance in Education: A Study of Pre-Service Teachers. *Computers & Education,* Vol. 52, No. 2, pp. 302-312. http://dx.doi.rg/10.1016/j.compedu.200.08.006

Wang, Y., et al., 2009. Investigating the Determinants of Age and Gender Differences in the Acceptance of Mobile Learning. *British Journal of Educational Technology,* Vol. 40, No. 1, pp. 92-118.

Wu, W.H., Wu, Y.C.J., Chen, C.Y., Kao, H.Y., Lin, S.H., & Huang, S.H., 2012. Review of Trends from Mobile Learning Studies: A Meta-Analysis. *Computers and Education,* Vol. 59, No. 2, pp. 817-827.

M-KINYARWANDA: PROMOTING AUTONOMOUS LANGUAGE LEARNING THROUGH A ROBUST MOBILE APPLICATION

Emmanuel Bikorimana, Joachim Rutayisire, Mwana Said Omar and Yi Sun
Graduate School of Information Technology, Kobe Institute of Computing
Kobe, Japan

ABSTRACT

Kinyarwanda, the national official language used by the population of Rwanda, was greatly affected by the tragic history that faced the country. The 13th annual national dialogue held at Kigali from 21st to 22nd December 2015, recommended the government of Rwanda, to put in place all measures to enhance and maintain the above mentioned language. This language, Kinyarwanda, holds the national identity and culture heritage values for the country, since its existence. This study proposes M-Kinyarwanda, an autonomous Mobile language learning application that will integrate multimedia techniques to teach and learn Kinyarwanda, in order to improve the efficiency in the language. The design and development of this mobile learning application will apply the prototype software development lifecycle approach, which requires more user involvement to allow them to see and interact with the prototype for better and more complete feedback and specifications. To measure the success of the developed system, evaluation will be carried out in the lab and expert-walk-through. Also, system field-testing will be conducted. We hope that M-Kinyarwanda will increase the motivation and efficiency of Kinyarwanda language learners, no matter where they are and when.

KEYWORDS

M-learning; Kinyarwanda Learning system; Mobile Assisted Language Learning; Autonomous Language Learning; E- learning.

1. INTRODUCTION

The Influence of English in the globalization movement (Rurangirwa 2012), and the fact that African languages are said to be neglected (Jordan 2013) , lead to the inefficiency in African languages (Herman M. Batibo 2005). Hence, Africa needs to promote African languages to enhance and safeguard the cultural and linguistic heritage of the continent, otherwise it will be threatened and perhaps it will be dissolved (Rurangirwa 2012).

From the above perspectives, Rwanda, a country located in central east Africa with a population around 11 million (National Institute of Statistics Rwanda 2016), where Kinyarwanda is the national and official language, faced a tragic history (Block 1994) that forced a considerable number of its citizens to leave the country and look for shelter in other countries. It was argued that language is always in the process of change, and when speakers of what was once the same language are separated by time and space, their pronunciation, vocabulary and syntax are likely to change in different ways (Wolfson 1989).

Actually, four million Rwandans who were repatriated after the 1994 liberation war, affected communication which was stable in Kinyarwanda before, and began to show features of a number of foreign languages brought into the country by the former Rwandan refugees (Habyarimana 2005).

Since then, there appeared varieties of sounds in Kinyarwanda because; only older people had kept their mother tongue as it was before they fled the country and their children either shifted from Kinyarwanda or learnt other languages, or spoke a little Kinyarwanda mixed with foreign languages they had already learnt abroad. In addition, from the 2015 reports, more than 300,000 citizens of Rwanda (International Organization for Migration 2016), lived outside their country of origin. This indicates that the Kinyarwanda language will remain affected, as long as those citizens living outside the country do not have any way through which they can learn or improve their national language.

Furthermore, the high number of Kinyarwanda speakers, around twenty five million (Drame & Paepcke 2010), including those beyond current borders in Democratic Republic of Congo, Uganda and Tanzania, raises the need to develop this language to improve its efficiency.

To assist those who do not have access to Rwandan education system, where Kinyarwanda is taught, we propose M-Kinyarwanda, an autonomous Mobile language learning system that is designed to incorporate multimedia technology. The goal is to provide tutorial services that support and motivate this language learning. We believe that the system will improve learners' motivation for Kinyarwanda learning, and by doing so, it will positively affect autonomous learning, and increase proficiency in Kinyarwanda.

2. OBJECTIVES

The main objectives of this study are:

1. To develop an autonomous & robust mobile language learning app that applies multimedia techniques;
2. To help learners to improve Kinyarwanda language proficiency from anywhere, anytime.

3. AUTONOMOUS LANGUAGE-LEARNING THEORIES

Learner's autonomy, as being the pre-requisite of productive learning (Paracha et al. 2009), has been an area of considerable research interest over the past decades (Dickinson 1995) (Esch 1994) (Godwin-jones 2011). It is a defining characteristic of all sustained learning that attains long-term success (Collentine et al. 2011) and principally an issue of students taking greater control over the content and methods of learning (Collentine et al. 2011). Autonomous Technology-Assisted Language Learning refers to (a) the development and use of technological tools to facilitate language learning, and (b) research on the development, use, and effects of such tools for language teaching and learning (Benson 2012). In recommending autonomy to learners, we assume that taking an active, independent attitude to learning and independently undertaking a learning task, is beneficial to learning; and that somehow, personal involvement in decision making leads to more effective learning (Dickinson 1995).

4. MOBILE APPLICATION FOR LANGUAGE LEARNING

Mobile applications (mobile apps) are software programs designed to run on mobile platforms such as Android (Google), iOS (Apple) and or Windows. According to (Son 2016), language learning applications are defined as applications dedicated to the learning (and teaching) of languages which can be used in and out of the language classroom. These applications can be developed as native apps, web apps and hybrid apps. He (Son 2016) further mentioned that these are Instructional apps, which are explicitly designed with language learning and teaching in mind.

5. THE ADOPTED DESIGN AND DEVELOPMENT APPROACHES

M-Kinyarwanda is expected to be a tool that will focus on closing the gap of proficiency between formal Kinyarwanda learners and those who do not have access to any formal education of Kinyarwanda. In this context, research revealed that motivation plays an important role within the learning process and its existence is essential in order to succeed in learning (Andersen & Brink 2013). This is the reason why we opted for mixing multimedia techniques to keep learners motivated (Andersen & Brink 2013) whenever they are interacting with the application.

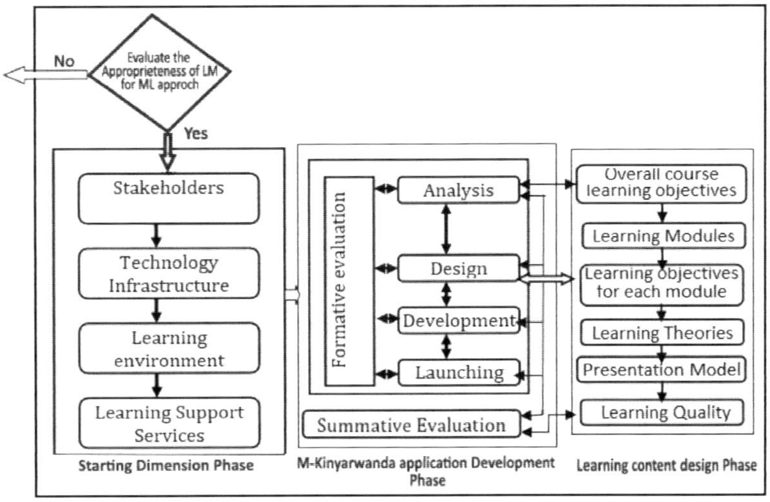

Figure 1. The adopted conception, design and development approaches (Al-Harrasi et al. 2015) for M-Kinyarwanda application.

About the starting dimension phase, as shown on figure 1 above, Kinyarwanda is being taught in the Rwandan education system from nursery schools to the university (Rwanda Education Board 2016) . The fact that it has the curricula and other educational materials, gave us the "Yes" answer to the appropriateness of proposing a mobile learning approach, given other factors as mentioned in the introduction. Stakeholders include the Rwandan Ministry of education, Rwanda Academy of Language and Culture, and all Kinyarwanda learners and users.

For M-Kinyarwanda application development phase, the problem statement has been clearly defined. We will make sure to develop M-learning activities that focus on the aspects of technology, learning content, learner and the learning context (Al-Harrasi et al. 2015). Our main target is the community of Rwandans living abroad, primarily those who did not get any chance to study Kinyarwanda at any schools, and later those who know the language but who wish to improve. For development, we are using Android Studio, as an integrated development environment (IDE) released by Google in May 2013 (SAMSUNG 2016). This is a popular framework for mobile application development, which uses Java programming language in order to get a dynamic, interactive, intelligent, adaptive, flexible and learner centered application. We have chosen the Google android mobile phone platform as one of the most anticipated smartphone operating systems (Holla & Katti 2012).

In the last phase, we will focus on the design and quality assurance of learning contents. At the beginning of each module, clear objectives and learning outcomes will be mentioned followed by rich content in the format of text, audio, image and video materials in order to ensure a motivating environment to the learners. We hope to make special contents based on the new competence based and learner centered curricula of Kinyarwanda, published by the Rwandan Ministry of Education through Rwanda Education Board in 2015 (Rwanda Education Board 2016). For the system pedagogy design process, the following factors (Xhafa et al. 2010) will be taken into consideration: (i) content of the course, (ii) learner's activities, (iii) mode and level of interaction, (iv) impact of new approach, (v) performance indicator, and (vi) learning outcomes.

6. METHODOLOGY

The following are the research questions from which the study will be trying to answer:

1. Whether or not M-Kinyarwanda increases the motivation of language learners;
2. Whether or not M-Kinyarwanda improves Kinyarwanda language-learning outcomes.

We will follow mixed method, both quantitative and qualitative approach, for requirements generation and system evaluation to get quantification of data and for gaining a deep understanding of underlying reasons and motivations. To conduct this research, the research sample will be made of 10 young Rwandans who grew up out of the Rwandan education system. They will be selected randomly to use the developed prototype of M-Kinyarwanda application. After a specific period, an assessment will be carried out to assess the impact of the developed application on improving efficiency in Kinyarwanda language and their level of motivation while they were interacting with the application.

6.1 The system development model

In order to develop a system, which will more likely to satisfy the user's desire for look, feel and performance, we opted for Prototyping software development model. This is an initial version of a software system that is used to demonstrate concepts, try out design options, and find out more about the problem and its possible solutions (Sommerville 2011). The prototype model places more effort in creating the actual application instead of concentrating on documentation (Sabale & Dani 2012). This way, the actual application could be released in advance. It requires more user involvement and allows them to see and interact with the prototype for further feedback that lead to the software requirements specification (SRS) document, for extra improvement until the desired product (Sabale & Dani 2012).

6.2 Evaluation strategy

With this research, the evaluation framework of the proposed M-Kinyarwanda success will be based on pedagogical, to determine learning outcomes, and technical aspects to address important issues (Son 2016) such as curriculum integration, learner engagement, collaboration, interactivity, feedback and personalized learning. Motivated strategies for learning questionnaires will be used to measure learners' motivation. We will opt for a modified version of the Motivated Strategies for Learning Questionnaire (MSLQ) (Pintrich et al. 1991) for our research. The reason behind MSLQ is simply the way it assists in investigating learners' eagerness and learning strategies in various subscales. Each subscale will consist of several questions to measure one particular factor. Each of those questions will state a specific learning exercise, and the participants will have to respond in relation to their appositeness.

On the technical side, the usability evaluation will be based on effectiveness, efficiency and satisfaction with which learners can perform tasks with the system. It will be evaluated on [1] user-based where a sample of the learners will interact with the system, and [2] expert-based for the usability dimensions. Experts will examine the presentation, hypermediality and application proactivity (Ardito et al. 2006).

7. CONCLUSION

This paper is about ongoing research on development of M-Kinyarwanda, a mobile application for Kinyarwanda language learning. The issues that most African languages, especially Kinyarwanda, are facing have been clearly mentioned and the proposed solution, design framework, development model and the methodology to follow have been indicated. At the current stage, we wanted to show that there is yet room and need to encourage research and development of language learning applications relating to African languages or for those countries that are facing a similar tragedy as the Rwandan case. The proposed application will provide immediate, customized instructions and feedback to learners, without any assistance from a physical teacher. This will be possible through the integration of various multimedia products and techniques within the current application under development.

M-Kinyarwanda should be considered as a contribution to the lifelong learning innovation that will consider all places where learning takes place. Requirements generation, the design and development of application prototype have been started, and hopefully, M-Kinyarwanda application will be widely available, accessible and benefited from many Kinyarwanda learners and users around the world. At the moment, the plan is to develop a prototype that will be about 70% complete. In the near future, we will implement the full system and allow more users to benefit from it.

REFERENCES

Al-Harrasi, H., Al-Khanjari, Z. & Sarrab, M., 2015. Proposing a New Design Approach for M-learning Applications. *International Journal of Software Engineering and its Applications*, 9(11), pp.11–24.

Andersen, B.B. & Brink, K. Van Den, 2013. *Multimedia in Education*, Moscow: UNESCO 2013.

Ardito, C. et al., 2006. An approach to Usability Evaluation of e-Learning Applications. *Universal access in the information society*, 4(3), pp.270–283.

Benson, P., 2012. Autonomy in language learning , learning and life. *Synergies France*, 9(1), pp.29–39.

Block, R., 1994. The Tragedy of Rwanda. *The New York Review of Books*, 41(17), pp.3–8.

Collentine, K. et al., 2011. Special Issue: Learner Autonomy and New Learning Environments Articles. *Language Learning and Technology*, 15(3), pp.1–136.

Dickinson, L., 1995. Autonomy and Motivation a Literature Review. , 23(2), pp.165–174.

Drame, A. & Paepcke, H., 2010. *diversity series diversity and global understanding* D. H. P. Anja, ed., Vienna: TermNet.

Esch, E., 1994. *Self-Access and the Adult Language Learner*, 20 Bedfordbury, Covent Garden, London WC2N 4LB, England, United Kingdom: Centre for Information on Language Teaching and Research.

Godwin-jones, R., 2011. Emerging Technologies: Mobile Apps for Language Learning. *Language Learning & Technology*, 15(2), pp.2–11. Available at: http://www.llt.msu.edu/issues/june2011/emerging.pdf.

Habyarimana, H., 2005. *Multilingualism and change on the Kinyarwanda sound system post-1994*. Doctoral dissertation, Faculty of Humanities, University of the Witwatersrand, Johannesburg.

Herman M. Batibo, 2005. *Language Decline and Death in Africa: Causes, consequences, and challenges*, Multilingual Matters.

Holla, S. & Katti, M.M., 2012. Android Based Mobile Application Development and its Security. *International Journal of Computer Trends and Technology*, 3(3), pp.486–490.

International Organization for Migration, 2016. World Migration. Available at: https://www.iom.int/world-migration [Accessed October 25, 2016].

Jordan, K., 2013. *"Language use in Rwanda. Multilingualism in public and private contexts."* Doctoral dissertation, uniwien.

National Institute of Statistics Rwanda, 2016. Key figures. Available at: http://www.statistics.gov.rw/ [Accessed December 20, 2016].

Paracha, S. et al., 2009. A Review of Basic Kanji Courseware. *Multidisciplinary Engineering Education Magazine*, 4(1).

Pintrich, P.R.R. et al., 1991. A Manual for the Use of the Motivated Strategies for Learning Questionnaire (MSLQ).

Rurangirwa, S., 2012. The Absence of Kinyarwanda in the Current Language Policy of Rwanda. *The Journal of Pan African Studies*, 5(8), pp.169–179.

Rwanda Education Board, 2016. Competence based Curriculum. Available at: http://reb.rw/fileadmin/competence_based_curriculum/index.html [Accessed November 17, 2016].

Sabale, R.G. & Dani, A.R., 2012. Comparative Study of Prototype Model For Software Engineering With System Development Life Cycle. *IOSR Journal of Engineering (IOSRJEN)*, 2(7), pp.21–24.

SAMSUNG, 2016. Overview of the Android Studio. Available at: http://developer.samsung.com/technical-doc/view.do;jsessionid=F300A29605C85CD58D06ECFF78D47CF9?v=T000000027 [Accessed January 15, 2017].

Sommerville, I., 2011. *Software Engineering* 9th ed., Pearson Education, Inc. publishing as Addison-Wesley.

Son, J.-B., 2016. Selecting and Evaluating Mobile Apps for Language Learning. In P. Agnieszka & A. Mohammed, eds. *The International Handbook of Mobile-Assisted Language Learning*. Beijing: China Central Radio & TV University Press Co. Ltd, pp. 161–179.

Wolfson, N., 1989. The social dynamics of native and nonnative variation in complimenting behavior. In *The dynamic interlanguage*. Springer US, pp. 219–236.

Xhafa, F. et al., 2010. *Computational Intelligence for Technology Enhanced Learning*, Berlin: Springer.

Posters

DESIGN OF MOBILE E-BOOKS AS A TEACHING TOOL FOR DIABETES EDUCATION

Sophie Huey-Ming Guo
Mackay Medical College, Department of Nursing
New Taipei City, Taiwan

ABSTRACT

To facilitate people with diabetes adopting information technologies, a tool of mobile eHealth education for diabetes was described in this paper, presenting the validity of mobile eBook for diabetes educators This paper describes the design concepts and validity of this mobile eBook for diabetes educators delivering diabetes electronic self-care.

KEYWORDS

Diabetes education, self-care, mHealth, eHealth, health literacy.

1. INTRODUCTION

While increasing the numbers of people with diabetes, mobile eHealth technology-driven solutions emerge to assist chronic care. A gap is still existed between current end users and these technology-driven solutions (Boren, 2009). To facilitate their adoption, the ability of using mobile eHealth technologies and application, as known 'mobile eHealth literacy', is required for all participators involved in the technology-based diabetes education programs. Clinical nursing staff and nursing students play a key role of patient education that teaches patients to perform self-care in outpatients or medical wards. However, they are not ever to instruct patients that how to use mobile eHealth technologies in their daily self-care. This paper describes the design process of a mobile eBook as for diabetes educators delivering diabetes electronic self-care.

2. DESIGN PROCESS

Content and concepts

The importance concepts of the study consisted of eight elements of eHealth literacy: traditional literacy, health literacy, information literacy, scientific literacy, media literacy, computer literacy, mobile literacy, and Internet literacy (Figure 1). A mobile eHealth literacy program was proposed for patient with diabetes in this study. Firstly, the partial content of the diabetes mobile eBook referred a toolkit for trainer original from by NIH Senior Health National Institute on Aging (NIA, 2010). This toolkit, an educational material, has been validated its effectiveness by Xie(2011). To enhance the ability of patients with diabetes on using diabetes applications (apps), this study also added new content in eBooks to provide the detailed instructional information of diabetes apps practice. The content validity index of the mobile eBook for diabetes e-healthcare was 0.86 performed by six experts. Figure 2 shows the screen shot of the mobile eBook designed in the study.

Development software

The eBooks was developed with iBook Author software built in iOS operational environment and deployed the eBook onto iPad. Advantage of iBook Author software are friendly interface, easy to use and interactive media.

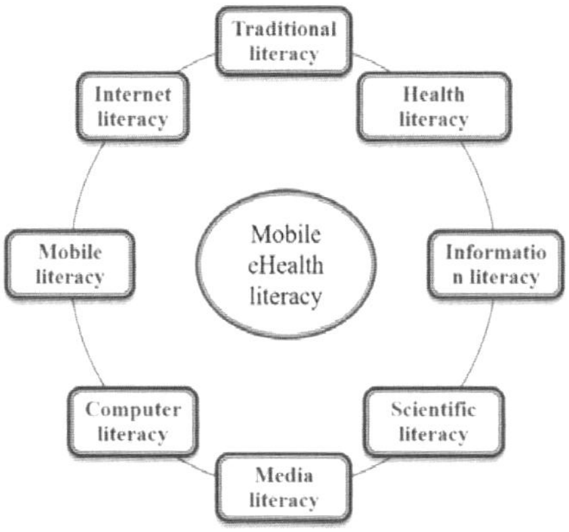

Figures 1. Eight concepts of mobile eBook.

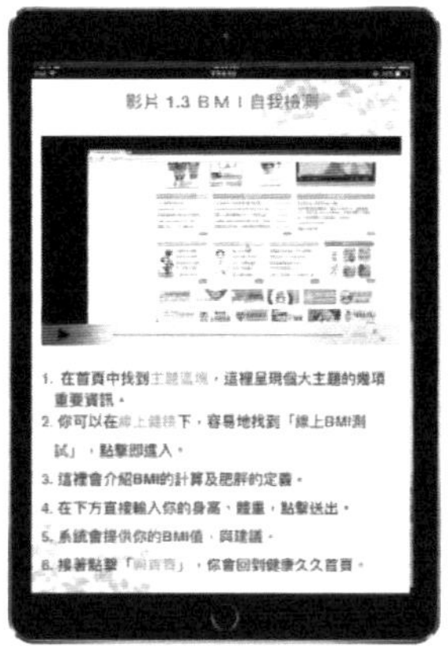

Figure 2. Screenshot of diabetes mobile eBook.

3. CONCLUSION

The potential benefits of the diabetes mobile eBooks can be a useful tool to enhancing eHealth literacy for people with diabetes and assisting clinical patient education. The performance of this programs is ongoing up-to-date.

ACKNOWLEDGEMENT

The project was partly supported by grants from partly supported by the Mackay Medical College (1021A10) and Ministry of Science and Technology (MOST 105-2511-S-715-001).

REFERENCES

Boren, S.A. (2009). A review of health literacy and diabetes: opportunities for technology. Journal of diabetes science and technology, 3(1), 202-209.

NIA. (2010). Helping Older Adults Search for Health Information Online: A Toolkit for Trainers.

Xie, Bo. (2011). Effects of an eHealth literacy intervention for older adults. Journal of medical Internet research, 13(4).

READING WHILE LISTENING ON MOBILE DEVICES: AN INNOVATIVE APPROACH TO ENHANCE READING

Aicha Rochdi and Jenny Eppard
Zayed University, Dubai, UAE

ABSTRACT

This poster session will describe a study that took place at a university in the United Arab Emirates. The study included a reading app that was downloaded onto each student' individual mobile device. Students could read while listening to the stories. The primary goal of the study was to determine how, if at all, listening while reading in a potentially ubiquitous manner impacted their reading ability, particularly fluency and rate. The study was mixed method and included in ABBA design as well as qualitative questions. Data is still being analyzed.

KEYWORDS

Reading app, reading ability, second language.

1. INTRODUCTION

This poster session will highlight a research study on the impact that mobile devices potentially have on reading fluency in a second language context (specifically the United Arab Emirates). The poster will be divided into several key areas: previous research on reading using mobile devices, trends in reading fluency, reading issues related to the population, the methodology and some of preliminary results. The study took place at a university in the UAE with students who were enrolled in a pre-sessional English program.

2. BACKGROUND

Much of the research on using mobile technologies to enhance reading has focused partly and often primarily on motivation (Hsu, et al., 2013; Wang and Smith, 2013). An exception to this, is a study by Hsu, Hwang and Chang (2013) who researched reading on mobile devices with English as a Second Language learners in Taiwan. Their study included a personalized learning system that catered to the students' preference and level. The reading comprehension of the experimental group increased in comparison to the control group. Even though this aspect of the study is positive, it is difficult to generalize the results to other populations such as the one under investigation.

Although the central issue in this paper is reading comprehension, the focus is less on the aforementioned reading skill and more on a specific reading component that is essential to reading comprehension namely reading fluency. The rationale of this focus is that a large body of research has shown that the higher-level processes that influence and determine effective comprehension do not become fully operational until the reader has acquired a reasonable level of fluency (Kuhn & Stahl, 2003). In other words, in order for a college student to read a text and achieve adequate comprehension, she should be able to read the text in question effortlessly and accurately.

Over the past decade, fluent reading has been recognized as a central component of skilled reading. This surge of interest is partially due to the identification of fluency as a major component for optimum reading development by organizations such as the National Reading Panel, the National Institute for Literacy, and the National Center for the Study of Adult Learning and Literacy through the Partnership for Reading and to a broader reconsideration of the role of oral reading in the development of skilled reading (Rasinski, 2006). In recent years, instructional methodologies have been developed that are aimed at achieving reading fluency.

Reading fluency can be fostered through a process called assisted reading (Rasinski and Hoffman, 2003). Reading fluency can be fostered through a process called assisted reading (Rasinski &Hoffman, 2003). Assisted reading, also called Listening while reading (LWR), involves having the student read silently while simultaneously listening to a fluent rendition of the reading passage. The auditory version of the reading can be performed by a fluent adult reader or by the utilization of various technological devices. Of interest to this paper is the investigation of the effect of assisted reading, specifically listening while reading (LWR), on reading comprehension on Arab learners of English as a Second language..

Academia and educators alike continue to grapple with areas germane to reading literacy in the Arab world. For one, there is a need for quality scholarly articles that explore aspects of reading such as reading strategies, the process of developing reading skills, reading rate, reading comprehension, and other relevant topics. One of the reasons why it is difficult to have a clear understanding of the true nature of reading in the Arab world is that reports often combine all Arab countries into one category or the studies are fragmented with one study conducted in one place, while other areas are not researched. This is not necessarily true. The region is vast and differs greatly even within the same country. What is true in one country or region may differ from another depending on factors such as demographics. The reasons for these disparities are not entirely clear.

3. METHODOLOGY

We used a commercial reading program that has an app on multiple platforms. The app allows students to listen while reading. There were several reasons for choosing this particular program: a) it has a rich collection of levelled books; b) it includes tests that allow to establish a baseline and monitor students' progress; c) it allows students to listen and read simultaneously. Even though the books in this program were geared towards young learners, the fact that they provided clear and interesting illustrations along with the reading text, and that their length allowed them to be read in one class period made them an adequate choice for the intervention. Using children literature to further adult literacy is a method that has been used in the ESL/ELL classroom and that has yielded positive results (Horwitz & Worthy, 2007).

Teachers and students alike are able to choose the learners' reading level based on results from pretests that screens for rate, accuracy and comprehension. The study was mixed method and included an ABBA quantitative design as well as qualitative questions. Eighty-eight students participated in the study as did four teachers. We had four experimental groups. Two groups read while listening for the first part of the semester and the other group read without listening. They swapped strategies mid-semester. We frequently tested students throughout the semester and at the end we interviewed both students and teachers. Our research questions included the following: (1) To what extent does reading on a mobile App impact the reading skills of ESL students enrolled in a university foundation English class in the UAE? (2) To what extent does reading while listening using a mobile app affect reading fluency development of ESL students enrolled in in a university foundation English class in the UAE? (3) What are students past experiences with reading? (4) Which types of text are students most interested in reading? (5) In which ways do students use technology for reading? (6) What are the benefits and challenges to using the iPad for reading?

4. PROJECTIONS

Most of the data analyzed thus far does not indicate a significant difference between the two experimental groups. However, as shown in previous research qualitatively students are motivated by the possibilities afforded to learning on mobile devices. We also asked students some background information about their reading habits and experiences with reading at a young age. We will include any findings that we have in the poster as well.

REFERENCES

Horwitz, E. K., & Worthy, M. J. (2007). Integrating children's literature into a college foreign language class: A teacher-researcher's perspective.

Hsu, C.K., Hwang, G.J. and Chang, C.K., 2013. A personalized recommendation-based mobile learning approach to improving the reading performance of EFL students. Computers & Education, 63, pp.327-336.

Kuhn, M. R., & Stahl, S. A., 2003. Fluency: A review of developmental and remedial practices. Journal of educational psychology, 95(1), 3. Literacy and adult education in the Arab world. (2003). Retrieved September 3, 2015, from http://www.unesco.org/education/uie/pdf/country/arab_world.pdf

Rasinski, T.V. and Hoffman, J.V., 2003. Oral reading in the school literacy curriculum. Reading Research Quarterly, 38(4), pp.510-522.

Rasinski, T., 2006. Reading fluency instruction: Moving beyond accuracy, automaticity, and prosody. The Reading Teacher, 59(7), pp.704-706.

Wang, S. and Smith, S., 2013. Reading and grammar learning through mobile phones. Language Learning & Technology, 17(3), pp.117-134.

Doctoral Consortium

HOW CAN TABLETS BE USED FOR MEANING-MAKING AND LEARNING

Liv Lofthus
University college of southeast Norway, Norway

ABSTRACT

The background for my research project is to look closer at how social sciences such as history, geography and civic life can be taught outside the classroom by using tablets as a tool. This paper looks closer into how tablets can be used as a learning recourse in an interdisciplinary project outside the classroom. I will follow a group of pupils that are used to using iPad in all subjects to see how they, in small groups, use their tablets outside the classroom. I will see how they use their tablets for orientation, collecting information and documentation. The methods used is observation, interview, and video documentation. The project spans from work inside the classroom to prepare for the task outside, and after the project has come to an end I will document how they work with it inside the classroom. The aim of the analyses will be to describe how the pupils use the tablets, from a socio cultural perspective, as a tool for learning.

KEYWORDS

Digital skills, ethnomethodology, m-learning, formal-informal learning.

1. INTRODUCTION

According to "The Norwegian Directorate for Education and Training" one of the five skills that are defined as basic to learning in school is digital skills." Digital skills involve being able to use digital tools, media and resources efficiently and responsibly, to solve practical tasks, find and process information, design digital products and communicate content. Digital skills also include developing digital judgment by acquiring knowledge and good strategies for the use of the Internet." (UDIR, 2012). The pupils are expected to learn technical skills, and also digital judgment. What are the best means to achieve these goals? There are great differences in the praxis used in schools to meet the aims of digital skills. Some have PC in separate rooms, in some schools the pupils each have a PC, and in more and more schools pupils have their own tablets, or other kinds of mobile digital tools. There are different opinions on these practices, on what works and what does not work. The usage of mobile digital tools in schools is especially debated. Critics argue that it can take away the focus from learning, and online bullying can be a problem. Some research show that pupils have a harder time focusing on school work with internet access, than without it (Christiansen, 2010). How teachers should set limits on its use can also be challenging. Some schools will total ban the use of cell phones during school hours. Arguments for the use of mobile tools in education, believes that banning them would be to not take advantage of the resources these can be in teaching, and that would be going backwards into the future (Nordstrand, 2015). Some seem to think that the best way to learn about digital judgment is to deprive the pupils from having access. In many schools digital judgment is more or less taught within a few occasions, rather than as an ongoing learning project.

Mobile digital tools is something the pupils are familiar with from other contexts than school. Mobile devices often have a more personal function than other digital tools and learning methods. They are easy to carry and to show to others. When working with tablets/smartphones it is relatively easy to produce good results in terms of student work such as images, movies, audio statement, and more, which in turn could increase students' motivation. Since the pupils use these tools in many different contexts, the usage of these tools can, ideally, enable a connection between various physical learning environments (Stewart & Hedberg, 2011). I believe that this link between physical learning environments, along with increased motivation through the use of mobile digital tools can lead to increased learning outcomes among pupils.

Many school subjects can be taught outside the classroom. In my project I will focus on social sciences (in Norway this consists of history and geography and civic life) as a subjects that can be taught outside of the classroom, within the society and environment that the pupils learn about in these subjects. The reason why I want to look closer at social sciences is my background from teaching these subjects in school and in museums. I find the need to go outside the classroom in these subjects, is important for the pupils to get a better understanding of the society they are a part of. They are used to using tablets or mobile phones outside the classroom, and they have knowledge about this that they have not learned in school.

In my project I will follow 9th graders that are used to using tablets to see how they do this, and interview them about their experiences.

2. THEORETICAL BACKGROUND

As a starting point for my research design, I will focus on ethnomethodology as a perspective to study people's everyday behavior and choices of methods for interacting with others. I will use this perspective as I will look into how students solve everyday activities, and what methods they use to approach the task, artifacts, their peers and their surroundings. I want to see what methods they choose and develop, when they use tablets both individually and in collaboration with the others in the group. I consider this to be a way to get aware of the pupils tacit knowledge. The tacit knowledge in my project will be some of the knowledge the pupils have about using mobile digital tools that they have learned informally. They may possibly know more about the operation than they can explain. One can well imagine that the knowledge we have acquired by verbalizing is easier to articulate than knowledge of a trial and error that the use of mobile devices will be. One does not know what one is doing before having done it. According to Polanyi tacit knowledge has a dimension related to culture, and a dimension related to the subject - knowledge is socially and culturally oriented (Polanyi, 1983). This consists with Vygotsky and sociocultural theories of learning, reviewing learning as socially and culturally oriented (Vygotskij, 1978). I have a sociocultural perspective on learning, and to illuminate my perspective on learning I will look closer into Polanyi view on tacit knowledge.

I will use the sociological perspective ethnomethodology to look at the pupils interaction with one another as they go about the using their mobile digital tools. I think this is a suitable way to look at the phenomenon of using this tools as this is something they are used to in their everyday lives. I want to look at what they do, and try to explain why. Try to make these common place scenes visible (Garfinkel, 1964).

Through my research, I will seek an understanding of the relationship between digital tools and learning. I will examine how pupil's skills and knowledge about the use of digital tools can be used as a resource in schools, in this case outside the classroom. The research aims to emphasize the importance and usefulness of pupil's contribution to their own learning. It also aims to increase awareness of how children's digital skills can be used in teaching, as well as bridging the digital home and on leisure time and school. I will also look at how teachers can find their place in this. On the bases of my research I will look at m-learning by focusing on the following elements: - informal learning – Ethnomethodology – digital skills – sociocultural learning perspective – outdoor education. Using this definition of outdoor education: "Outdoor education is a way to work with the school's content on the part of school life moved out in the community. Outdoor education thus implies regular and purposeful activity outside the classroom." For a closer look at the activities and interactions that take place between pupils, between pupils and the physical space and between pupils and artifacts. I be based on an ethno-methodological perspective on interaction (Vom Lehn, 2014).

Although there is controversy about the use of mobile tools in schools, the usage is increasing. Mobile learning (M-learning) involves the use of mobile technology, providing excellent opportunities for learning outside the classroom (Kukulska-Hulme, Sharples, Milrad, Arnedillo-Sánchez, & Vavoula, 2009). M-learning can be said to be the use of digital tools that are easy to bring, and that can be used anytime and anywhere (Crompton, 2013). This can help to make learning easy, accessible and interactive (Kukulska-Hulme, 2006) (Burden & Maher, 2014). Use of mobile devices can also connect formal learning that happens in schools with informal learning that happens in the pupils spare time (Kukulska-Hulme et al., 2009). Several theories about m-learning is postulated. Marguerite Koole has put forward a model to describe m-learning. The model explains how mobile learning takes place at the junction of the technical aspect (mobile device), the social aspect and the learner (Koole, 2009). Laurillard have based conversational theory (Pask, 1975) to create a "conversational framework" which sets m-learning. Conversation theory is based on the idea that learning happens through conversation (Pask, 1975). Laurillard notes that conversation is important in all forms of learning, and in m-learning there are more opportunities for pupils to gain ownership of what they learn through conversation (Laurillard, 2007). Several other studies of mobile learning in recent years has placed "mobile education" under socio-cultural approach to learning (Kearney, Schuck, Burden, & Aubusson, 2012). There is no clear agreement on the theoretical approach that best suits m-learning (Crompton, 2013). Within my research I will focus on the sociocultural aspects of m-learning.

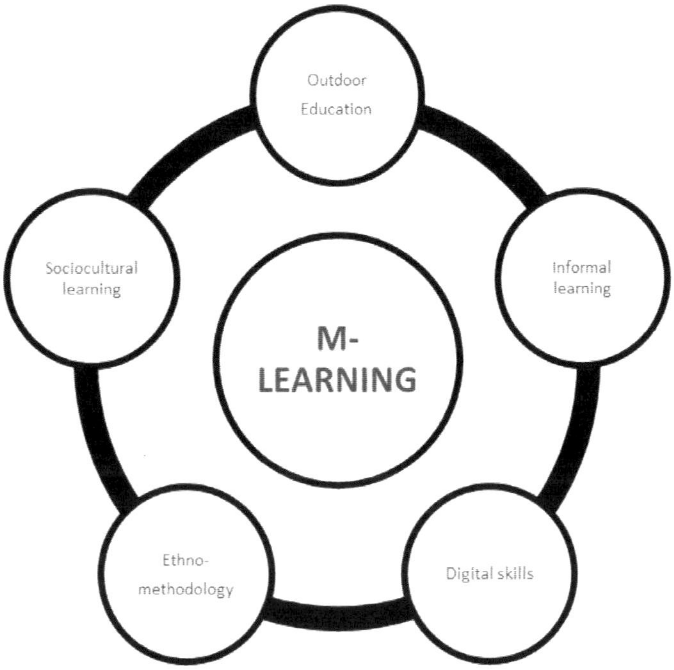

Figure 1. Research perspectives.

3. METHOD

Areas of focus for the project will be to test and analyze educational resources on the basis of empirical studies of learning processes in secondary schools. Furthermore, I will look at how these educational resources are included in the activities taking place in schools, but outside the classroom, and how they put into play through individual and collective learning processes.

The collecting of data has taken place in November of 2016. I have studied a group of 9th graders that are used to using iPad in almost all school subjects. I want to look closer at how this works within a group of pupils that are used to working with iPads. The field work started with observation in the classroom to see how they work with the iPads. After this I will followed the group when they did a project initiated by their teacher. The project involved using the iPad outside the classroom for orientation, documentation and to gather information in an intersubjective project consisting of history, geography and civic life in the pupil`s nearby community. The school project started in the classroom where the teacher divide into small groups of 2-3 and give the pupils information about the project. I will gathered data through video filming in the classroom. The next part of the data collection was to go outside where the pupils did the major part of the project. Here some of the groups wore go-pro cameras so they could film what they were doing. After the work outside was done we went back into the classroom where I will film what is happened in the classroom after the pupils went through their work and showed the rest of the class what they had been doing. I interviewed groups of students about how they worked with the project. I also interviewed the teacher about how they work with the iPads.

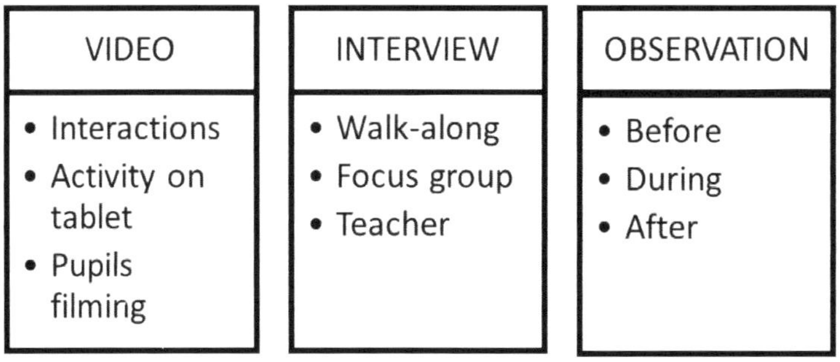

Figure 2. Goals in the different methods in the multi-methods approach.

4. CONCLUSION

The project is timely and can generate information on how to use tablets within the school and take advantage of what the pupils already know. This is applicable for schools and pupils, and important as digital skills now are of great importance- in this case, not mainly technical, but pedagogical. The project is still wide, and needs a more specific aim.

REFERENCES

Burden, K., & Maher, D. (2014). 15 Mobile technologies and authentic learning in the primary school classroom. *Teaching and Learning with ICT in the Primary School*, 171.

Christiansen, V. (2010). Førsteklassinger med mobiltelefon i skoletida. *NRK Hedemark og Oppland*. Retrieved from http://www.nrk.no/ho/mobiltelefon-i-skoletida-1.7087629

Crompton, H. (2013). Mobile learning: New approach, new theory. In Z. L. Berge & L. Y. Muilenburg (Eds.), *Handbook of Mobile Learning* (pp. 47-57): Routledge.

Garfinkel, H. (1964). Studies of the Routine Grounds of Everyday Activities. *Social Problems, 11*(3), 225-250. doi:10.2307/798722

Kearney, M., Schuck, S., Burden, K., & Aubusson, P. (2012). Viewing mobile learning from a pedagogical perspective. *2012, 20*. doi:10.3402/rlt.v20i0.14406

Koole, M. L. (2009). A model for framing mobile learning. *Mobile learning: Transforming the delivery of education and training, 1*(2), 25-47.

Kukulska-Hulme, A. (2006). Mobile language learning now and in the future. In P. Svensson (Ed.), *Från vision till praktik: Språkutbildning och Informationsteknik* (pp. 295-310). Sweden: Swedish net university.

Kukulska-Hulme, A., Sharples, M., Milrad, M., Arnedillo-Sánchez, I., & Vavoula, G. (2009). Innovation in mobile learning: A European perspective. *International Journal of Mobile and Blended Learning, 1*(1), 13-35.

Laurillard, D. (2007). Pedagogical forms of mobile learning: framing research questions.

Nordstrand, Ø. (2015). Mobilforbud i skolen=å pisse i egen bukse.

Pask, G. (1975). *Conversation, cognition and learning*: Amsterdam: Elsevier.

Polanyi, M. (1983). *The tacit dimension*. Glouchester, Mass: Peter Smith.

Stewart, K., M. , & Hedberg, J., G. (2011). The Pedagogy of Mobility. In N. Wan (Ed.), *Mobile Technologies and Handheld Devices for Ubiquitous Learning: Research and Pedagogy* (pp. 259-278). Hershey, PA, USA: IGI Global.

UDIR. (2012). *Framework for basic skills*. http://www.udir.no/contentassets/fd2d6bfbf2364e1c98b73e030119bd38/framework_for_basic_skills.pdf: Norwegian Directorate for Education and Training Retrieved from http://www.udir.no/contentassets/fd2d6bfbf2364e1c98b73e030119bd38/framework_for_basic_skills.pdf.

Vom Lehn, D. (2014). *Harold Garfinkel : the creation and development of ethnomethodology*

Vygotskij, L. S. (1978). *Mind in society : the development of higher psychological processes*. Cambridge, Mass: Harvard University Press.

AUTHOR INDEX